Frank Pace

SYSTEM vs. CULTURE

NORTH AMERICAN EDUCATION AND SOCIETY IN THE BALANCE

Copyright © 2014 by Frank Pace
First Edition – May 2014

ISBN
978-1-4602-4226-1 (Hardcover)
978-1-4602-4227-8 (Paperback)
978-1-4602-4228-5 (eBook)

All rights reserved.

No part of this publication may be reproduced in any form, or by any means, electronic or mechanical, including photocopying, recording, or any information browsing, storage, or retrieval system, without permission in writing from the publisher.

Produced by:

FriesenPress
Suite 300 – 852 Fort Street
Victoria, BC, Canada V8W 1H8

www.friesenpress.com

Distributed to the trade by The Ingram Book Company

Table of Contents

Acknowledgements..i

Introduction..iii

1 – From Personal Experience to Broad Perspective..............1

2 – Issues, Obstacles and Problems in Education................57

3 – Education and Society..113

4 – On Teachers and Teaching...153

5 – Imagine the Future...181

6 – Directions..217

About the Author..229

For my wonderful daughters
Adrienne & Nathalie
and
For all who hope to attain self-actualization
through meaningful learning experiences.

Acknowledgements

Many thanks to my partner Wendy and her children Blaine, Craig, Amanda and their partners just for being in my life. Also thanks to my parents Carmel and Nellie and my sisters Lynn, Esther, Shelley and their families for their support. I especially want to thank my daughters Adrienne and Nathalie for being the special individuals that they have always been and always will be. Many thanks to numerous friends and colleagues, especially my brothers Tony Westerink and Dave Dowling, my most influential teacher Anne Marie Walkey, Dan Chappell for arranging my first teaching opportunity, friends and colleagues including Paul & Shannon, Gabe & Darlene Denis, Dave & Bev Lockwood, Rachel Schmitt & Charmene Vega.

I would like to extend special thanks to my friend, casual editor and critic Joan Robertson for taking the time to comb through this work and make some valuable suggestions as well as providing encouragement and support. Also, I would like to thank the many wonderful students and educators I have had the opportunity to know and work with over the past three decades in both Canada and the United States. You all know who you are. And finally, I would like to thank anyone and everyone willing to engage in discussion about the many aspects of North American education that needs to change -- whether it is prompted by this book or any other medium. Let real discussion begin. Let real change happen.

Frank Pace

Introduction

"The only thing that interferes with my learning is my education."
Albert Einstein

Everyone has a stake in education and eventually learns this at some point in their lives. Education is the process whereby we are supposed to learn essential skills for living successful lives in both social and economic terms. It is supposed to be, and is actually touted to be, about self-actualization, yet this is often only the case with a very small percentage of the people who go through the system.

Throughout history we have primarily learned about how to live successful lives through interaction with others. Parents, siblings and peers teach us the bulk of the many things we learn in life, especially in our early years, but as we progress beyond infancy and early childhood, we come to learn that formal education plays a huge role not only in what we learn but in what we think we can learn. Through competition, testing and grades we come to learn our place in the world – one that not only fits us accordingly into the niche we fill as we progress through the modern schooling process, but also the one we will likely fit into throughout our lives. Whether we excel at the formal learning process or experience bumps along the road, the system itself is an effective generator of human material to fill whatever spots are needed in the economy that exists – both good jobs and not so good jobs. If this is satisfactory and we aspire to nothing more than that, then there is no reason to analyze, criticize or attempt to change the current North American education system. We already have what we want and need. However, if we all recognize that we have a vested interest in education and have come to see that the current education system not only produces a lot of graduates (many of whom can neither function capably as literate or numerate individuals once they actually graduate), but also produces a significant amount of dropouts (numbers consistently and statistically up to 30 percent of all students who enter the formal schooling system), then we may also appreciate the idea that we could probably do much better than that.

System vs. Culture: North American Education and Society in the Balance is about looking at the current education system in a very different way than we have been taught to look at it. It is about recognizing why the problems in our educational system exist. It is also about presenting ideas for creating a more equitable education culture where everyone can participate, benefit and move toward real self-actualization. Understanding problems in education – the process we use to prepare for participation in the real world – is also key to understanding why we have some of the problems that exist in society as a whole. The two are inextricably connected. Therefore, if we want to change the world to make it a better place, we need to look at the root of the system as it exists in the process of education. If one does not change, then how can the other? If what we want is a culture which emphasizes the importance of accumulating more than one's neighbours and which disproportionately benefits corporations and the top one percent, then the education system we already have in place is an excellent one for advancing such economic objectives. Significant change is necessary to progress from where we are now. Despite all of the technological and social advancements of the past two centuries, we have come no closer to reducing crime, violence, unemployment, poverty and many other problems that have been with humanity since the dawn of civilization. If the promises we make about compulsory schooling as presented in school district mission statements were really true and applied to everyone, then wouldn't the many problems in our society eventually be eradicated? How much closer to such a goal have we come with the 160-year-old education system that prepares us all for the society we live in?

This book outlines the many specific issues, problems and obstacles that exist in North American education systems today while mapping an alternative for what could and should become an educational culture. Many of the things we have come to believe as being essential components of our education system often serve to disenfranchise a significant number of those who go through the system. An educational culture would go much further in embracing all members of society through pragmatic methods.

Many other books have focused on problems in one area or another and develop suggestions for improving the system that exists. This book is different in the sense that it recognizes that no amount of change within the current system will really improve it. It is the system itself that inherently perseverates issues, problems and obstacles that prevent many from benefitting from the promise of education as worded in the mission statements of our educational institutions. This is true both at the level of compulsory schooling during elementary and high school years and even at the university level. The very things we have come to see as integral parts of the system – grades, testing and large classrooms full of students being, for the most part, taught directly in the same old lecture form that has been around for over a century and a half – all contribute to the many problems that persist year after year, decade after decade. We are a society that finds it very difficult to see out of the educational box we have placed ourselves in over the past century and a half.

It is important to note that this book really just begins to touch on the direction(s) we could navigate toward. An initial template is suggested but it will take thinking and acting along new lines by everyone who participates in the education process for it to really evolve into an ideal form. Education is something much bigger and more important than schooling and should be part of our life plan at every stage of that plan. This is both an individual and collective process. We need to imagine our future as it could be and not as a continuation or extension of what we have today. The difference between the industrial model promoting impersonal competition and an educational culture that promotes interpersonal cooperation is this: one has a corrosive influence on society; the other has a cohesive influence on society. Once the difference is recognized, we need to choose between the one we already have and the one we could attain. Educators, parents, students, politicians – anyone involved in the educational process needs to think about questioning current practice and supporting many new ways to deliver quality education for all.

Frank Pace, January 11th, 2014

1

From Personal Experience to Broad Perspective

"Much education today is monumentally ineffective. All too often we are giving young people cut flowers when we should be teaching them to grow their own plants."

John W. Gardner

In my grade ten English class in 1972, students were asked to prepare a presentation about William Golding's *The Lord of the Flies*, a book about civilized British school boys who are marooned on an island and rapidly degrade into savages. I enjoyed this book just as much as most books presented throughout my school career and finished reading it on my own time a few days after it was handed out to us. Then I went through it again and again in my English class as students were methodically reading it aloud every day over a period of several weeks as required. It was necessary for me to continue reading through the book just to deflect boredom while classmates trudged through it one-by-one. Other students in the same situation simply fell asleep. Language arts classes often operate the same way to this day. Many teachers believe that every student should have to read aloud on a daily basis in order to improve their reading. One difficulty with this approach is that students who are poor readers are more conscious of their deficit in this area and end up hating literature because they are embarrassed to be targeted in front of their peers. It does little to promote an appreciation of good writing or storytelling. Another problem is that those students who are proficient readers become bored and often end up disliking the course. Then by extension, many also come to believe that literature itself is boring. On several occasions, this teacher asked me to take my turn only to discover that I had no idea what page the class was on. She probably assumed I was simply disinterested. It is true that I wasn't paying attention, but that was simply to evade boredom by reading the text over and over. The story itself was far more interesting than listening to my fellow classmates struggle just to read it. Like watching a film more than once, you pick up extra little things you may not have noticed or quickly forgot during the first read. You remember more dialogue and detect subtle clues about upcoming events more readily. In the process, I had learned much more than my teacher thought. Fortunately during this particular course, I had the opportunity to prove it with the final project. The handout for the assignment provided some suggestions such as defending or criticizing the actions of various characters, discussing the power of symbols in the novel, or regurgitating some other information disseminated through the lecture/discussion process – typical language arts procedure. There may have been a total of four or five specific, sanctioned ideas, but it was the final, surprisingly flexible offer at the end that appealed to me: "…or develop a presentation idea of your own."

I thought about this for some time and came up with a few ideas, but in the end I relied on my increased knowledge of now-familiar passages as I had read through it several times over the two months or so we spent on the book. On the day I was expected to do my presentation, I walked up to the podium without a paper in hand and introduced myself as Ralph, one of the main characters in the book. I proceeded to tell 'my story' in great detail and described my thoughts and feelings about the progression of events and the loss of humanity to savagery. At the end of this discourse, I even took questions from classmates about 'my experience' of barely escaping alive. The duly surprised teacher gave me an 'A' grade for that presentation, but I'm sure she never realized that my seeming lack of interest in her class had nothing to do with my interest in literature. I was often chided for not paying attention, but the teacher never asked me why or took any real interest in any of her students other than to impose her lesson plans – one size fits all – or to engage in disciplinary efforts against any student whom

System vs. Culture

she believed had committed one of many possible transgressions. She never found out that reading was actually a passion of mine or that I had purchased and read other books like Shakespeare's *Othello* or *Antony and Cleopatra* on my own. I bought these plays (which were not being taught in class) with allowance money simply because I had enjoyed the bard's *Julius Caesar* which had been introduced to us that same year. It would not have mattered anyway, at least as far as my grade in her class was concerned. I was not being graded for any love or appreciation of literature that I might have privately. My grade depended on how well I followed the daily lesson plan. In other words, I was being graded for jumping through the specific hoops she had arranged for the class as a whole to jump through within the time frame of the school day in which her class occurred on the schedule. Just like every other student in that class, I was being evaluated for how well I accepted schooling without any knowledge or consideration of what I knew or was learning. Regardless of the fact that I knew Golding's book as well as anyone and probably enjoyed and appreciated Shakespeare more than any other student in the whole school, at year's end, I was awarded a grade of 64 percent.

Almost seven months later, I dropped out of high school. It had been planned for weeks. My sixteenth birthday happened to be the first day back to school after the Christmas holidays. I arrived before the first morning bell rang, emptied my locker and proceeded to the main office. The assistant principal was behind the counter and overheard me telling the secretary that I was handing in my textbooks because I was quitting school. He must have been confused on a few counts: First, it is possible that he may have known my name because of recent absenteeism, but he had only spoken to me once or twice the whole time I had attended that school and likely did not remember me. I was not someone who registered on his radar with any regularity. Second, it was probably unusual for a student to be responsible enough to come into the school and formally resign rather than just avoid coming to school, especially after weeks of excessive absenteeism. Except for absenteeism, there was no indication that leaving school might have been on my mind. Third, my hand-ins included textbooks for French, German and Latin. What struggling student would have been found in a trio of elective classes like that?

The assistant principal asked me to wait in his office while he looked through my file. Within a few minutes, he came in with file in hand, sat down and proceeded to try and convince me that I was making a mistake. I was obviously a capable student and my grades were generally decent until I started skipping school and missing due dates and tests that semester. He wanted to know what I planned to do instead. I laid out my plans with confidence stating that I intended to work full-time and had already arranged full-time hours at the job I had held for eight months. It wasn't a great job but I didn't expect to be there forever. He gave me the expected lecture that I was not living up to my potential and that I could be finished high school in less than two years. Why would anyone consider throwing away his future by turning his back on education? What made me think I would ever find a better job than the one I had now? His admonitions fell on deaf ears. I had made my decision and walked out of that school never to return.

Although it would be almost ten years before I even heard of philosopher and social critic Ivan Illich, I soon learned his dictum that "Most learning is not the result of instruction. It is rather the result of unhampered participation in a meaningful setting." [1] There were many meaningful settings to be explored. I soon moved out of my parents' house preferring to share apartments with friends or living in rooms on my own. Living with friends, acquaintances and even strangers met through newspaper rental ads took some getting used to. Not everyone shares the same ethics about any of a number of things – like doing dishes, keeping bathrooms clean, taking out garbage or paying bills on time. One begins to learn about making compromises and also knowing where one may not be willing to compromise. You learn about yourself. Living independently at an early age meant having to figure out my own transportation, making due with limited furniture and finding the resources to pursue the kinds of entertainment that were important to me. Reading always remained important to me but I can't deny that other forms of entertainment and lifestyle were not necessarily as positive a part of my life at the time. Nonetheless, it was all a grand learning experience. I worked in the fast food industry making burgers, chicken and pizza. I painted houses, factories and commercial buildings. I worked for others and organized painting jobs to do on my own. The transition from the world of school to the world of work also meant that I drifted away from old friends who were still in school to new friends who also worked full-time. The real difference between these two worlds was that in school it was possible for many to simply be passive participants, but in the so-called "real world," as many adults called it, one had to be an active participant in order to progress, not merely survive. In this real world, so to speak, I had to pay attention to the kinds of interactions I would have with people who might be my boss or coworker. Rash decisions to quit jobs provoked greater thought about doing the same thing in a similar situation the next time. Many more decisions and actions led to greater evaluation and analysis about which direction was better than another. This was how I learned to pick my battles and when to fight them if need be. It also led to more thoughtful planning and a profound realization about life in general: freedom and responsibility were closely tied together.

Responsibility sometimes requires a little more than just verbal admonishment. I managed to buy a car when I was seventeen, but I had much to learn about taking care of it. Unlike many of my friends growing up, I had little interest in cars or things mechanical. Consequently, even simple maintenance procedures like changing the oil rarely happened with any regularity. I sure loved driving that car and traveled hundreds of miles on a whim either by myself or with friends. It allowed me to go into Toronto and become familiar with its urban sprawl providing access to more than what was available back in Oshawa. I also traveled to Ottawa and even New York. The car gave me an increased sense of freedom, but it wasn't going to last. Within a year, various mechanical problems began to arise. This cost me more and more money as I had no idea how to perform even the simplest maintenance tasks. That put a strain on my finances and I found it difficult even to maintain my insurance. Nonetheless, I continued to drive that car into the ground until finally, during a bout of freezing rain one January afternoon, I had an accident that totaled it. I was lucky not to lose my life. Since I had not paid my insurance premium for some time, that meant paying for a car I no longer had. It was a tough lesson for sure. More than two years would pass before I could even consider buying another one.

Without a car, exploration and discovery were going to require another mode of transportation. Over a period of several years, I hitchhiked approximately 22,000 kilometers across Canada and lived in many places in various provinces. I picked fruit, worked as a stock boy, found private jobs painting, learned fine cooking in an upscale restaurant and how to operate a forklift and other machinery in a lighting factory. When a friend offered to have an accountant teach me to keep a ledger so I could work as a night auditor in a Toronto hotel he managed, I took the opportunity. And when I thought it would be fun to work as a waiter because it offered me flexible hours and a constant income of fast cash, I talked my way into a position at a busy restaurant in downtown Toronto's Eaton Centre, despite the fact I had never even worked as a busboy before.

Throughout all of this, I maintained my passion for reading and was slowly developing a small library of books. I went through a period of reading several classics. Titles I enjoyed included Homer's Iliad and Odyssey, Ovid's Metamorphosis, Cicero's Letters to Atticus, Collections of Japanese literature by various writers known and unknown, Plato's Republic, Tolstoy's Anna Karenina, Dostoyevsky's The Brothers Karamazov, Kafka's The Trial, Sartre's The Age of Reason as well as writings by other philosophers and classical writers like Aristotle and Herodotus. By reading and collecting biographies, I came to know more about scientific figures like Newton, Darwin, Einstein and Edison as well, yet most of what I learned about science itself came from more popular sources like Scientific American or Popular Science magazines. I also studied the Bible and delved into both Hebrew and Classical Greek, the languages utilized to write the Bible. I had a collection of six texts called Alford's Greek Testament which prompted me to try and translate some of the New Testament's Gospel of John from the original language. Over a period of months, I managed to translate a number of chapters, although probably quite poorly. I concede that they would not have had any chance of being taken seriously by anyone who really did study Classical Greek professionally, but it was an interesting undertaking I have never regretted. Even as an agnostic, I believe it is essential to have a good understanding of the Bible in order to better comprehend Western culture and cultural references. The translation project also helped to perseverate an interest in languages I had developed earlier while still at high school.

In 1982, I got the idea that I wanted to learn how to speak French. Although I had taken French in school for over four years and knew how to conjugate verbs, there had never really been any opportunity to learn the language conversationally. I realized how poorly I was able to communicate in that language while working at the hotel. For months we had a contract with the government to house many of the so-called "Boat People" who were arriving in Canada as refugees from Southeast Asia. They spoke French as a second language and it would have made communication a lot easier if some of us English Canadians had known French as well. It was the first time I really felt that I had some kind of obligation as a Canadian to know both of the country's official languages. So I decided to move to Montreal.

It would take a lot more to convince an employer to hire me as a waiter in Montreal than it had been in Toronto, even when that employer was an affiliate of the restaurant where I worked at the Eaton Centre in Toronto. While waiting for my interview in the days after arriving in the city, I spent a lot of time sitting in Westmount Library in west-end Montreal with the French version of that menu and a French-English dictionary. There I sat for days, hours at a time, translating and memorizing every possible phrase I would need to know as a waiter based on my experience in English Canada. When my potential employer finally interviewed and then tested me, I fell painfully short. The manager admired my determination but turned me down. It wasn't a good idea for a downtown Montreal restaurant to hire a waiter who couldn't speak any French in Premier Rene Levesque's Quebec. Although she offered me another chance in a few months if I could improve on my French, I'm sure she never expected to see me again.

Knowing I could not live in Montreal without contacts or language, and resolved not to return to Toronto, I decided to hitchhike one last time across the country. Within a week, I was in Calgary where I found a job the first day I arrived, despite then Mayor Ralph Klein's recent admonishment to "eastern bums and creeps" [2] to stay out of his city. As fate would have it, I met two French girls from Rimouski, Quebec. They had come to Calgary for the summer to learn how to speak English. Linda and Denise needed someone to share their apartment expense and so I took advantage of another excellent opportunity. Within days, a French-English dictionary we shared looked a decade old. We had lots of laughs and all three of us were well on our way to achieving our summer language objectives. I hitchhiked back to Montreal at the end of August and promptly walked into the same busy downtown restaurant at Les Terrasses to speak to the manager. She was quite surprised to see me return and to hear of my summer adventures. This time she hired me and I ended up living in Montreal for almost seven years.

A McGill University student used to work at Les Terrasses part-time. Bill and I often carried on interesting intellectual conversations during work that would pick up and leave off all night as we entered and exited the waiter's station in between serving tables. He often commented at how surprising it was to meet a high school dropout so well-read and began badgering me about going back to school. I defended my position by declaring that I had absolutely learned much more outside of school than I had ever learned "on the inside." He acknowledged that I knew much more than a high school diploma could ever certify me for, but asked what I was going to do in the future without a formal education. This comment was suspiciously similar to one presented to me by the vice principal on the day I quit school many years earlier, but somehow it resonated a little longer. It's funny how someone's perspective changes between the ages of sixteen and twenty-five. I acknowledged that as a dropout my choices were limited, but I steadfastly declared that I had no intention of going back to complete high school. He kept badgering me and finally suggested that I apply to McGill University directly as a mature student. This idea seemed ludicrous to me. McGill is one of the most reputable universities in Canada. Formally speaking, I was only a dropout.

This seemed to be a strategic opportunity to end the badgering. I suggested that Bill bring me an application to fill out. Then when I was formally turned down by the university as I surely expected I would be, he would have to cease all harassment about going back to school forever more. Bill agreed and brought me an application the next time he was scheduled to work. He insisted that I make a written request for an interview at the bottom of the application. This seemed a little bold as well as ludicrous, but it was a harmless suggestion. Once an admissions official read that I had only completed grade ten, it was inevitable that a form letter would be sent to my address regretfully informing me that they could not accept me at this time. I was most profoundly surprised when a letter did arrive at my address, but it didn't turn me down outright. I was actually offered an interview.

System vs. Culture

Right up to that appointment I was skeptical enough about my chances to consider not going to the interview at all. At best, I might be offered a conditional acceptance if I took make-up courses to prove basic skills, but I fully expected to be turned down and embarrassed by the thought that I had actually believed it was possible. When I first sat down in the interviewer's office, he asked me how I came to my decision to apply to McGill. Already feeling foolish, I proceeded to tell him that I didn't have grand illusions about the possibility of going to his school, but that it was a means of closing an argument that had been going on for some time. He asked me what kinds of things I was into. When my response focused on two activities -- listening to music and reading books, he asked what book I was reading right now. I answered that I had a few going but that I was currently into Friedrich Nietzsche and Hermann Hesse, both German authors. Although he claimed never to have read any of philosopher Nietzsche's works, he was familiar with at least some of Hesse's novels. He was curious to know "which one I had read." I told him I was reading Magister Ludi: The Glass Bead Game at the time, but I had read most of Hesse's work. It was hard to tell whether he was surprised or not or whether he believed me at all, but he asked me which one was my favorite. As it turned out, he had also read Narziss and Goldmund and enjoyed it immensely. I soon felt less nervous and inferior and opened up. We got along quite well and conversed for some time about specific scenes in the plot and the contrast between the thinker and the artist as expressed in the personalities and lives of the two main characters. Just as I was about to walk out the door at the end of the interview, he told me that he would make sure I received an acceptance letter in the mail within the next two weeks, but advised me to maintain a good GPA if I accepted the offer. I thanked him and left dumbfounded at what I had just heard.

That acceptance letter really did come in the mail within a couple of weeks and that changed my life – not because it was an opportunity to get "back on track" as many would have viewed it, but because it was an opportunity for a new challenge and adventure on a grand scale. It wasn't a matter of going back to school to get a diploma to get a job. It was a chance to achieve a few more immediate objectives: to major in English for the purpose of improving my writing skills; to explore teaching methodology as a means of improving how I share my ideas; and to explore new areas of interest through the use of elective classes. I immersed myself in this experience. Of course I still had to take care of myself and maintain an apartment, buy groceries and clothes as well as books and other materials. This meant that I had to juggle shifts at the restaurant to accommodate my studies, but it all became part of the challenge.

In addition to my main course of study, I took classes in anthropology, psychology, Anglo-Saxon and film, but I developed a particular interest in linguistics and northern studies. Most of my electives were in these two areas. At the end of three years, I had taken every northern studies course available at McGill, several classes in linguistics including a graduate course I was given permission to take, and completed my Bachelor's degree in education, majoring in English. Even before graduation, I sought out teaching positions in the far north, but was only offered one in Labrador that did not suit my interest. So instead, I decided to go to graduate school in the area of education psychology. The three years I had already spent at McGill seemed to fly by and perhaps I wasn't ready to give it up just yet.

One of the first things I had to decide was whether to pursue a course of study that focused on experience through the internship process or to pursue a thesis-based diploma. I chose both. I did two year-long internships to help me decide what area of special education I might want to focus on as an area of expertise. In the first year-long practicum, I worked at a school with kids who had various disabilities including autism, Asperger's syndrome, Down's syndrome and various physical disabilities. In the second, I worked exclusively with kids who exhibited "emotional disturbances." This seemed to be right up my alley as I had always considered myself a little bit different and probably even a little disturbed to boot.

Outside of school, I made some changes as well. I had lost interest in working as a waiter, even though the flexible hours and quick cash were more conducive to my university lifestyle. I decided to pursue yet another area of interest that I had first acquired a few years earlier. When I walked into Theo Lubber's studio in the Monkland district of Montreal during the last year of my Bachelors program, I had little experience in stained glass. Although I spent my childhood Sunday mornings admiring every detail of various windows in church, it wasn't until I lived in Toronto and met a young woman who owned a nice piece of antique stained glass that I realized this beautiful art form could also be secular in nature. That piqued my interest and I remembered it when I sought out a new line of work. Theo was in the process of painting while he interviewed me and rarely even looked away from his work the whole time we spoke. He was not particularly impressed by my reasons for wanting employment in his studio, but he did take an interest in what I was doing at McGill. For whatever reason, he hired me. The pay was difficult to live on, but I had an opportunity to learn from someone I later discovered was probably the best craftsman at his trade in North America. He had made windows for many prestigious cathedrals, churches, libraries, mausoleums, private collections and Kennedy Airport in New York. During my three years working with him, we even received an old panel from Switzerland to be repaired. This was surprising to me because Europe is where the craft originated and flourished for hundreds of years. One would have thought that the window could have been repaired across "the pond." Theo was self-educated in much more than stained glass himself and he seemed to attract other employees with varied intellectual interests. Without a doubt, some of the most stimulating conversations I ever had in my life were in that stained glass studio, and so I stayed there for three years until I finished my university studies and left Montreal.

During the time I was working on my Master's degree in education psychology and working in between at the studio, I also got married. Making this decision altered another decision —going north to teach. My new wife did not want to live in an isolated community and preferred to live in a major city like Montreal where she grew up. Just around the time I completed my Master's degree, my brother-in-law announced that he was moving to California as he had taken a position with a high tech company in Temecula. Once there, he and his wife sent a job listing clip from the Los Angeles Times highlighting several special education positions that I might be interested in. Although I had never considered moving to the United States, my wife encouraged me to send out a few resumes. She had always wanted to live in a warmer climate and this seemed like a good opportunity. I was contacted within days and offered a position at a unique school, which I accepted on a whim.

Despite the excellent learning experience that McGill afforded me, nothing I learned there could have prepared me for Hathaway. My second practicum at Hugessen Hall School associated with McGill gave me my first exposure to working with students labeled emotionally disturbed. That was valuable but my experience in Los Angeles was absolutely enlightening. It was where I first realized that many rules did not apply and traditional methods of teaching were inadequate.

Hathaway Children and Family Services was a unique place to begin my professional career as a teacher. The school where I would work for seven years was part of a residential treatment campus for severely emotionally disturbed, abused and neglected children that provided classes from kindergarten to grade twelve. The students at Hathaway were referred by State departments of children and family services, probation and mental health. Our population of students were widely recognized as being the most difficult to work with in Los Angeles County. Many were hardcore gang members from the San Fernando Valley communities of Greater Los Angeles. The school itself was situated somewhat apart on a 300-acre ranch donated to Hathaway by the DeMille Foundation after famous American film director Cecil B. DeMille died in 1959. It was located in the San Gabriel Mountains just eight miles from the community of Lakeview Terrace where the Rodney King incident occurred and later sparked the Los Angeles riots. Although the San Fernando Valley area of Los Angeles was only a ten minute drive away, the ranch itself was in the Angeles National Forest. The schools (elementary and high school), student residences (known as cottages), and administrative buildings shared the land with a plethora of creatures. These included coyotes, various lizards and snakes, tarantulas, wolf spiders, foxes, bats and so on, all of which were sighted regularly by staff and students alike. Part of the responsibility of full-time "ranchers" was to make sure that no dangerous animals, especially rattlesnakes, remained on school grounds. When found, as they were quite often, they would be captured and relocated.

The students themselves were an interesting and assorted microcosm of Los Angeles itself. Although we had a few Asian students at Hathaway, most were Caucasian, African-American and Latino. Many were gang members, which is not a surprising fact since Los Angeles is home to 26,000 gang members divided into some 250 gangs. [5] The Crips and the Bloods are the dominant gang entities (made up of smaller gangs with different names associated with one or the other); members of both alliances existed at the school. This often caused tension amongst students from rival gangs and was a significant and serious threat to overall safety concerns. The "ranchers," were trained in social work and like all staff at Hathaway, had current P.A.R.T. (Professional Assault Response Training). They would sometimes have to intervene using such techniques. This was a last resort in conflicts between students that often began as the result of gang rivalry.

Life and work at Hathaway could certainly not be described as tense or difficult most of the time however. In many ways, staff and students were a big family as there were rarely more than 125 students being served from kindergarten through grade 12 at any given time. Many students were there for years and developed excellent rapports with many staff who were both dedicated and nurturing. The personal histories of many of the students were sad and sometimes horrific. Students had to have individualized educational programs (IEPs), with a designation of severely emotionally disturbed to qualify for services at Hathaway. That was interpreted by some as good reason to reconsider a position there, especially first-year educators, but I loved that place. In my 25-plus years of working with so-called "difficult" students, I have never enjoyed a teaching experience as much as I enjoyed working there.

It was often problematic for Hathaway to recruit teachers capable of effectively working with students labeled "emotionally disturbed." These students often exhibited multiple issues. Some teachers worked at Hathaway for several years, but it was not uncommon for new hires to last only one day, a few days or a couple of weeks. Long-time residential and administrative staff sometimes joked about how common it was to see newly hired teachers' smoke rise up behind their vehicles as they sped back down the hill. Over the years, there were many individuals who decided that this line of teaching was not for them.

There were also times when Hathaway had to make decisions to dismiss new hires within similar time frames. Since most teachers did not consider a career working with children who were considered "difficult," job openings were often filled by teachers who didn't find jobs they wanted and felt they had to settle for an interim job until their prospects looked brighter. These same teachers would be hired (reluctantly), with the expectation that they had to complete other university courses as well as Hathaway inservices to meet requirements for working with such a population of students. Sometimes teachers who fell into this category did not work out well. The extra courses they had to take did little to help them meet some of the challenges that inevitably arise from working with a population of students that often exhibited many more complex behaviours than so-called "normal" populations of students. A relatively high percentage of these teachers would find such challenges overwhelming. Sometimes they reacted in ways that were not conducive to a healthy classroom environment either for themselves or their students and Hathaway's administration was compelled to replace them.

Shortly after being hired by Mickey Shriner, the original teacher and then principal at the school on DeMille's ranch, I learned that I was the only teacher there to have a Master's degree in Special Education at the time. California and other southwestern states had a shortage of educators with graduate degrees in education psychology/special education. That explained the quick response to the few resumes I mailed off to schools and districts in Los Angeles County. Mickey had a good impression of McGill University and that may have been the reason Hathaway was interested in sponsoring a working visa for the United States on my behalf. Neither Mickey nor I knew the bureaucratic mire we would have to wade through. Hathaway had to prove that they could not find an American with equal or better qualifications to fill the teaching position they were offering me. Despite the paperwork and extensive documentation for Hathaway and me, required background checks and "getting in line" with numerous other applicants for American working visas, mine came through in three-and-a-half months.

Unlike the United States Government in this particular situation, I don't believe that one's university education alone is enough to qualify someone over and above someone else who might have a lesser degree but extensive experience for a position in a classroom like the one I was hired to teach at Hathaway. One can jump through whatever hoops might be required to achieve the desired qualifying piece of paper, but that piece of paper cannot ensure success in a real classroom. Interestingly, my years of travel and experience when I was still considered just a high school dropout did much more to prepare me for my professional career than formal education ever could. During my youth I explored some interesting and somewhat alternative paths. I managed to meet and befriend people from many walks in life. Many of these could be considered people on the fringes of society, but many others would fit into the everyday, normal (whatever that means) parameters of society. All in all, my life experience was "well-rounded" so-to-speak and I consider myself fortunate to have met most of them. It taught me to be open-minded and accepting of people who did not necessarily fit the mold of mainstream society. All were colourful in their own ways and taught me that no matter what niche in life one occupies, most people are basically the same. They just want to live a valid, meaningful lifestyle. They have definite ideas about what is right and wrong although many of their ideas might differ from one another. They value friendships and making positive connections with others. Most were very intelligent in individual ways and that provided me with my most poignant experiences in understanding multiple intelligences.

The theory of multiple intelligences was first proposed in 1983 by Howard Gardner.[3] He argued that intelligence as it was traditionally defined did not effectively describe the wide range of cognitive abilities that humans exhibit. The currently accepted list of intelligences includes: spatial; linguistic; logical-mathematical; bodily-kinesthetic; musical; interpersonal; intrapersonal; naturalistic and existential.[4] One type of intelligence that Gardner did not discuss and is not on any list of accepted intelligences – that of a sense of humour – is something that I have found many students to possess in unique variations. It is a type of intelligence that has turned out to be a gold mine to tap into when working with youth at risk. It can be great for diffusing potential situations and for highlighting issues that do not warrant taking seriously. In order to produce or comprehend humour, it often takes significant intelligence because one must grasp subtle nuances and contradictions in what is being stated, especially in wit and sarcasm. Topical humor requires intelligence and retention of information in order to be successful, but in a classroom situation, that can be built upon like any other body of knowledge. In small classes like special education settings where students, teacher and aide often become surrogate families and get to know one another especially well, humour can be an incredibly powerful tool for attaining camaraderie and maintaining focus among the members of the group.

All classes at Hathaway were self-contained with a teacher and one teacher's aide. Being self-contained meant that students stayed in the same classroom all day with a teacher who was responsible for teaching them every academic subject. So even though my undergraduate degree was in English and my forté was history, I had to teach many other subjects including Physical, Life and Earth sciences, various electives and even that most dreaded of all subjects: math – basic, algebra and geometry. In retrospect, this was somewhat humourous as well as downright ironic since I never thought that after high school I would ever have to be so involved in math again. Making sure I always kept ahead of my students, I borrowed texts from school and studied all of those subjects I felt less confident about until I became proficient. I came to realize that perhaps the best way to learn is to have to teach. Being assigned to a senior high school grade 11/12 split class meant having to cover twice as many subjects too, but it was exciting. I guess I ended up finishing high school after all.

Despite the hard work involved and the population of students to be served, everything went well. I had never been so engaged in a variety of learning experiences and I loved it. The challenge this presented became a major motivating factor and pushed me forward continuously. One of the best concepts I learned early on was that being creative and engaging students' interest yielded much better results than relying on punitive measures. At a school where keeping students in class was often the main objective, any ideas a teacher may have to engage them in actual learning was not only welcome, but almost revered. It didn't make sense to send students back to their cottage units for time outs for every little infraction of the rules. A lot of school rules never even made sense to me and so one of the first things I thought made a lot of sense was to keep it simple. I created just one rule in my classroom at Hathaway: No B.S.

As most people are aware, B.S. is an abbreviation with multiple meanings. The students certainly had a very specific idea of what it meant as it is a common English language expression. That was just fine with me as it served the intended purpose. Officially, I claimed the abbreviation stood for "No Bad Students." Its practical translation was as follows:

> If you aren't doing something that gets in the way of acquiring your education, then you aren't breaking the classroom rule; if you are doing something that gets in the way of acquiring your education, then that's B.S. The rule also applies if you are doing something that prevents

a classmate from acquiring their education. The rule only applies in this classroom.

It was simple; it was something they could understand and accept; and it was posted at the front of the class. Students were quick to point out that wearing a hat or chewing gum in class did not get in the way of acquiring their education and I agreed. A more challenging objection was the use of certain types of language within the classroom context. After discussing the matter with the students at length, we agreed that language like "Fuck you" would not be tolerated because it was focused against another individual. It was an expression of anger on the part of the user and the source of offense and possible hurt to the person the expression was spoken to or intended against. Since it could quite easily be a springboard for an escalation to violence as well, everything about using swearing to direct anger would get in the way of acquiring an education. Therefore it violated the B.S. rule. However, if a student was working on assignments, felt some frustration and uttered an expletive not usually tolerated within the classroom context, it could and would be overlooked. There has been plenty of evidence over the years to support the idea that cursing curtails anger by relieving stress. Every so often, studies [6] supporting this notion even earned mention in the mainstream media. Without an intended target based on anger, even "fuck" is just a word.

Once students realized they were able to participate in the evolution of guidelines that governed their classroom, they were much more likely to abide by them. The rapport between the students and I increased significantly because I listened to, and empowered them, and that in turn legitimized my opinions in their minds as well. Respect became mutual. The classroom environment, despite the fact it contained the oldest and most potentially disruptive students in the school, started to become a model of learning, innovation and mutual purpose.

At first this began very modestly. Behaviour issues were significantly decreased because of the personal rapport I was able to build with my students. With less behaviour issues, there was more time for learning. It usually began casually in the morning, but it always began right on time. As soon as the bell rung I would begin with a description of various current events being reported in the news for that day. It was a little like a Johnny

Carson monologue (for those who still remember Johnny), in the sense that I often made humorous comments to highlight points I thought were worth discussing. Stand-up comedian and social critic George Carlin has spoken about engaging his audience "in forward movement, from a familiar place to an unfamiliar place" using humour with the objective of teaching them something: "I have to do it with marvelous language or some other attention-getting element that transfixes them and moves them along to their destination…That gets away from the most formal definition of the word "teaching," but in a way that's what it is, laying it out for them in an amusing and entertaining way, taking them on an instructional tour. Because there's something you want them to know that they didn't know, or didn't know they knew when they sat down in their seats." [7]

Students would often ask questions during these newslogues and conversation would meander from one topic to the next. It was all worthwhile and students were made aware of events that happened locally, nationally and internationally. I often thought about the international stereotype that Americans knew little of occurrences outside their own country and was determined that would not include any of my students. Allowing them to interrupt with questions and voice their opinions about any topic brought up in the morning "newslogue" made for great discussion and the students were always kept up to date. These sessions lasted anywhere from 10 minutes to half-an-hour, depending on the level of interest in what was going on that day. It was fun for me too. I have always found news and politics interesting and routinely kept abreast of international events and issues. Canadian, American and British politics were of particular interest and came up in discussion often. As the students became more news-aware, they were more inclined to share their opinions and ask better questions. Even though most of the students lived at Hathaway, it was common for issues at the cottages to prevent them from coming to class on time. Yet most of the students wanted to be there for the morning newslogue and knew it would start promptly when the morning bell rang.

Another difference between how I conducted my classroom and how most other teachers managed theirs was that I never gave tests of any kind except compulsory State Exams that I had no control over. Tests only tell an examiner how a particular student performed at the time the test was taken and demonstrates little if anything that the student has actually learned.

The two facts that some students don't take tests seriously and others have increased anxiety about taking them are good reasons why test validity is questionable at any time. There are many other reasons for this but they will be explored later in more detail. To this day, I do not believe in the validity of most testing and think that learning should be organized around problems and questions, and then explored through projects. Most of the time I worked at Hathaway, activities in my classroom were almost always project-oriented and often integrated different subjects.

One particularly successful project that integrated most subjects my grade 11 and 12 students were taking came to be known as Planet 9. It lasted the entire school year. The premise for the project was that the students were going to be traveling to a distant planet for the purpose of colonizing it. Since each of them were going to be "in charge" of developing a specific geographical area once they arrived, they had to pick a team of twenty people whom they thought would be best suited to the mission. This required careful consideration. The students had to think about what kinds of skills their team members should have. In order to complete their "proposals" to NASA, they had to include documentation packages for each of their "applicants." They had to create fictitious individuals with detailed backgrounds and appropriate educational histories to support their qualifications for the job. This meant that the students were engaged in writing stories about their characters, creating at least three detailed resumes as samples of their team's qualifications, and writing recommendation letters for at least three of their team members.

We created a giant fictitious map of the land surfaces on Planet 9 (named after our classroom number). The map occupied most of an entire wall in the classroom. The continents and islands were given only outlines as the students themselves would later determine land formations on their territories. Once we "arrived on the planet," we pulled numbers from a hat to determine who would be responsible for each territory. We did not assign the entire map to the students who were in the class from the beginning of the year. That way we could accommodate any new students that might join us as the school year progressed.

Planet 9 became a wonderful vehicle for active-learning. It provided a scenario that the students accepted as their own to explore and build upon. Assignments were handed out both individually and to groups for various activities and products that often lasted the duration of a week or more to perform. Students would be given various projects that still covered material expected to be gleaned from textbooks. But instead of going to page 47 or 212 or 365 in a text on any given day, students were given problems to solve that ultimately encouraged them to seek the information they needed.

This was certainly preferable to sitting as a captive audience and being expected to show interest in dry facts without context. For example, in high school biology, students are expected to learn about genetics, heredity, ecosystems and plant anatomy. Imagine students working on the topic of molecules and cells. They could expect to sit in their seats and be asked questions like: Are cells alive? Why do you think this? Where are cells located in your body? Where do cells in your body get energy... and so on. At the end of any given unit in their text books, students could also expect to be given a unit test. This test would not expect them to know everything that was covered in class; it would only ask questions covering the main points of each lesson. Then students would only have to get anywhere from 50 to 60 percent to achieve a passing grade. If they manage to pass all of the exams by the minimum required, they will still pass the class – even though it is unlikely that two months after taking the class, they would remember much if anything at all. Even by the measurement that the testing process can afford, only a small percentage of information provided is actually gleaned. Furthermore, the information assembled is a collection of loosely-connected facts not particularly absorbed in class, but stuffed into short-term memory while studying for a test they will soon forget the contents of once it is written.

For the Planet 9 project, students were expected to provide taxonomies of plants found on their territories. After all, as chief colonizers, they had to know what resources their territories had for present and future use: raw materials for developing products or use in trade with other territories; assessing the value of what is available for medicines and other uses. Students were allowed to create entirely new plant forms if they wished, but their scientific description had to correspond with known classification systems and descriptions "here on earth." Students often created unique forms of trees, cacti, herbs and vegetables but these had to be described and classified as angiosperms, gymnosperms or whatever group they

System vs. Culture

might be classified as "on earth." The Planet 9 project happened before computers became part of classroom landscapes and so the students did not have Google to look up information. Hathaway had a very limited collection of books and so the main resources for looking up information came from encyclopedia or text books. By engaging in this project, students were using their text books as resources to look up information that would help them achieve their own objectives. They were also enabled to be creative by having to classify unique forms of their own making. Rather than just giving them dry information out of context, students now could understand the advantage of classification techniques for determining resources and other reasons. If students came up with questions that could not be answered by means within the classroom, they could make lists of what they needed to know. I would then draw on resources from off campus — local libraries, books I had at home, and the emerging computer resource that afforded online information through services like Prodigy or CompuServe before most people ever heard of the Internet. In this way, the students and I became a team in developing their territories and learning was collaborative. Assignments and projects were coordinated so that all of the concepts that might be covered in textbooks were actively discovered within the context of Planet 9. By the end of the year, they had developed governments, economies, trade agreements, explored ways of averting crime and poverty, created businesses, and negotiated peace treaties. The students employed various writing techniques to produce business contracts, resumes, speeches, histories, advertisements and even fictional stories that characterized the uniqueness of the lifestyles people might lead on their "new" territories. They named their lands, gave them flags and national animals, birds and emblems. They drew geographical and topographical maps and created works of art for numerous purposes. They had fun and learned about all of the things expected of students in regular high school classes. Perhaps the best outcomes of all were learning how to ask questions, how to collaborate, how to create and how to think for themselves.

I also learned valuable lessons from the Planet 9 project. One was that students learn best when they are engaged, active learners. "There is no way to help a learner to be disciplined, active, and thoroughly engaged unless he perceives a problem to be a problem or whatever is to-be-learned as worth learning, and unless he plays an active role in determining the process of solution." [8] Another lesson I learned was that a teacher is more effective when acting as a collaborative coordinator than as a traditional teacher. The traditional teacher usually asks questions and coordinates lesson plans to look for specific answers that are often unrelated and expected to be memorized; the collaborative coordinator or teacher/mentor guides the learning process through meaningful exploratory tasks that: a) have contextual meaning; b) allow the students to have original input and be creative; c) encourages the asking of meaningful questions; and d) affords the students a reason to search for and find more information. Interestingly, when I tried to look up research to support the idea of teacher-as-collaborative-coordinator, there was nothing to be found. Several articles discussed collaboration, but the collaboration intended and referred to was not teacher-student collaboration, it was teachers collaborating with other teachers to determine better ways of teaching learners – without learner input.

Perhaps the best opportunity for a teacher-student collaboration project came with the advent of computers making their way into schools. In 1991, this was, for the most part, still a future phenomenon. Most public schools did not have any computers in their buildings at all let alone for student use in individual classrooms. This was certainly true at Hathaway. At the time when some ideas were being bounced around about employability skills, the principal had asked the Board to purchase some typewriters to at least help some of the senior students gain marketable abilities. One of the organization's administrators raised the standard and suggested trying to get some computers. This was a tall order as individual computers were still retailed at two-thousand plus dollars per unit. Some months later after a concerted drive for funding the project, Hathaway was able to put together enough cash to purchase nine computers. These were to be placed in a single lab and a computer tutor was to be hired to come to Hathaway on a part-time basis. The idea was to teach basic word processing skills and to let students use a paint program called KidPix to become familiar with using a mouse and seeing what the computer could "do." The tutor had to be hired because none of the teachers on staff even owned a computer themselves; we had no idea how to use one let alone teach students how to use them. Despite this problem, there was no thought about how the tutor and the service she worked for would be paid beyond the first year.

System vs. Culture

Since I taught the senior class, my students were given first priority to learn word processing skills. At first I was apprehensive about the whole thing because of a personal experience a few years earlier. In the early 1980s at McGill University, one of my instructors decided to take his class to "the computer lab." Most students did not use the computer lab because it was there for students who took a course or were majoring in this new field of study. Few would have had any idea what to do with one if they had access to it anyway. Personal computers were still in their infancy and only had command line interfaces (That's where the user issues commands to the computer in the form of successive lines of specific text which can be recognized by the computer. The user must know the right syntax for it to work as well). There were no graphical user interfaces like the now familiar Windows or Mac platforms. When a person turned on a computer, he would see a small flashing cursor waiting for a command from the user. Most "users" in the class my professor took to the lab had no idea what "command" they would consider typing because they were unfamiliar with the possible uses of a computer. Computers were portrayed in the media as some advanced form of mechanical intelligence that could be used or abused to get instant answers to questions or control of resources – usually for some inane scheme like world domination – but that was the stuff of celluloid fantasy. In real life, computers were not very user-friendly and most people found them frustrating. This was also our experience. Our teacher wanted to introduce us to using these new machines, but his explanation was lacking and we had limited time in the lab. Few of us left with any real sense of a computer's usefulness or how to use one.

In another example, I had to take a course in microcomputers through UCLA in Los Angeles as part of my qualification requirements to acquire a permanent teaching license in the State of California. The course took place over four Saturdays and much of what we learned involved being able to "load" and run a program called 'The Oregon Trail' on Apple II computers. Again, the computers only had command-line interfaces, even though both Mac and Windows had early graphic user interfaces available on the market by that time. The students in that class were happy when the four weeks were up and their frustrations were over. I am sure that very few, if any, students left that course with the intention of buying a personal computer. Never in my wildest dreams could I have imagined at that time what an impact computers were about to have on me and my career let alone society at large.

My experience at Hathaway did motivate me to buy a personal computer. It was top of the line at the time: a 286 computer with Intel processor and a 40 MB hard drive (not enough space to hold one song in mp3 format these days and well before the gigabyte was developed); a 1200 baud modem (that's right: dial-up when it was state-of-the-art); two floppy drives — an 'a' and 'b' drive that supported both 5 ¼ inch floppies and 3.5 floppy disks; a graphic shell called GeoWorks that looked similar to early versions of Windows available for DOS-based IBM compatible machines; and finally, a dot-matrix printer with continuous-feed paper guided through the machine. Once you were finished printing, you had to cut the paper with your printing on it by hand along a perforated edge. Every page printed had to be separated in this way. This might seem low-tech by today's standards, but it was exciting at the time. All of a sudden, I was able to do things I had never done before — acquire information and communicate with others without watching television, speaking into a telephone or speaking to someone in person. I could also produce documents that could be saved electronically and unlike a typewriter, could be corrected easily as you went along. Back when I was at McGill and used a typewriter for all of my papers including a 100-plus page thesis for my Master's program, if I made an error on a particular page, I had to scrap it and start over again. This alone was a liberating advance in helpful document-producing technology that is easily taken for granted today.

When I bought that computer, I might just as well have caught a virus that infected me completely. I became obsessed with, and absorbed into, a new world of possibilities. I wanted to learn everything that could be learned about computing and related activities. Being mechanically-minded was never a personal attribute and to this day I can do little more than change a tire on my car. The world of computing was different. It required less hands-on tinkering and more problem-solving activity to correct issues, solve enigmas and meet challenges to progress. Along with a healthy dose of patience, most issues could be solved using software or rewriting lines of code in primary files like the autoexec.bat, config,sys or through batch files that would perform user-determined functions to execute customized commands. Within weeks I was buying and borrowing manuals, learning the ins and outs of established programs like WordPerfect, new programs like AutoCAD (still in version 2 back in 1991), and finally programming. Efforts at programming began by simply using GW-Basic, a command-line programming language that came with DOS operating systems before 4.0, but I eventually progressed to C++, a multi-paradigm, compiled programming language.

Within a short amount of time, my knowledge of computers and computing increased exponentially. This influenced my teaching practice considerably. The importance of ongoing learning to be a dynamic and effective teacher never became as poignant in my mindset about teaching as it did during that period of my life. There was an obvious and direct correlation between the energy I expended on learning and the energy I expended on teaching. When I became energized by what I had learned, it had to be expressed. In the computer class that my students attended four times a week, I became as proficient as the tutor who was hired to teach the students. She soon recognized this and so did Hathaway's administration. Within six months of learning how to turn a computer on, I was asked to take on supervision of the school's computer program. This was an enormous opportunity and I relished the thought of taking advantage of it.

There were two problems that I felt were important for the program as a whole. Since Hathaway had limited funds, it was important to figure out a way to be less reliant on a tutoring service to provide our computer instruction needs. There was no guarantee that any money would be available the following year as the entire organization was highly dependent on fund-raising ventures. The cost for this service was just under $33,000 for a couple of hours a day during the first year. Along with the cost of the original nine computers, this exhausted our entire funding resource without taking into account the cost of repairs, acquiring new software, updates, licenses, or the cost of continuing the program into the following 1991-1992 school year. The other problem was that only about 30 of Hathaway's 120 students were benefiting from the computer lab.

Although I had been mulling over various ideas for a few weeks, it wasn't until I went out to the desert for a hike with my brother-in-law one day that it all came together. I drove 140 miles out from Santa Clarita at the north end of Los Angeles to the Joshua National Monument in the Mohave Desert. It has since become a national park. We hiked to the top of a hill overlooking a sea of Joshua trees on the desert floor below. I have never seen a place that made me feel like I had gone back in time to a prehistoric location, but the Joshua Monument made me feel just like that. Surrounding hills were like mounds of rubble and there was no one else to be seen for miles around. It was a perfect place to have some peace and quiet from the hustle and bustle of the city. We sat there for some time watching two hawks circling above in search of something to eat. Eventually, my thoughts came out in conversation and we discussed the problems I wanted to solve. Then everything seemed to click and a plan took shape. On our way back down, I felt like an enlightened Moses coming down from a mountain in the wilderness. That night when I returned home, I wrote a proposal.

In the original rationale for the school's computer program, it was suggested that proficiency in computer-related skills would allow our most senior students to overcome many educational deficits caused by their neglected and disrupted personal and educational history. The ultimate goal at that time was to provide them with the opportunity and resources to rejoin the community with marketable entry level job skills. The proposal I put forth had much broader objectives. The quotes are taken directly from the original proposal and were as follows:

1. "To introduce the students to well-established and newly developed programs which are widely used in the business, industrial and artistic communities."

2. "To facilitate learning by introducing programs which make the useful operation of computers and various software easier for all." This was a specific reference to purchasing Microsoft Windows software as an interface instead of the DOS command line. Windows was still years away from becoming an operating system and was itself still a DOS program. Its function was to provide a graphic user interface that would allow users to point and click with a mouse to initialize other programs resident on the computer rather than remember specific commands to execute specific functions.

3. "To utilize the computer room not only for objectives outlined in the original rationale and goals for the program, but also as a tool for enhancing the studies conducted in all of Hathaway's classrooms

in other subject areas." The idea was to acquire the Prodigy online service which at the time claimed to be the first online consumer service. It offered a graphical user interface which differentiated it from CompuServe, the first service available to consumers; therefore it would be easier for both staff and students to use. Although this was before the Internet became available, Prodigy did offer a wide range of networked services that included news, weather, some expert columns and communication between Prodigy subscribers.

4. "To maintain, upgrade and introduce new hardware and software into the program." It was pointed out that computer education is more prone to becoming obsolete faster than any other area of education simply because of the rapid developments in the field. There was little point in having a computer program if we were going to let it become obsolete. We wanted to emerge on the cutting edge of what was possible.

5. "To look ahead and maximize the computer program by assessing its value to Hathaway staff as well as students." This was a specific reference to offering staff inservices so that they could at least learn how to word process. Teachers were eventually going to be expected to conduct their own classes in the computer lab as we phased out our need for a tutoring service. It was also intended to consider the fact that support staff like the school's administration and secretaries could utilize computers for record-keeping that was less paper-dependent.

A specific schedule for phasing out the tutoring service was outlined in the proposal. I immediately took control and responsibility for teaching my own class and would provide in-service training for the rest of the staff both in groups and by classroom teams. The money that was saved initially gave us some room to move forward in very positive ways. Two thousand dollars of that saving would immediately be spent to buy a new computer (As already mentioned, the going price for individual computers was much higher in the early days of personal computing). The computer was to be purchased from a small business in Burbank that taught its clients how to build the machine from its component parts. Therefore, I spent just one Saturday learning how to build the computer Hathaway purchased. In terms of its potential, this provided an invaluable advantage. It would reduce the cost of acquiring more machines in the future because now Hathaway could buy components and we were capable of putting them together ourselves. Furthermore, this new knowledge could be used to repair machines at minimum cost as various issues arose. Within two years, every classroom had two computers. Each was equipped with a modem and a printer. All classrooms could also schedule the computer lab with the original nine computers for lessons where it was advantageous for each student to work on their own machine. Hathaway realized that there were more advantages to the program than outlined in the proposal as well. It became a highlight of this nonprofit school and a means for attracting more donations. It could now be argued quite successfully that any incoming funds and resources were being used efficiently, wisely and creatively.

Hathaway had a long tradition of being supported in various ways by elite figures and organizations in the entertainment industry. Perhaps most notably, actress Julie Andrews had donated much to the organization over the years and often supported a trip to Disneyland for our residential kids at Christmas time. Actor Hervé Villechaize, known best for his role as "Tatoo" on the television program, Fantasy Island, was also a member of our board of directors until shortly before his death in 1993. Other entertainers like actresses Drew Barrymore and Sara Gilbert came to shoot movies on our grounds. The DeMille Foundation offered ongoing support in many ways for years. Famous Hollywood heyday director Cecil B. DeMille left several film artifacts at his former ranch anyway. These included wagons and even the "Gates of Jerusalem" that were used in the original production of The Ten Commandments. At one point, I was asked to introduce and explain the direction of our computer program to Joey Travolta (actor, director, producer, writer and brother of John Travolta), Katey Sagal (actress known best for her role on Married with Children), and film legend John Voight within the space of a month. A couple years later, the computer program was also featured in the game handout of a professional football exhibition match between the Pittsburgh Steelers and Miami Dolphins to benefit Hathaway.

SYSTEM VS. CULTURE

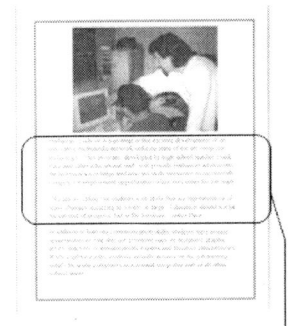

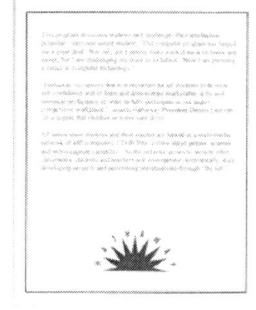

> Hathaway's school is a pioneer in the exciting development of an innovative multimedia network utilizing state of the art computer technology. The program, developed by high school teacher Frank Pace and other educational staff, will provide Hathaway adolescents the technical knowledge and relevant skills necessary to successfully compete for employment opportunities when they enter the job market.
>
> "We are providing our students with skills that are representative of many changes occurring in society at large. Education should not be at the tail end of progress, but at the forefront," states Pace.

Hathaway may have had reason to be excited about the program as a whole because it became a high profile attraction, but it was really the students and teaching staff that benefitted from the computer revolution within our school. More teachers began to buy computers for their home as they became comfortable with using them at work. From kindergarten on up, students had online access although it was still in the early days of mass information sharing; the Internet would not explode onto the scene in a big way until 1994. The students were excited by the changes they saw occurring around them and there was a general buzz around the ranch about the rapid advances being made. The students were also enthused about little side projects I worked on as I continued to explore the possibilities of what could be done. By the end of 1993, I had written a little program in GW Basic that simply showed Santa Claus riding his sleigh in the night sky above a snow-covered house. The animation was somewhat choppy as the program had to read each line of code one-by one and the computer itself was still a 486 with 4MB of RAM memory. The whole program took less than 15 seconds to run through the 4,000 plus lines of code that had to be created to make it work. The students were impressed and wanted to learn how to develop their own programs. It seemed like a good idea as it would give them a chance to develop even advanced math skills in a practical setting. I started off by teaching them the rudiments of command-line programming.

Programming in GW-Basic was very unforgiving in the sense that if a programmer made a "syntax" error when writing even the simplest code, the program would not function when it reached the command line where the error existed. We started off simply with an explanation of the screen resolution; it was important that the students understand the workspace environment they had to work in. The screen resolution was 1024 by 768 which meant that the number of pixels (points of light) displayed on a computer monitor from left to right was 1,024 per line. Since the number of pixels from top to bottom was 768, that meant that there were 786,432 individual points on the visible screen. In order to even create the simplest of drawings on the screen, one had to calculate the x and y coordinates of any object from starting points to ending points. For example, to draw a simple straight line somewhere in the middle of the screen, students would have to identify these points and state them correctly using the syntax inherent in the program. This would be as follows: Line (x,y)-(x,y) Line (400,200)-(500,200)

The first x and y represent the location of the coordinate where the line starts. The second x and y represent the location of the coordinate where the line ends. X and y are given specific values that specify location. The 400,200 refers to 400 pixels to the right and 200 pixels down as the starting point of the line. Since both y coordinates are the same, this means that the line will have a straight horizontal orientation that looks like this:

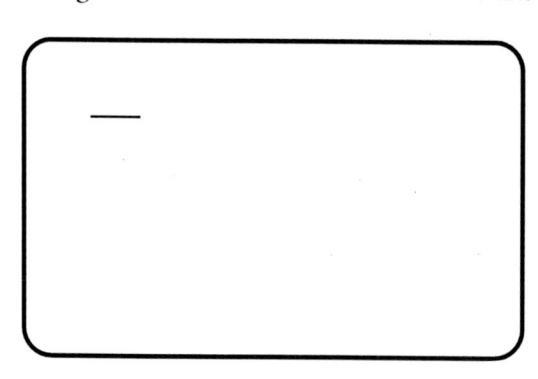

Beginning coordinates

Ending coordinates

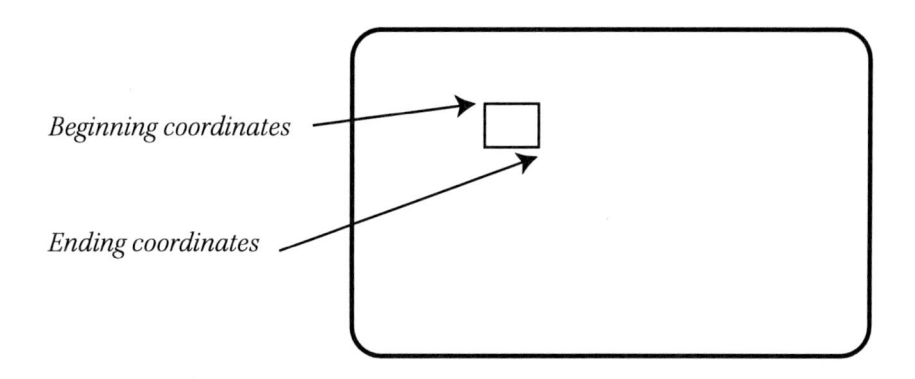

In order to create a box, the programmer would have to specify the beginning and ending coordinates (with the ending coordinates referring to the furthest point to the right and down), then add "b" for box to the syntax. Therefore, the command to create the little box on the screen would be as follows: line (400,200)-(500,300),b. The second y coordinate has to be changed from 200 to 300 to tell the computer that the height of the computer was 100 pixels. As the reader will begin to detect, command-line programming was labour-intensive, even when producing something as simple as a stationary rectangle on the computer screen.

All commands in a GW-Basic program had to be ordered according to the sequence the programmer intended the program to display actions. Therefore, every command had to be numbered. Protocol determined that line numbers be designated by tens. That way, if the programmer wanted to add something in between commands later, they could add up to nine more commands in between previously written ones. The command line numbers were given in order vertically and the commands written horizontally. If the programmer simply wrote a short program that drew three lines, it might look something like this:

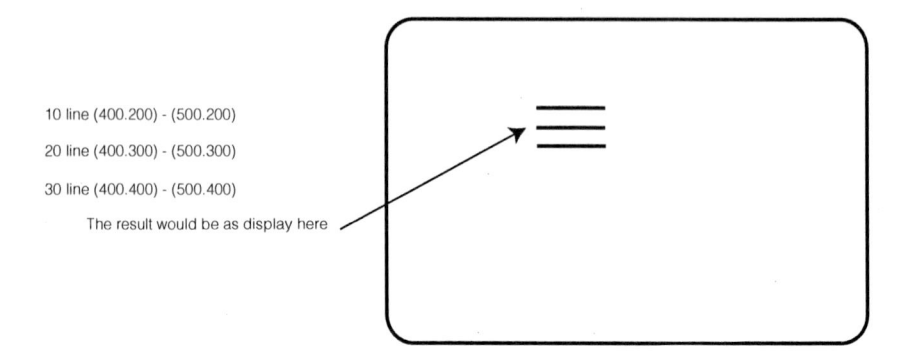

10 line (400.200) - (500.200)
20 line (400.300) - (500.300)
30 line (400.400) - (500.400)
The result would be as display here

Keep in mind that so far, all we have done is show how the potential programmer can draw three lines. They do not move, display text, or have any other function other than what has been described in perfectly-written syntax recognized by the programming language itself. In order to create anything more complex, more complicated programming is required. The moving Santa Claus program which took me over a month and more than 4,000 plus lines of code to write, had to specify the starting and ending coordinates of every identifiable point on the screen and determine their movement one pixel at a time. Just drawing the Santa and sleigh required hundreds of lines of code even before any movement could be calculated.

If the students wanted to use text, sound or create movement, we had to figure out as a team how to solve various problems. We had only a single manual to assist us and explanations were general. Specific uses we might conjure up required brainstorming. This was a great example of working as a collaborator with the students. I was only a couple of months ahead of them in learning this new skill but it was exciting for all of us. Within a short time, we learned quite a repertoire of commands and how to use them. Math skills expanded to include not just basic algebraic functions, but the students learned about algorithms, cosines, tangents and the uses of employing random variables. Most importantly, it made sense to them. They saw math in action and manipulated mathematical concepts to create actual products.

The students required some very advanced techniques to develop their ideas for even small programs. They came to understand that programming statements generally take one of three forms: assignments, loops and conditional branching. Most possible programs can be written using these constructs. Some of their ideas demanded that students consider what actions would be performed if other actions were made conditional. This required what is called an "if-then" statement. In this scenario, one action is performed if another action is activated or executed. The code would have to describe the conditions under which actions would occur. For example, it could be stated as a command that "if x = x+3, then print x." Only under that condition could x be printed. At other times, students might want to create sets of commands that are used together to perform specific functions. However, the specific functions could only occur under specific conditions. They had to create "goto" commands that would redirect the execution of certain commands from points in the program that may be before or after where the functions themselves were described in code. There were no modules as there are in newer programming languages. The students all learned how to use these and many other complex commands to create their own programs. They were also learning other real-life skills like thinking about both the big picture and the sequence of steps one must take to advance logically from one point to the next. These are practical tools that students can utilize throughout their lives in a) unique, unforeseen circumstances to solve problems of many kinds; and b) as the mechanism for life-long learning in the direction of their own choosing.

During the second semester that year, I challenged every student in my class to develop a program that could even be used by a grade one student. They were encouraged to think of unique ideas and to avoid having any two students doing the same kind of project. Since some grasped different concepts at different speeds or explored different concepts than others, the students were also encouraged to help one another when individuals encountered obstacles. Therefore, each student came up with a unique idea, but everyone helped one another. Not only did our skills advance more rapidly than expected through the collaborative process, but we developed a close bond that was tied in with our ongoing exploration and shared successes. It was very exciting.

All eleven of the students in that class came up with wonderful ideas. One student, Aaron, was particularly clever because he used his own musical knowledge to have his program play Led Zeppelin's song, Stairway to Heaven, as a reward for going through a sequence of questions and answers correctly. It was an impressive feat because the method for making sounds in GW-Basic was hard to use effectively. It required that the programmer specify first frequency, then duration of each individual sound to create notes. Remember that this required writing code using perfect syntax for each separate command in order for the program to be executed successfully. Once a sequence was described at length and without errors, loops could be created to repeat where necessary, but it was a tedious process that required at least as much editing, trial and error as it did forethought and brainstorming. People familiar with that song will know that it runs just over eight minutes long. It wasn't necessary to do so, but would have taken dozens of typed pages to print all the lines of code necessary to produce it.

For me, one of the most memorable projects that semester was created by a student named Monica. She had been at Hathaway for at least a year before she came to my class. Her previous teacher informed me that although Monica was 17 years old at the time, her academic functioning was at a grade three level. Furthermore, she rarely spoke or interacted with either staff or peers and other students tended to ignore her as well. She chose to sit at a desk that was nearer to my own desk than any other student. At first, she did not speak but certainly seemed to be interested in classroom discussions. Within a short period of time, Monica began initiating conversation with me when I was seated at my own desk about class discussions that just concluded. As she became more comfortable, she began participating during class discussions as well. Monica became more confident in her abilities and proved to be a highly intelligent individual. I remember our first meaningful conversation being about art, a topic she was passionate about. It soon became apparent that she was knowledgeable about current events, could formulate logical arguments about a wide range of topics, and was very enthusiastic about learning, especially when she was given opportunities to express her ideas. She produced a great deal of work in relation to the Planet 9 project and excelled in the computer programming project as well. She developed a program called "Sammy and the Fish" after a story her mother used to tell her when she was a small child. The program began by telling the story of Sammy on screens that had various coloured backgrounds. At the end of the story she programmed a question and answer sequence that allowed the user to provide responses. If a user response was incorrect, the program allowed that user another chance to answer the question. If a user response was correct, fireworks would erupt on the screen until the user pressed enter to continue. At the end, the program would also tally the user's score. To create the fireworks, Monica had to manipulate calculations using advanced concepts: sines, cosines and tangents, the three main functions in trigonometry. These calculations were then executed using loops that created the visual bursts in various colours. In the end, Sammy and the Fish had almost a thousand lines more code than my Santa Claus program.

During 1993 and 1994, I had an opportunity to participate in a minor role at a few sessions of the Industry Council for Technology in Learning (ICTL), a temporary advisory council to then California Governor Pete Best. The council met every three months. Representatives of many American and Canadian telecommunications and related corporations were involved. Meetings were usually held at interesting locations in various cities including NASA's Jet Propulsion Laboratory in Pasadena. A typical day at the council usually involved a main presentation, then separating into groups to discuss various issues, and regrouping to summarize objectives and conclusions. Most topics of discussion were centered on practical considerations that included the laying of fiber optic cable throughout the State to support digital networking, software tools for supporting new mediums of learning, and ideas about the establishment of a means to assist schools to implement technology. Such assistance was eventually given to schools in the form of the Digital High School education technology grant program, passed in 1997 by the California State Legislature.[10] Only once was I involved in a discussion of developments in the public school system. It was then that I discovered that my program at Hathaway was unique. It was the only one in the State of California that participants in the Governor's Council knew of at that time that had a classroom network with plans and a timetable to connect an entire high school. Granted, Hathaway only had a six classroom high school, but if those council members were correct, then Hathaway still achieved a major accomplishment.

As exciting and time-consuming as the computer program was, I also enjoyed being involved in other projects. During a two-year stint as Hathaway's curriculum coordinator, I was able to offer some new electives that included French and Future Studies as summer school courses available to all students in the high school. Working with other staff on teams to develop specific objectives also produced Hathaway's first school library and a multiculturalism awareness program. There was also one area where I benefitted from learning about something I had never known or cared much about: sports. Hathaway's gym teacher knew this and was determined to "help" me develop a sport awareness. He did this by insisting I assist him with coaching the school's football, basketball and baseball teams in their respective seasons and managed to convince me to do this for at least three years. All in all, I was very busy during my first seven years of teaching but that time was nothing short of magic. I really came to understand that the combination of learning and teaching was the balance that made my career as a teacher enjoyable as well as successful.

After achieving that level of involvement and success at Hathaway, I decided to leave in 1995 for a position with the La Cañada Unified School District. I was hired for a position working with special education students at the high school but also to participate in the district's technology plan which was just getting under way. La Cañada High School was located near Pasadena's Rose Bowl and interestingly, just down the street from the Jet Propulsion Laboratory, NASA's facility that I had visited just a year and a half earlier with the ICTL. La Cañada proved to be a completely different situation than Hathaway. "La Cañada High School has been named both a California Distinguished School and a National Blue Ribbon School. The U.S. Department of Education has recognized LCHS for "high achievement and exemplary programs", for rich extracurricular activities, and for strong community support." [11] The school has often been near the top of school rankings nationally and as recently as 2009, was ranked by U.S. News and World Report as the eighth best public high school in the United States and 80th best high school overall. [12],[13] Although it may have had a few gang "wannabes," La Cañada was an oasis of little to no gang activity in this upscale Los Angeles bedroom community just thirteen miles from the civic center downtown. Parental involvement was much higher than the average high school and the community as a whole had a surprisingly small town feel to it.

My involvement in technology development at this district was also extensive. My arrival there coincided with the beginning of LCUSD's computer-related advances and the Internet revolution that was spawned that year. As part of a three-man team, we developed the district's first computer network and websites for each of the district's five schools and district office. I wrote the initial web pages for each of these, a technology handbook, various individual program tutorials for use throughout the district, and participated on the grant-writing committee that brought California Digital High School Grant funding to the district. I was also involved in staff development conducting in-service training for district teachers and administrators on using WORD, EXCEL, ACCESS and PowerPoint in the earliest versions of Microsoft's Office suite as well as basic training in the use of the first laptops that the district issued to all teachers. These new skills were passed on to students as well. I taught a class on Writing HTML and Web Design to students as part of a special transition program. It was cutting-edge education at the time as we were one of the first schools in the State to have web pages or web design classes. In 2000, the year I left that school, the Institutes for the 21st Century honoured me with a special recognition and appreciation award for "5 years of service as a Visionary Mentor to the Students of La Cañada High School." (14)

A great deal of time and effort may have been spent working on district technology initiatives, but my heart and mind was still focused on working with the special education population at the school and within the SELPA (Special Education Local Plan Area - La Cañada belonged to the Foothill SELPA that included the adjoining communities of Burbank and Glendale. The SELPA coordinates with school districts and the County Office of Education to provide a continuum of programs and services for students with various disabilities). Most of my involvement at this level was in promoting transitional initiatives for students within these three school districts.

The La Cañada High School special education program was set apart from most of the rest of the school. An old automotive shop class had been converted to house three separate classrooms, one of which was being used for students with multiple disabilities. The other two classes were occupied by myself and a teacher named Charmene Vega. We both began working at La Cañada in 1995. We were responsible for most of the special education students at the high school level. Most students were mainstreamed into several regular classes and only came to "Room 610" to take courses in areas where they may have had diagnosed disabilities. As we gained a rapport with our students, a "610 culture" began to develop. In a small school district, word spread and eventually, some families who had children with disabilities even relocated into the district from Burbank or Glendale so that their children could be part of our program. Charmene and I became a great team over the years and we divided up responsibilities according to our personal strengths. Therefore, any students from either of our caseloads who came in for math or science went to Charmene's room; any students who came for English or history came to mine.

Some of our students were completely mainstreamed but it was common for them to come to 610 for assistance with their schoolwork, advice about how to proceed with various assignments, perhaps some intervention in their mainstream situations, or for transition planning. One area where we managed to excel was in preparing our students for college or university. A full year before La Cañada High School's regular students were expected to complete personal portfolios, our special education students were creating portfolios that would highlight personal accomplishments and academic achievement, but also feature resumes, awards, transcripts, future planning, thank-you cards or letters others may have given them, ideas the students themselves may have had for presenting information featuring a unique personal quality, and a cover letter. An added feature was that students were to create digital copies of their information and store them on disk. The students then had a physical portfolio displaying all of their self-promotional information in an organized presentation, but also a portable, endlessly-reproducible miniaturization of all their information that could easily be sent by snail mail or electronically to potential employers. In order to do this, the students had to scan all physical material, produce documentation in MS Word or Excel, and include any other digital information like photographs into organized, easily accessible programs. In many cases, html documents were created to produce indexes of their information and link them all together with a point and click. At the end of the 1999 school year, the 18 seniors on Charmene and my caseloads not only graduated, but went on to higher study. Of these 18 students, 16 went on to four year universities and 2 to two-year colleges. [15], [16]

This was something new, even for a school that was used to accolades for achievement and was a source of pride in the community. The culture of special education at the high school had truly changed. Students with

System vs. Culture

IEPs formerly preferred to keep their status quiet and resented being considered "SpEd." By the end of the 1990s, high school special education students referred to themselves as "610ers" and were proud of it. The last year that Charmene and I were there, the students even produced their own yearbook and called it "610 Fa Life."

However, various issues arose over the years and some were never resolved. Until Charmene and I came to this district, most special education students were not really expected or encouraged to prepare for the possibility of attending a university. Furthermore, these students were not even encouraged to participate in testing that ultimately determined the school's achievement ranking. This was not unusual at the time either. I truly felt that many schools and school districts paid only lip service to being concerned about all of their students because the truth of the matter was that it could make a difference to them if special education students were skewing their overall standardized testing scores downward. Expectations for many students with IEPs were not as high as they were for students without them.

By 1998, Charmene approached me about helping her establish a charter school in the district. She had already been in discussion with several parents who were enthusiastic about the possibility. At the time, we thought that it would better service the special education high school students in the district and provide a means for the high school to focus on what it did best – work with the regular students pursuing the high standards that included university preparation. We did not anticipate any objection or controversy.

The Charter School project became both interesting and controversial but evolved in various stages. During the first stage, Charmene and I did a considerable amount of research and met with several parents to see what kind of support there might be for such a project. As it turned out, once the idea was mentioned, most parents of our special education population were very enthusiastic about it and encouraged us to move forward on the initiative with their support. In the planning grant abstract outlined in our application to the California Department of Education, we stated that "our Educational Vision entails providing a curriculum that is both rigorous, relevant and empowers these adolescents to enter today's competitive job market. The use of technology will be the central thread linking all curricula with a strong emphasis on technical reading and writing. Mathematics, science and language arts will be presented in real world, practical applications, not theoretical or laboratory based." [17]

The National Education Association of the United States defines a charter school as "publicly funded elementary or secondary schools that have been freed from some of the rules, regulations, and statutes that apply to other public schools, in exchange for some type of accountability for producing certain results, which are set forth in each school's charter." [18] California charter school law was passed in 1992, [19] but the idea had yet to take off in the state by the late 1990s. Interestingly, early critics feared that charter schools would only lure the highest performing or most gifted students from the public school system. However, charter schools have tended to attract low income, minority, and low performing students. [20] Our school targeted a population somewhere in between as La Cañada is an affluent community, but we wanted to serve all at-risk students, not just the special education students we were already working with.

As mentioned above, we did not anticipate any objection to, or controversy about, the plan. Parents were enthusiastic and we imagined the school district would prefer to have the community's special education students benefit from highly individualized/specialized programs while it focused on achieving academic accolades without the possibility of testing scores being compromised. We were wrong. The LCUSD apparently saw the proposal of a charter school within their jurisdiction as a challenge to their perceived effectiveness working with special education populations. The district wanted to quell any suggestion that they were not effectively servicing that population. The charter school initiative became a major controversy because the school district had to be involved. California law stipulated that all funding for charter schools had to be funneled through the existing school district in the area where the school was to be established. In effect, any school district that might be willing to function as a "charter agency" for such a purpose had a say in how funding was spent, even though such funding was being directed toward a school that was technically independent. The fact that the LCUSD had to be involved in the creation of Charmene's charter school meant that they had the means to effectively block it if they chose to – and they did.

SYSTEM VS. CULTURE

At first, the district simply tried to ignore Charmene's request to present her proposal to the School Board. In April, 1999, when it was first presented to the district, they rejected the idea outright because they did not realize the extent of parent support. Therefore it was impossible to go ahead with a planning grant that would have been the first step toward the establishment of an actual charter school. To appease the many parents who became vocal about their decision during that long period of time, the district commissioned an at-risk task force chaired by the assistant superintendent. Very little to nothing was actually accomplished by the task force. As parental support gained momentum and the controversy hit the local newspapers, the district realized that we were not going to give up so easily. After fourteen months of stalling, the Board eventually had to cede some ground and allow for the plan's presentation. Even then, the assistant superintendent "emphasized that the proposal is for a planning grant, not for an actual school." [21] It became apparent that the school board members had no intention of allowing a charter school within their jurisdiction, regardless of how much public support there was for the initiative. This heated up for months and then it got both personal and ugly.

It is not my intention to relive the details of every incident that happened in relation to the charter school initiative at the time; suffice it to say that it profoundly affected my opinion of how even a reputable school district can lose sight of what is important. Eventually, Charmene and the LCUSD entered into legal conflict which was not settled for another two years. Frustration mounted high and the charter school never materialized in the La Cañada-Flintridge community. It was a pyrrhic victory for the school district as everyone lost. The students who were most affected were the 610ers. As events played themselves out in the newspapers and the district threatened to transfer me to another school, the students organized and marched themselves up the main street and over to the district office to protest. That too ended up in the newspapers, including the following observation by a La Cañada resident who witnessed the event:

> "Suzie Kelley, a resident of LCF who has a child with special needs, was driving down Foothill Boulevard last Friday morning when she saw the students walking up the street with their signs. She learned later why the

– 41 –

students were picketing and outraged by Pace's transfer. "I have never been vocal about this, but going to that Board meeting in May opened up my eyes. I was amazed that the Board and the school district aren't using that kind of passion (that Pace displayed at the meeting) to help the kids. This was the first clue (seeing the students with their signs) that the man who had spoken with such strength and passion at the meeting was being punished. They are going to move that man because he had the courage to try and bring about wonderful changes for the children. It's political. I am ashamed of the Board and the school district for displaying this kind of behavior," Kelley said." [22]

Others apparently shared the same opinion. Every Board member but one who supported Charmene's initiative, were voted out in the next election. The district superintendent, despite having been there for only a short term, was soon replaced as well. Nonetheless, I was demoralized by witnessing some of the personal attacks on Charmene that continued in the year after the controversy had climaxed. I had seen enough and decided to resign and move up to the high desert area of the Antelope Valley in north Los Angeles County, some 40 minutes away from inner city Los Angeles. Over the years, various students have kept in touch with both Charmene and I by email, invited us to their weddings, and shared pictures of how their families are doing. This is the real measure of any impact we may have had in that community. Although I regret that our charter school initiative never came to fruition and we weren't able to continue what we accomplished in the six years we worked in La Cañada, it is interesting to know that we haven't been forgotten either. It came to our attention that in one last newspaper article ten years after the events, it was mentioned in a story outlining that it happened 10, 20, 30, 40 years ago, that ten years ago, the students of La Cañada marched up Foothills Boulevard to protest their teacher's transfer. [23]

The Antelope Valley Union High School District was as different in comparison with La Cañada as La Cañada was from Hathaway. When I first applied for a position there, they were interested in hiring me for my technological experience and expertise, but they were also looking for someone who could successfully work with a severe population of students with behavioural issues. The special education position was the one I wanted and was then hired for. The previous teacher in my new position had little to no control over the classroom and there had been several daily interventions involving the school's security and on-site police just before I was assigned to the classroom at Lancaster High School. Most of the students placed there were involved heavily in gang activity.

At the time, Lancaster was one of the newest schools in the district. Before settling on the school's name which was the same as the city of Lancaster it was located in at the top of Los Angeles County, several names had been bandied about, including Frank Zappa High School. Frank Zappa, of course, is the famous composer, singer-songwriter, electric guitarist, record producer, and film director best known for his work with the Mothers of Invention in the late 1960s and early 1970s. In the 1950s, he had attended Antelope Valley High School where he also met his friend Don Van Vliet, better known as Captain Beefheart. It isn't much of a surprise that Lancaster High School was not named after Zappa however, as he was an ardent critic of mainstream education. [24]

The city of Lancaster itself, along with the neighboring community of Palmdale, was the hub of north Los Angeles County at the edge of the great Mohave Desert. It is actually about 70 miles northeast of the Los Angeles Civic Center and is separated from the Los Angeles Basin by the San Gabriel Mountains. The city had grown rapidly from a population of 37,000 residents at the time of incorporation in 1977 to almost 140,000 by the time I arrived in 2001. It was quite hot in the Antelope Valley with an average summer temperature of 95 degrees, although it often went into triple digit temperatures.[25] Lancaster and Palmdale were criminal microcosms of the metropolis just down the highway. Gang activity was common and the Antelope Valley community was becoming notorious for growing numbers of meth labs that were being discovered and busted in the area. This, of course, trickled down to the student population as well and drugs were a major concern at all of the schools in the district.

Security was always a matter of interest at the high school. There were usually six to eight full-time security staff and one or two full-time police officers assigned to the school at all times. Fights often broke out at lunch between rival gangs and sometimes riot police were called in en masse to secure the school. There have been times when even helicopters were employed to surveillance disruptive situations as they unfolded. Knives and guns were often carried by students and confiscated when found, but the district never moved to have metal detectors installed during the six years I worked for the AVUHSD (Antelope Valley Union High School District). Unfortunately, my P.A.R.T. (Preventative Assault Response Training) was necessary at times and there were occasions when knives and even a gun had to be confiscated during serious incidents that broke out between students in the classroom. It was at such times that I wondered how more Columbine situations did not erupt in the United States. There were many communities with crime rates way out of control. The rough nature of the population of students I worked with at Lancaster rivaled that of Hathaway, but it cannot be said that the administration or staff in general were as nurturing there as that which I had experienced at my first California employer. Indeed, administration was quick to try and expel students for even first infractions against rules. The volatility of the population along with safety concerns were important factors in this policy and many could argue the benefits of a hard-line approach. Nonetheless, I did not agree with many administrative actions against students assigned to my caseload and often found myself in conflict with the powers that be over what I considered to be overly punitive measures.

The truth of the matter was that almost all of the students I ever met while working there were students who could be reached one way or another if one spent the time to do so. I understood the concerns that many in the district and the community at large may have had about potential violence, but did not see the need for punitive measures to be the first line of defense. It all came down to the same thing I had already recognized for well over a decade: Positive human interaction would always trump punitive rules and harsh measures when trying to mold young individuals into responsible, contributing members of society.

The student population in my class ranged from grades 9 through 12 and so I often had a busy schedule juggling the various subjects each had to complete toward graduation requirements. This was no different than the situation I worked in at Hathaway except that it covered all four high school grades, not just grades 11 and 12. The first couple of weeks were challenging because it takes a little while to develop a rapport with students and establish a classroom culture that promotes real learning. It required a careful balance between many variables that were needed to change that classroom culture from what was effectively a free-for-all before I arrived, and the structured-but-student-friendly environment that I wanted to develop it into. I remember a rather shy grade nine student starting at Lancaster the same year I began working there. This student was not a gang member but had some distinctive personal issues that made him a significant "at risk" individual nonetheless. On the second day of school, his father came to express concerns about his son's placement in such a rough class. He stated that he would give me two weeks to straighten out what he understood was not my fault but still a difficult situation for his son to be placed into. If things did not work out to his satisfaction, he was prepared to withdraw his son from the school if necessary. Fortunately, I was able to gain that parent's confidence and ended up having his son in my class for his entire four-year high school career. That student graduated in 2005 and I still hear from him on and off to this day.

In order to turn things around, I returned to my old Hathaway policy of having a "No B.S." rule in the classroom. It definitely helped pave the way for less and less interventions to be required by administration. Within two weeks, my two classroom aides and I were enjoying a civil situation where students were learning and moving toward much more positive goals than inevitable arrest and incarceration. There were some students who had a penchant for getting into trouble, and I might add that trouble had a way of finding them as well. Students knew that I would "go to bat" for them when they needed support, and in return, their parents or guardians supported my efforts to run an unusual but successful classroom. It even became a drop-in center at lunch. Students who were not in the special education program could often be found there mingling with students and staff.

Getting involved by making real connections was an essential component for success with many of these students. Sometimes it was necessary to branch out and extend this connection outside of the five-day-a-week school schedule. For years, I arranged to take groups of students out to the desert or the mountains one weekend a month. It never ceased to astonish me how many students had lived in the Antelope Valley their whole lives but had never been outside of their "hoods" to see the beautiful wilderness areas close by. This was a real tragedy because the desert and mountain areas were wonderful places that the students really enjoyed when they were exposed to them. It afforded them some peace as well as beauty that stood out in stark contrast to their everyday lives on the streets. Many had no idea of life outside what they were familiar with. Their lives were ongoing challenges. Whole communities were affiliated with either the Crips or Bloods. These gangs often included not only the students, but their whole families – parents and sometimes grandparents too. These young people frequently got into trouble outside of school for tagging (doing graffiti on both public and private buildings, objects and spaces), theft, or various acts of violence. Except for the time I worked at La Cañada, my years working in the Los Angeles area were filled with sad stories. Many students ended up being incarcerated for both short and long periods of time. Others acquired injuries from stabbing or gunshot wounds and some even died from rival gang activity or altercations with the police. Some girls ended up in prostitution rings – some of which were local but others that required traveling to Las Vegas on weekends to be "working girls." It often amazed me that some of these students came to school at all.

One thing that needs to be stated again and again is that most of these kids were good kids in tough circumstances. Unlike what many people might think, it was possible to establish a rapport with them, gain their trust and trust them as well. They understood and upheld codes of honour, practiced loyalty, and looked out for younger siblings. One student I had was often targeted by administration for even minor infractions because they wanted him out of their school. He was a known gang member, but he came to school despite such harassment when he could and certainly tried his best. This young man was barely literate. He missed many classes because his mother was a crack addict who often left her children at home unattended. This student often stayed home because he was determined to make sure his youngest sister was taken care of. That was a familiar situation for many of these kids. They were caught in a world where they were still children themselves but expected to be adults. They were caught in a world where they grew up in, and under the influence of, crime-ridden neighbourhoods but expected to look and act like members of picture-perfect families. They were caught in a world where they were expected to be enthusiastic about school when in reality, many of them had more important things to worry about. And they were often caught in a world where loyalty to family, friends and fellow gang members was paramount, even when each of these fell short in providing the basic means that would help these young people become successful. Many times these students were quite simply and literally, hungry and tired. It should be no surprise that the only support some of these young people ever felt they had were the gangs they were affiliated with, but such associations estranged them from the very mainstream supports that are supposed to be buffers against such dangerous affiliations. Many teachers and administrators could only see the gang-related activity students were associated with and not the human beings in difficult circumstances themselves. I often wrote letters of support or testified in court on a student's behalf, sometimes successfully, sometimes unsuccessfully. The system itself, including schools and entire school districts, more readily saw potential solutions not in means of providing supports, but by means that were punitive and exclusionary. Many teachers and administrators truly believed that using the legal system to its fullest extent was the best way to teach important life lessons. The irony of this approach is that regardless of how many expulsions were made or charges laid, the activities administrators were fighting against never seemed to diminish. The outlook was depressing and actions undertaken by school officials constituted little more than an education-to-prison pipeline for some students.

In 2007, after nineteen years living and working in California, I decided to return to Canada. After enjoying a year off, I took a teaching position with the Calgary Board of Education and have enjoyed working with students with behavioural issues in Calgary up to the present. My experiences and observations, as well as the many books and articles I have read across various disciplines over the years, have combined to form a very definite view of public education in my mind. Over a period now spanning almost fifteen years – from the time the charter school project met obstacles from the School Board at La Cañada, arguably one of the best high schools in the United States, through my six years working at Lancaster High School, arguably not one of the best high schools in the United States, and finally coming full-circle by returning to Canada where my career as a professional educator began, I have come to believe that the idea of public education has lost its way. In Western Society, we believe that public education is a necessity, but we are more concerned with statistics produced by "educating" our young people than we seem to be about the young people themselves. We have come to see our children as commodities that represent attendance figures utilized for payment transfers from governments to educational institutions. We have learned to declare with great conviction that our "students come first" but we practice policies that place our educational institutions and their curriculums first. We have come to believe that test scores tell us what we need to know about our young people's progress and that the testing process is a legitimate and viable way to measure preparedness for life after formal public education. We believe that we are teaching our children valuable information that is relevant to their preparation for life in the modern, interconnected, electronic, information-society that we have become. We are wrong.

There is much to criticize about public education. Yet I believe that public education could be transformed into the most powerful force for personal and collective enlightenment and empowerment ever conceived. Many have criticized public education for its many deficiencies over the decades; many have offered ideas for new methods of teaching or improving programs; and many have outlined new theories of learning; but few have proposed any alternative to the big box of education that encompasses all of these in Western Society. We need a new paradigm to correct the inadequacies of education as it currently exists and to encompass the possibilities and challenges of the society we are building for ourselves in the 21st century. In short, we have outgrown the structure that exists. We have to reevaluate our very ideas about what education is and what it is supposed to do, what form or forms it can take to meet our needs, and to plot a course for achieving these objectives.

In my life, learning has been a varied experience. Reading and writing were the greatest and most important skills I ever learned through formal education. My grade eight teacher, Mrs. Walkey, motivated an interest in writing stories and gave me an appreciation of the structure of language. Writing stories evolved into my ongoing interest in using writing as a means of personal expression and my interest in the structure of language eventually led to my interest in linguistics at university. I trace these interests to a particular school year and teacher but could not state or verify that any of my classmates that year became as interested in those two aspects of language as well. Many saw reading and writing as mundane and schools in general often do little to help develop a different viewpoint. Indeed, most subjects seem tedious to young people and if asked if there was something they would rather be doing than going to school, most would come up with something, anything to get out of class. Schools somehow manage to make reading and writing "assignments" seem dull rather than something interesting and gratifying. Mathematics too could be learned in exciting ways but is often the most reviled of subjects at school. If the topic of math is brought up in conversation among adults, there will be a predictably high number of groans, directly attributable to most people's experience with math when they were in school. There is no reason why this should be the case. Educator Richard Gerver recently wrote "that it would be interesting to ask one of the world's giant advertising agencies to create a campaign that marketed learning to children" and wondered aloud why learning couldn't be as interesting as going to Disneyland. He goes on to state that "we need to find ways to make education the new rock 'n' roll." [25] Possibilities for learning are endless and this fact alone gives public education the potential to be more interesting, motivating and beneficial than any other human activity. Yet most people who have been through the public education system are unlikely to describe it as interesting or motivating; and now it is possible to argue that it may not even be beneficial.

The idea of public education is a good one in theory. It is the process that modern society intentionally uses to convey the knowledge, abilities and ethics it believes the next generation needs to successfully move society itself forward. In Western culture, this refers, at least in principle, to: expanding and protecting democratic principles; advancing individual freedoms and rights; promoting free markets and expanding the economy. In order to accomplish this, the work force must be literate, numerate, and have the skills required to function successfully in an industrialized, information-based culture. Today, the skills required are numerous and expanding rapidly. In fact, with the rise of social networking and the ongoing introduction of new and more powerful technologies to communicate, the skills required today for many jobs are already different than they were just five to ten years ago. The problem is that in practice, public education can no longer claim to be preparing the next generation for the world that already exists, let alone the one that will be there when many of them graduate from the education system. This book is not the first to identify deficiencies in public education; many voices have been crying in the wilderness for decades. Social critics and prominent educators have been the loudest of these voices, but in 1970, a massively popular book was published and eventually sold over six million copies. In Future Shock, a book about "too much change in too short a period of time," [26] futurist Alvin Toffler dedicated an entire chapter to education. The millions who read that book were informed that "What passes for education today, even in our "best" schools and colleges, is a hopeless anachronism. Parents look to education to fit their children for life in the future. Teachers warn that lack of an education will cripple a child's chances in the world of tomorrow. Government ministries, churches, the mass media – all exhort young people to stay in school, insisting that now, as never before, one's future is almost wholly dependent upon education. Yet for all this rhetoric about the future, our schools face backward toward a dying system, rather than forward to the emerging new society." [27]

The process of education has not changed much since Alvin Toffler made those statements and I was in formal public schooling. Students still come to class and are expected to be seated in properly aligned rows. They are also expected to be quiet, attentive and interested in each day's lesson. Students are expected to do homework, which is often supplementary but only loosely connected to what was done in class. They are expected to be respectful toward staff and peers in all interactions but highly competitive in their pursuit for marks and grades. The marks and grades students "earn" are usually measured using tests that rarely ever give educators accurate information about what the students have actually learned or what they are able to do with the information they have been given. Furthermore, the information itself is divided into categories (English, science, history, math, etc.) and classes not only separated from other categories and classes, but from life experience itself, therefore making the information simply a collection of bits and chunks of trivia. Students are expected to prepare for future experience in a system that is separated from experience. This is why early 20th century educator and philosopher John Dewey openly questioned the true meaning of preparation in the educational scheme. He stated that "when preparation is made the controlling end, then the potentialities of the present are sacrificed to a suppositious future. When this happens, the actual preparation for the future is missed or distorted. The ideal of using the present simply to get ready for the future contradicts itself. It omits, and even shuts out, the very conditions by which a person can be prepared for his future." [28]

Claims that formal public education prepares students for their future is questionable at best. There is minimal preparation for the future. Students are admonished on a regular basis that they are "future citizens" of society and that is how we treat them. It is not particularly surprising that many drop out of the process – either literally by leaving school when they are legally entitled to, or through non-compliance by acting out in class, not handing in assignments, or being generally disengaged. There are many variables that contribute to such disengagement but often the only learning that is truly well-communicated in a classroom is non-academic in nature. Postman and Weingartner have described this learning as being communicated by the structure of the classroom itself. Among many things, they point out that some of what students learn is that:

- Passive acceptance is a more desirable response to ideas than active criticism.
- Discovering knowledge is beyond the power of students.
- Recall is the highest form of intellectual achievement, and the collection of unrelated "facts" is the goal of education.
- The voice of authority is to be trusted and valued more than independent judgment.
- One's own ideas and those of one's classmates are inconsequential.
- There is always a single, unambiguous Right answer to a question.
- English is not History and History is not Science and Science is not Art and Art is not Music, and Art and Music are minor subjects and English, History and Science are major subjects... [29]

Award-winning former New York educator John Taylor Gatto stated his role as an English teacher that worked in the public school system most eloquently: "I don't teach English; I teach school – and I win awards doing it." [30] There is a considerable body of literature to support the ideas that what we teach in school has little to do with real learning and that it does not actually prepare our young people for the rapidly-changing world that exists in the 21st century. What is worse is that many see the structure of schools as being harmful to the well-being of our young people because intimate primary relationships (between teachers and learners in a traditional learning experience) have been supplanted by an impersonal bureaucracy. "Students and teachers do not relate to one another as whole persons, but in narrow circumscribed roles. Communication is restricted to what one can and must do in a 50-minute hour where a highly structured setting is a sanction against all but teacher-directed behaviour." [31]

The development of a culture of learning is both important and necessary. Narrow circumscribed roles for both teachers and learners need to become a thing of the past. Our students must be encouraged and allowed to be citizens in the present so that they can be truly prepared for a perpetually changing future. If education is to meet the needs of the globalized digital information world we are creating, then it must adapt to the changes that are rapidly developing. There are ways in which this can be accomplished, but it will take a complete restructuring not only of educational practice but of the ideas we have about learning itself. The problems with education today are systemic and must be addressed not only at individual school and program levels, but from national governmental and legislative initiatives right on down to where each and every student is affected.

The focus of the ensuing chapters in this book is twofold:
- To provide an outline of the specific issues, problems and obstacles that exist in education theory and practice today;
- To provide an alternative for both individuals and society as a whole; and

The longer we wait to make necessary changes, the more obsolete our education system will be. We claim that we want the best for our children, but we have not really considered the best way to prepare them for their future. That is because we have continued to separate the future from the present by making learning something apart from life experience itself. We need to understand that interest, relevance and real human connections are essential to the learning experience more so now than ever before. This brings us right back to the opening quote in this chapter by John Gardner: "Much education today is monumentally ineffective. All too often we are giving young people cut flowers when we should be teaching them to grow their own plants."

References and Footnotes

1. Illich, Ivan (1970), <u>Deschooling Society</u>, Marion Boyars Publishers Ltd., London, New York, reissued 2002, pg. 39.

2. CBC archives (1982), first broadcast on CBC's Nightly News on January 7th, 1982.

3. Howard Gardner (1993), <u>Multiple Intelligences: New Horizons</u>, Basic Books (Perseus Book Group), New York, pgs. 8–18.

4. Robert Slavin (2009), Educational Psychology, pg. 117. Reference taken from Wikipedia, <u>Theory of Multiple Intelligences</u>, http://en.wikipedia.org/wiki/Multiple_intelligences.

5. Taken from the "Los Angeles Police Department Gang subsite," Lapdonline.org retrieved on April 13th, 2010, http://www.lapdonline.org/get_informed/content_basic_view/1396.

6. Bates, Simon (2009), <u>Study Finds Swearing Therapeutic: Cursing Curtails Anger</u>, reported on CBS Up to the Minute, September 3, 2009. Retrieved January 12, 2011, http://www.cbsnews.com/stories/2009/09/03/uttm/main5287050.shtml.

7. Carlin, George (2009), <u>Last Words: A Memoir</u>, with Tony Hendra, Free Press, a division of Simon and Shuster, New York, N.Y., pgs. 249-250.

8. Postman, Neil and Weingartner, Charles (1969), <u>Teaching as a Subversive Activity</u>, Dell Publishing Co., New York, pg. 52.

9. Schiff, Tamara W., and Solmon, Lewis C. (1999), <u>California Digital High School Process Evaluation Year One Report</u>, Milken Family Foundation, online at http://www.mff.org/publications/publications.taf?page=258, February 5th, 2011.

10. La Cañada High School official website, taken from http://www.lcusd.net/170220930124912990/site/default.asp, February 5th, 2011.

11. La Cañada High School, an article published by Wikipedia.org, taken from http://en.wikipedia.org/wiki/La_Ca%C3%B1ada_High_School, February 5th, 2011.

12. <u>America's Best High Schools: Gold Medal List</u>, article in U.S. News and World Report, posted December 9th, 2009 online at: http://education.usnews.rankingsandreviews.com/listings/high-schools/california/la_canada_high_school.

13. Award mounted on a wooden plaque and presented by Emma Sanchez, the first director of La Cañada Unified School District's Institutes for the 21st Century program in April, 2000.

14. Thach, Jim (June 1st, 2000), <u>Governing Board Takes First Steps Toward Charter School Planning Grant</u>, La Cañada-Flintridge Outlook: This was the first public reference made about Charmene preparing 18 students for university.

15. Reidel, Barry (July 6th, 2000), <u>Foothills School</u>, La Cañada-Flintridge Outlook: This was the second public reference made to Charmene helping these 18 students.

16. Vega, Charmene (1999), <u>Charter School Planning Grant Application</u>, pg. 1.

17. <u>Charter Schools</u>, National Education Association, retrieved online February 9th, 2011, taken from http://www.nea.org/home/16332.htm.

18. Selected Charter School Laws and Policies, EdSource, <u>Charter Schools Act of 1992: Senate Bill 1448</u> (Hart), retrieved online February 9th, 2011, from http://www.edsource.org/iss_charter_laws.html.

19. Radcliffe, Jennifer and Gary Scharrer. (December 17th, 2006), Decade of change for charter schools / Experts say spotty success keeps them from competing with traditional system, Houston Chronicle,

section B1 MetFront. Retrieved on February 9th, 2011 from: http://www.chron.com/CDA/archives/archive.mpl?id=2006_4249236

20. Green Light for Charter School Study (June 29th, 2000), article submitted to the La Cañada-Flintridge Outlook by Cissboom (Consensus in Support of a School for a Broadening of the Open Mind), pg. 25.

21. Saenz, Ralph (July 29th, 2000), Special Ed Students Protest Pace Transfer, La Cañada Valley Sun, a three-page story highlighting several statements of opposition to the transfer.

22. What Happened 10-20-30 Years Ago? (July 28th, 2010), article in the La Cañada Valley Sun mentioning that "Ten Years Ago, Several La Cañada High School special education students, upset that their teacher, Frank Pace, was being transferred to Foothills School, staged a walking protest on Foothill Boulevard." Retrieved online, February 13th, 2011, from: http://www.lacanadaonline.com/entertainment/tn-vsl-102030-20100728,0,1208152.story.

23. Frank Zappa, article found on Wikipedia, retrieved on February 15th, 2011, from: http://en.wikipedia.org/wiki/Frank_Zappa.

24. Lancaster, California, article found on Wikipedia, retrieved on February 15th, 2011, from: http://en.wikipedia.org/wiki/Lancaster,_California

25. Gerver, Richard (2010), Creating Tomorrow's Schools Today, Continuum Books, London and New York, pg. 21.

26. Future Shock, an article retrieved from Wikipedia on March 6th, 2011 at: http://en.wikipedia.org/wiki/Future_Shock.

27. Toffler, Alvin (1970), Future Shock, Random House, Inc., New York, pgs. 398, 399.

28. Dewey, John (1938), Experience and Education, taken from the Kappa Delta Pi lectures, this edition published by Simon and Shuster, New York, pg. 49.

29. Postman, Neil, and Weingartner, Charles (1969), Teaching as a Subversive Activity, Dell Publishing, New York, pgs. 20-21.

30. Gatto, John Taylor (1992), <u>Dumbing Us Down: The Hidden Curriculum of Compulsory Schooling</u>, New Society Publishers, Gabriola Island, B.C., Canada, pg. 1.

31. Brendtro, Larry K., Brokenleg, Martin, and Van Bockern, Steve (1990), <u>Reclaiming Youth at Risk</u>, Solution Tree Press, Bloomington, Illinois, pg. 13.

2

Issues, Obstacles and Problems in Education

"Human history becomes more and more a race between education and catastrophe."

H.G. Wells

All four of my grandparents were born between 1888 and 1908. They acquired their education in the dying years of the 19th century and the early years of the 20th century. My own daughters Adrienne and Nathalie were born in the 1990s, the fourth generation in just over one hundred years. They are acquiring most of their education here in the early years of the 21st century. The kinds of lives my daughters will live compared to the kinds of lives my grandparents have lived are amazingly different. However, the generations who were alive before my grandparents were born experienced similar lives for hundreds of years. The Industrial Revolution that began a little over two centuries ago has accelerated change in our collective lifestyle from that which once occurred at a glacial pace to a rate of change that futurist Alvin Toffler already described by 1970 as inducing "Future Shock." Even in the 40 years plus that have passed since that declaration, the world has changed so much that people like my grandparents, all of whom passed on by 1975, would not recognize the world that exists now compared to the one they departed just decades ago.

Frank Pace

At the beginning of the twentieth century, the telephone and the light bulb were a few years old, but they did not become common household items for another few years. Modern cities beginning with New York were building the first electrical lighting systems to illuminate streets at night. Public telephones only became common sights on street corners after World War I. Flight was first achieved in 1903 and cars, trucks and buses did not roll off production lines until 1904. The first highways were developed in the 1920s and commercial airlines gained prominence in the 1930s. These three aspects of modern life: lighting, communication and transportation, quickly changed how people lived, worked and interacted with one another on a mass scale. Technological advances fuelled economic advances and these in turn created social change. The age of empires came to an end and nations became identified more by sociopolitical ideas than they did by Royal houses. Capitalism, communism, varying forms of socialism, democracy, fascism, and dictatorships have dominated the political global landscape of the 20th century – all profoundly affecting the lives of the planet's human inhabitants. World wars, ongoing regional conflicts, economic depression and boom times have dispersed millions of people. Globalization was already evolving rapidly when my grandparents were young and it has accelerated continuously to this moment. People's everyday lives have been modified by rapid changes in our societies, ideologies, technologies, medicine and many other factors uninterruptedly from the time my grandparents were born to the present. These changes have continuously restructured how we live our lives, communicate, raise our children and even how we think about and perceive ourselves. These changes have also profoundly affected the opportunities we could take advantage of and continue to affect how opportunities themselves are made available to our populations as a whole. In short, the incredible change to all aspects of our lives has been unprecedented and nothing short of remarkable – except in the area of education. (One simple way to illustrate how education has changed little throughout the 20th century which can also be seen as the new age of film documentation, might be to look at how school and classrooms have been portrayed on film. Whether you are watching To Sir With Love in black and white, or Educating Rita and Dead Poets Society in colour, schools and classrooms are portrayed similarly. Everyone knows the rules that are not to be broken, the authority invested in administrators and teachers and of course, student expectations).

"The institution we call "school" is what it is because we made it that way. If it is irrelevant, as Marshall McLuhan says; if it shields children from reality, as Norbert Wiener says; if it educates for obsolescence, as John Gardner says; if it does not develop intelligence, as Jerome Bruner says; if it is based on fear, as John Holt says; if it avoids the promotion of significant learning, as Carl Rogers says; if it induces alienation, as Paul Goodman says; if it punishes creativity and independence, as Edgar Friedenberg says; if, in short, it is not doing what needs to be done, it can be changed; it must be changed." [1] These words were published by Neil Postman and Charles Weingartner in 1969 but are even truer today. Change in education is needed because education has become increasingly irrelevant, even counterproductive to what individuals and society need as a whole.

The numbers themselves clearly show the inadequacy of education today. In the United States alone, about 7,200 students drop out of high school every day. That adds up to approximately 1.3 million students dropping out of school every year. Nationally, Newsweek magazine reports that only about 68.8 percent of students who start high school actually graduate four years later. These are the most recent figures available at the time of writing this and were published in 2010.[2] The actual figures for 2010 may be worse because there is a delay in data collection. The report which was produced by Editorial Projects in Education [3] is based on graduation data from 2007 which predates the recession that began in 2008. Therefore, the economic downturn in recent years was not even a factor in the statistics produced. Educational research and policy analyst Chris Swanson, who is also vice president of Editorial Projects in Education, stated in the Newsweek article that "the roots of the drop-out crisis are longstanding and persistent." This view is consistent with observations made by numerous educational experts and analysts for decades.

In Canada, the numbers aren't quite as damning as they are in the United States, but nationally, about 10.2 percent of high school students drop out of school. There is significant variation between the provinces and territories. For example, British Columbia had the lowest dropout rate in the country between 2007 and 2010. Approximately 6.2 percent of students who begin high school drop out (and do not return to complete high school even by the time they reach the age of 24). This still translates into over 19,000 students who do not complete high school per year in B.C. The province with the highest dropout rate during this same period is Quebec, with 11.7 percent of students who begin high school but drop out and do not return to complete their studies by the age of 24. With a much larger provincial population, this translates into more than 55,000 dropouts per year. Overall, Canada's dropout rate averages just under 200,000 students per year, a considerable drop from what it was in the early 1990s when more than 315,000 -- one third of a million -- students were dropping out annually.[4]

The difference in dropout rates between the United States and Canada are only a matter of degree. The point is that it is unacceptable for average dropout rates to be one out of ten students in Canada and just under one out of three students in the United States. Ultimately, the questions that arise are significant: How can we justify a "success" rate in education that leaves behind so many students? Why are dropout rates this high and so consistently poor from year to year and decade to decade? How will this affect the individual lives of the students dropping out? What strains on our society and economy are directly affected by these numbers? These and many more questions will have to be addressed by us as they continue to impact society as a whole. They can either be addressed proactively by re-evaluating the education process; that is, by reconsidering how we do what we do to prepare our young people for their adult lives, or it can be reacted to by the "fix-its" we develop to band aid each of the multitude of problems that arise in all aspects of our lives largely because of the failure of our schools.

So why are students dropping out of high school at such alarming rates? It would be a mistake to oversimplify because there is no single reason why students drop out. Research does indicate that prominent barriers to graduation include deficiency in basic skills, lack of engagement and difficult transitions from junior high to high school.[5] Most of the students who drop out of high school were already on a path to failure in their middle school years. Various behaviours and specific risk factors such as low attendance and failing grades are good indicators of future drop outs. In some cases, this begins to occur as early as grade six.[6] According to an article in Education Week, an American newspaper covering K-12 education, the ninth grade is somewhat of a bottleneck year for students in general. They arrive at high school only to find that their academic skills are not sufficient to keep up with high school-level expectations and work. In cities with the highest dropout rates in the United States, as many as 40 percent of ninth grade students have to repeat much of that year. Of these, only 10 to 15 percent actually go on to graduate from high school. [7] Academic success or failure in the ninth grade is highly predictive of potential graduation – even more so than demographic characteristics or academic achievement in previous grades.[8]

Even before the ninth grade, there are several indicators that our students are choosing not to engage in their classes and education. Many do this: by not concentrating in class; by not doing their homework; by acting out; by getting high at school; and through truancy, especially as they progress through junior high and high school. For two years, I worked in a special program in Calgary, Alberta where junior high students whose educational opportunities were being jeopardized by pronounced academic difficulties, persistent behavioural and/or emotional difficulties or family struggles were sent for 20 days for observation and assessment. At any given time there might be as many as ten students being assessed by our team of one teacher and two behaviour specialists. Many of these students came with "canned" descriptions of their behaviour that stated transgressions such as: lack of motivation, disrupting class; exhibiting defiance toward teachers and administrators; and rising incidences of truancy. When I say that many descriptions of student behaviour are "canned" prior to the intake process, that is exactly what I mean. My colleagues and I often marveled that the wording in these descriptions were routinely identical – that the very incidence of individual student behaviors could be so similar and common that a canned blurb of student behaviour was produced to be used indefinitely to describe new "individual" cases. If so many individual cases could be described so similarly using common verbiage about what each student is allegedly doing wrong in school, then maybe it isn't the individual students we should be looking at to address these common problems, but the schools themselves. The common pattern may simply be a common reaction. If we are losing anywhere between one out of ten and one out three students before they can graduate from high school in North America, then perhaps we should be looking at the problem more comprehensively.

Schools and those who support modern schooling often point fingers at the students, their families, society at large, lack of funding, and the need for improved standards, but rarely, if ever do they stop to take a serious look at what they themselves are doing. Schools and school districts do not believe that there is even a possibility that they are a contributing factor to the failure of their own system to produce better results. Yet at the program where I worked in Calgary, we saw this often. Principals, assistant principals or guidance counselors would attend intake meetings for students slated to come to our program. They would talk about all of the bad things that a particular student has been doing: speaking out of turn; asking questions when they were supposed to be quietly engaged; not completing assignments; being unmotivated and truant. Sometimes students did exhibit more serious problems, but most of the students sent to our program were referred to us for reasons which we saw as frivolous. Interestingly, the students often came with tracking records which were supposed to be used to record ongoing behaviours over a period of time. Rarely, if ever, did a tracking record ever come to us that highlighted anything positive. It was always: "...and he did this" and "she did that..." It often reminded me of a classic scene from the film 'One Flew over the Cuckoo's Nest' starring Jack Nicholson. Nicholson's character Randall McMurphy is sitting quietly during a doctor-patient interview listening to the list of transgressions he has committed that led first to incarceration and then to admittance for observation in a hospital for patients with emotional and mental issues. When the doctor finishes his list and looks up at McMurphy for a response, McMurphy simply looks back with a smirk on his face and replies with a question: "Chewing gum in class?" The point was well made and followed by McMurphy's admonition that the hospital needs to get down to what makes Randall P. McMurphy tick. And this is what we need to do with our schools and students as well: Find out what makes them tick. Utilize their interests and lead them to further discovery.

Richard Gerver, a British educator and Head Teacher of the internationally respected Grange Primary School states that "if school isn't working we can have only ourselves to blame. If our young people are leaving their formal education unable to thrive in their adult lives the system needs to look hard at itself." He goes on to compare problems that our young people are exhibiting in the workplace when they reach that stage in their lives with how we have prepared them at school. It isn't surprising that there are problems at all. For example, Gerver points out that one of the most common criticisms that target young people new to the workforce is that they "lack initiative." They don't seem to be able to solve problems for themselves and always need to be told what to do. This shouldn't be too surprising because as students, they are expected to know which class and lesson to attend, are expected to be prepared with their books, note paper and pens, and seated in their assigned desks. Furthermore, students are expected to sit quietly while their teacher takes the time to explain the objective of the lesson, set the context, perhaps refer to a specific page and concept to be taught, and then provide either an assignment or ask questions to which there are specific right or wrong answers. The teacher may use tools like the blackboard or, if modernized, an interactive "smart board," but these will almost exclusively be monopolized by the teacher before defining the task at hand and determining the amount of time given to complete it. Creativity, or the need for it, are rarities; schools are often about regimentation. Gerver points out that "schools are in many ways closely related to prisons; even the architecture of large school buildings with their high walls screams of internment. Schools are worlds of their own, divorced from reality of everyday life. Routines are exactly that: inflexible, repeated day in day out." [9]

Of course there are many questions and debates about whether particular common practices we use to educate our young people are effective. These questions and debates are important to make sure that our education system remains relevant during times that are constantly in flux. What is more important is that we act on them. This isn't only a question or debate about schooling. It is about how we organize our society and create opportunity. Meaningful education is not something that can only occur in schools; it is something that should not be restricted to schools. Education is something much bigger than schooling; it could and should be part of our life plan at every stage of that plan. Furthermore, it should be accessible to all of us in a variety of ways from when we reach school-age to when we achieve old age.

The case for developing a blueprint to deliver accessible, relevant and cost-effective individualized education is enhanced when the presentation of what is wrong with our present system is made clear. The purpose of this chapter is simply to look at the issues, obstacles and problems that make the current system inadequate and make the need for change all the more pertinent.

Testing

The earliest tests I can remember taking in school were spelling tests as early as grade one. Since they were often an extension of the spelling bees that would routinely be conducted in elementary school, I didn't mind them. Spelling bees were oral tests that seemed like competitive games. Students could see how they measured up to one another in the same way as they did on the school ground playing baseball or soccer. Each word correctly spelled was like scoring a goal or a run and the exercise which eliminated individuals for spelling a word incorrectly could be as exciting as a hockey playoff – at least for those who did well. For those not particularly competitive or not particularly good at spelling, the exercise may have been a more harsh measure. In fact, it may have contributed to poorer development of spelling skills by reducing many students' confidence to be a "winner" of a spelling bee or a written test. If a spelling bee or written test were held once a week over the period of one school year, there might be as many as sixty spelling bees/tests for students to compete in. This was normal when I attended elementary school and may continue to be an activity in elementary classrooms today. Given the array of individual differences in any given classroom, it is fair to expect that some students have a higher aptitude to be successful in that particular area of study and that some students have a lower aptitude to be successful in that particular area of study simply because of individual differences. It then follows that the chances of ending up in, let's say, the last five students standing -- or winning the whole thing -- will fall to those whose aptitude is higher in this area. Once patterns emerge, the students themselves will make judgments about their own abilities and those of their peers just like their teachers do about them. The ensuing expectations, or lack thereof, will assist in strengthening these observations and outcomes. Long before the end of the school year, a few students will "learn" that they are good spellers and most will "learn" that they are poor spellers. These self-perceptions can last for years, even lifetimes, and contribute to self-fulfilling prophecies about student capabilities for the remainder of their school careers.

Anticipation about an upcoming test can cause a significant amount of stress in many students. Perhaps it is directly related to early experiences where some students learned that they were not as capable as others. Expecting difficulty and possible failure can be a powerful deterrent to doing well on any kind of test. The fact that test anxiety has actually grown into a subfield of educational psychology is indicative of the strong reaction students have about testing generally. If such a reaction is so prevalent, then to what extent can we believe that tests are providing accurate appraisals of what students really know or can do? Furthermore, when tests are made to count for determining funding of schools as well as individual student's success or failure, the stakes are raised higher, the anxiety is commensurately increased and the less valid the scores gathered from the testing process become.

Aside from the anxiety question, it is very difficult to determine how well prepared for a test a student could be at any given time. Everyone knows that if something pressing is on one's mind, it can be very difficult to focus on something else. If a student experiences this at the time he or she is expected to write a test – and it is always expected that students write tests at specific times not usually determined by the students themselves – why would the scores achieved be assumed to represent the best effort any and every student could make? Of course there would be an obvious problem with allowing students to choose the time they take a test themselves; many would write the test and then inform peers of the test content. Although this only presents two issues so far, it already becomes possible to see that testing is not particularly favourable either to the person who is being tested or the person conducting the testing. One can't participate in choosing the optimal time to write the test and the other can't determine the validity of the test scores achieved.

The validity of test scores is the most important issue here. In fact, if tests and testing aren't valid, then the measurement derived from them has no meaning. The questions that must be asked include these: Can tests and testing provide an objective measurement of what a student knows and the skills he or she has developed over a given period of educational instruction? Are tests effective predictors of future success either academically or professionally? Can tests be good indicators of students' thinking processes? The short answer to each of these questions is: No. The scores on a test, let's say 70 or 80 or 90 can't measure the amount of information learned by a student like the measurement of a litre or a quart can measure the amount of liquid in a container. Neither can test scores measure the amount of skills a student has developed in the same way as one might use measurement in inches to calculate height or measurement in pounds to determine weight. Testing isn't an exact science; it isn't even an objective one.

Testing in schools has been around for so long that we as a society simply assume that tests are accurate, objective measurements of what our students can do. Have we really asked ourselves the hard questions about what these assumptions mean? Over the past twenty years educators have become familiar with the idea that students often exhibit intelligence in different ways. Howard Gardner's book on multiple intelligences has revolutionized many educators' ideas about how different individuals learn. Yet how we measure what we call intelligence in school does not reflect our evolving ideas about learning in general. Tests still tend to measure all students' capabilities the same way. If we really do understand that different students may learn in different ways, then why would we think that one method of measurement is accurate for all or even most? Students don't have the option to demonstrate competency in any way other than what is determined by the format of the test. The format of many tests these days is multiple choice because they are more efficiently scored by machines.

The problem with multiple choice tests – and in fact most kinds of tests – is that they usually only determine that a student has answered a question correctly. Student understanding of the process is often not measured in any way and where it is, as is often the case in mathematics testing, a specific process is expected to be followed even if there may be others that could lead a student to the same correct answer. It is not unusual for a mathematics teacher to declare that a correct answer is invalid because a student did not follow the specific steps taught in class – calculating an answer in one's head is absolutely forbidden. When one thinks about this issue, it becomes clear that tests not only fail to measure creative process or individual ingenuity, but it does measure compliance with set directions, even if they are not the only path to success. In other words, students are often being tested and graded more for obedience or acquiescence than they are for thinking originally.

The disturbing reality about much of the testing conducted is that students are routinely rewarded for regurgitating right answers without having to comprehend why their answers may be correct; other students are being penalized for being creative thinkers by the testing process because they did not regurgitate the specified response expected – even if they clearly understood the underlying process in the response they gave. In an interesting article published by the Journal of Education Psychology in 1988, researchers noted a distinct statistical correlation between high scores on standardized tests and relatively superficial thinking by students of different ages.[10] Interestingly, superficial thinking was positively correlated with high scores on the Comprehensive Test of Basic skills (CTBS), a norm and criterion-referenced achievement assessment for students in kindergarten through 12th grade that is widely used in the United States. It was developed by CTB, a Macmillan/ McGraw-Hill Company and has been used to measure student achievement in mathematics, study skills, science, and social studies. [11] In Canada, there is a similar battery called the Canadian Test of Basic Skills (also referred to as CTBS) published by Nelson Education. [12] It should be noted that the findings by Meese et al in 1988 are only statistical correlations. The fact of the matter is that there may be many students who are not just superficial thinkers and who score well on tests such as the CTBS, but as Alfie Kohn, educator and outspoken critic of grading and test scores, points out: "As a rule, good standardized test results are more likely to go hand in hand with a shallow approach to learning than with deep understanding." [13]

It can also be stated that as a rule, good test results are also more likely to go hand in hand with a shallow approach to teaching as well as learning. If tests are given regularly to collect information about students, it takes time away from actual student instruction. Rarely are test results used to further understanding of concepts already covered, even if it is clear that many students only grasped small percentages of what was taught in the previous unit of instruction. Tests are usually only used to measure what each student was able to answer correctly about that unit on the particular day the test was administered. And if tests are considered particularly important, like standardized State testing in the United States or provincial testing in

Canada, then a considerable amount of classroom instruction time is being utilized to teach to the test. Such testing does not improve the quality of instruction, but places an emphasis on knowing "the right answers" to typical questions likely to be asked. Understanding the "why" behind the answers is not necessary to scoring well. Furthermore, when the tests are actually taken by students, they are timed. This places an important emphasis on speed as opposed to creativity, logical process and even quality of response. As Kohn effectively points out: "If one small part of the test were timed, this would indicate that the ability to do things quickly and under pressure was one of several valued attributes. But if the entire exam must be taken under the gun, the logical inference is that this ability is prized above others." [14] If speed is prized above other attributes of testing, then there is another reason to believe that testing itself is not a valid measure of what a student can do. Testing not only ignores the fact that students may exhibit varying intelligences more strongly than others, but it also ignores the fact that most students do not learn at the same pace.

Testing is supposed to be a tool that gives us some kind of measure of a student's capabilities, but most tests place an important emphasis on remembering isolated facts with an added emphasis on the speed it takes to remember them. Knowing facts is not the same as being smart and a "Jeopardy" approach to teaching and learning has nothing to do with understanding what was taught or learned. As someone who has watched the television game show Jeopardy on and off over the years, I can state without hesitation that the program tends to recycle some questions with the intention of garnering the same answers. This allows fans at home who may watch the show regularly to have an added advantage in trying to compete with on air contestants. For example, every so often, a Jeopardy category will provide a clue that hopes to elicit the name of former Ethiopian emperor Haile Selassie. Those who have watched the program often enough will recognize that "answers" relating to Ethiopia routinely require Haile Selassie to be referred to in the form of a question. All a regular viewer has to remember is that when Ethiopia comes up in the line of Jeopardy questioning and the name of a prominent Ethiopian figure is required, then Haile Selassie is more often than not going to be the correct response. Contestants or home viewers don't actually have to know anything about Haile Selassie and probably actually do know very little about him. This is not much different than standardized testing as it is conducted in both Canada and the United States. If students do not answer a question correctly this year in a State or Provincial test, they are likely to be asked the same question (perhaps using slightly different wording), or a very similar question in next year's round of testing. If one is conditioned properly (which is what teaching to the test is designed to do), it becomes possible to recognize the similarity and answer it correctly next time. This also contributes to "improved test scores" without emphasizing that the improvements are at least partially achieved by conditioning responses -- perhaps over several years during the time period that a particular type of test might be given or repeated. And this is how and why such a huge industry has developed around SAT and other test preparation. Each year new editions of SAT and other test preparation manuals are published. They review recent lines of questioning for the purpose of preparing potential examinees for future lines of questioning. It is a lucrative extension of the concept of teaching to the test.

Of course there are many significant arguments that can be made against the use of testing in schools, especially the kind of testing that has occurred for decades and continues to be considered a significant, "accurate" representation of measurement. No such accuracy exists. To summarize the few arguments made in this section:

- Testing is, more often than not, a significant and destructive means for both teachers and students to make comparative judgments that can often lead to lifelong, inaccurate self-perceptions.
- Tests and testing are significant producers of stress that considerably reduce optimal conditions for accurate measurement. Test anxiety has actually become a subfield of educational psychology.
- Tests and testing are invalid markers of actual student capability. Neither multiple choice or essay exams allow for objective measurement and they are not effective predictors of future competency or success.
- Tests and testing continue to use a one-size-fits-all approach even though we have been aware of multiple intelligences and different learning styles now for decades.
- Students have no way of demonstrating competency or creativity in any other way than what is determined by the format of the test.

- Multiple choice tests, the ones most commonly given, can only determine that a student has answered a question correctly; actual student understanding or capability is not measured in any way.
- Tests and testing often penalize creativity by reducing marks for achieving a correct answer in any way other than what was pre-taught. Tests and testing do more to measure compliance and regurgitation than they do to measure creativity or problem-solving ability.
- Tests and testing go hand in hand with a shallow approach to both teaching and learning as evidenced in the common practice of teaching to the test. Teaching to the test does nothing to improve the quality of instruction or learning.
- Tests are almost always timed which places a higher emphasis on speed under pressure as a desirable attribute of testing than any other attribute it is trying to measure.
- Tests and testing encourage a "Jeopardy" approach to both teaching and learning but knowing facts and being able to intelligently use what has been learned are two very different abilities.
- Tests and testing are inaccurately used to determine both individual and school "improvement" even though they are invalid measurements of ability in the first place.
- The most important reason to continue testing has little to do with measurement of student ability and much more to do with continuing a lucrative corporate industry in capitalist societies.

Some of the reasons mentioned here as well as the many more arguments that can be presented may be why even Jean Piaget, the Swiss developmental psychologist and philosopher best known for his theory of cognitive development once stated that "Anyone can confirm how little the grading that results from examinations corresponds to the final useful work of people in life." [15]

Rather than employ a method of regurgitation that emphasizes the importance of speed under pressure, we should be giving our students opportunities to demonstrate their learning and capabilities over broader periods of time. As described in the first chapter, a project-based approach to teaching and learning would eliminate pressure, allow for creativity, enhance a more meaningful approach to learning through collaboration as well as competition, take into consideration multiple intelligences and different learning styles, and would not determine a student's capability based only on what could be produced within a narrow time slot. Furthermore, a project-based approach to learning would provide a hands-on method of participation in the learning process, not just an attempt to regurgitate it and then call it measurement.

Meaningful Curriculum and Instruction

We have now seen that the measurement of what is being taught in schools is not particularly valid, does nothing to improve the quality of instruction or learning, and does more to measure compliance and regurgitation than it does to measure creativity or problem-solving ability. But what about the content of what we are teaching in the first place? To what extent does curriculum prepare the students of today for the world of tomorrow? In what ways are the skills needed for the future embedded in the teaching processes we use today to help students develop what they will need? These are critical questions for determining quality of life and work in the future, but they are particularly pertinent for planning how to prepare our students for that future in the present.

As New York State Teacher of the Year, John Taylor Gatto, once stated that "reading, writing and arithmetic only take about one hundred hours to transmit as long as the audience is eager and willing to learn." [16] Interestingly, public schooling is compulsory for several years in both Canada and the United States, yet illiteracy is a significant problem, even at the end of that compulsory education. According to a 2010 report by the Conference Board of Canada, a not-for-profit applied research organization, "seven million working-age Canadian adults—about 4 in 10—do not have the literacy skills necessary to function in the workplace." [17] In a 2003 report published by the U.S. Department of Education's National Center for Educational Statistics, "an estimated 32 million adults in the USA – about one in seven – are saddled with such low literacy skills that it would be tough for them to read anything more challenging than a children's picture book or to understand a medication's side effects listed on a pill bottle." [18] These statistics have become much worse in just a few years since the 2003 report. According to a 2007 publication by The Education

Portal in California, 42 million American adults cannot read at all and 50 million are unable to read at a level that is expected of a fourth or fifth grader. Furthermore, the number of adults that are classified as functionally illiterate increases by approximately 2.25 million every year. The most damning statistic is that "20 percent of high school seniors can be classified as being functionally illiterate at the time they graduate." [19] How is it that 13 years of formal public schooling (kindergarten through grade 12) cannot achieve basic literacy standards for so many people when it should only take 100 hours to do so?

The deeply disappointing aspect of this is that we live in a society that does not prepare its youth to participate in the society we have produced and are continuing to develop. What does it say about our education systems in Canada and the United States – which are supposed to prepare students for life in our democratic and capitalist societies – if the institutions designed to prepare students to participate in standard values that include freedom, responsibility, productivity and efficiency cannot meet even the basic requirements themselves? If school superintendents were corporate CEOs, many would be fired. If school districts were corporations, almost all of them would be restructured to meet current demands or dissolved completely. It is true that at both the national and local levels in both Canada and the United States, educational restructuring takes place all the time. However, the new programs to do this or the initiatives to do that are rarely ever more than facelift enterprises. The basic structure of how we organize and deliver educational curriculum is very much the same in the second decade of the twenty-first century as it has been throughout the twentieth century.

The content of what we learn in schools is delivered in a set of courses referred to as curriculum. Although the idea of teaching basic concepts that are believed to be essential for the proliferation of society has been around as long as people have been able to communicate ideas, formal notions and design of what should be taught and why is not even a century old. The first book ever published on the subject was simply titled "The Curriculum" by John Franklin Bobbitt in 1918. [20] According to Bobbitt, the point of having a curriculum was to determine what had to be accomplished. He felt that curriculum was an arena for social engineering. There were two outstanding features of his ideas. The first idea was that scientific experts should design curricula based on their presumed knowledge of what qualities were desirable for functioning adult members of society. Bobbitt also believed that these experts were best qualified to determine the types of experiences that would generate these desirable qualities. The second idea was that curriculum was defined as "the deeds-experiences" students should have in order to become the adult each person should become. [21]

Herein is the basis for the idea that experts know what is best for everyone else in society and that schooling is to prepare students for life in the adult world. Anyone who has gone to school in North America over the past hundred years knows that there is very little self-determination within the context of curriculum designed for compulsory schooling. For the most part, learners are told what to learn and have very little choice themselves. There is no choice whatsoever in elementary school, extremely limited choices in junior high, and a somewhat expanded list of choices in high school, but even these are narrow in scope. Diversification at the high school level involves a little more independence and responsibility, but barely. For example, in the 2010-2011 registration guide of a high school considered one of the best high schools in Calgary, Alberta, independence and responsibility are described as follows:

Independence and Responsibility
- Students are more independent in high school. Each student has a different timetable and a different set of teachers. Each of these teachers has his or her expectations regarding behavior, homework, etc. and students are expected to take responsibility for knowing what these expectations are and for following through. High school teachers are helpful and want their students to be successful, but they do expect that students ask for help and be involved in their own learning. [22]

Diploma requirements are very similar from high school to high school. In four-year high schools (which is the norm across most of North America), students are expected to take English all four years, mathematics at least three years, history at least three years, science at least three years, and physical education at least two years. There are often choices for electives but the choices are narrow. The number of credits required for electives are even specified. For example, in the same registration guide where the description of independence and responsibility were found, students were allowed to choose their electives, but they had to choose three within the category of career and life management and another twenty from among career and technology studies, fine arts, second languages and physical education. Given the wide array of job categories a student might want to consider as an adult, preparation within the context of compulsory schooling is significantly limited. Yet this all fits in with what Bobbitt seems to have considered as the purpose for developing curriculum: to guide and mold expected outcomes. American school leaders widely adopted Bobbitt's early ideas that stressed the certainty of social efficiency and he is still recognized predominantly as an advocate of scientific, efficiency-based curriculum management. [23]

So to what extent does the curriculum in North American public school systems prepare students for living, working and succeeding in modern society and culture? Regulatory government agencies responsible for public education publish content standards that are supposed to determine what is taught and what outcomes are expected. The planning details are precise and specific. One could easily see and agree that the whole process is micro-managed from the top. For the most part, curriculum is determined at the top of the chain of command. This is done mostly by people who are no longer in a classroom and in some cases, have never been in a classroom. If you were to look up the credentials of the top education minister in each Canadian province or education secretary in the United States, would you also find education credentials to match? The answer is no. Yet the dictates that proceed from the desks of ministers or education secretaries are very specific and precise. For example, in a section of California's Common Core Content Standards outlining Reading Standards for Informational Text for grades 6 to 12, the key ideas for grades 6, 7 and 8 are as follows [24]:

System vs. Culture

Grade 6 Students	Grade 7 Students	Grade 8 Students
1. Cite textual evidence to support analysis of what the text says explicitly as well as inferences drawn from the text.	1. Cite several pieces of textual evidence to support analysis of what the text says explicitly as well as inferences drawn from the text.	1. Cite the textual evidence that most strongly supports an analysis of what the text says explicitly as well as inferences drawn from the text.
2. Determine a central idea of a text and how it is conveyed through particular details; provide a summary of the text distinct from personal opinions or judgments.	2. Determine two or more central ideas in a text and analyze their development over the course of the text; provide an objective summary of the text.	2. Determine a central idea of a text and analyze its development over the course of the text, including its relationship to supporting ideas; provide an objective summary of the text.
3. Analyze in detail how a key individual, event, or idea is introduced, illustrated, and elaborated in a text (e.g., through examples or anecdotes).	3. Analyze the interactions between individuals, events, and ideas in a text (e.g., how ideas influence individuals or events, or how individuals influence ideas or events).	3. Analyze how a text makes connections among and distinctions between individuals, ideas, or events (e.g., through comparisons, analogies, or categories).

These standards represent what students are expected to learn by the end of each of these grades. Content standards have been in place for decades, yet almost one in four adults in the State of California – 23 percent – are functionally illiterate. [25] Although percentages may differ in all American

States and Canadian Provinces, discrepancies exist between what is determined by the content standards issued by any educational governing body and actual outcomes. For the most part, procedures and mechanisms for adhering to the content standards do not exist. In other words, the standards for what should be taught are outlined in detail as above, but there is no structure for ensuring that individual school districts, schools or teachers follow them. In essence, they are simply guidelines. The exception to this may be in the area of special education. Every student who receives special education services must have an individualized educational plan. In each plan, known as an IEP, goals, benchmarks and timeframes are specified for student progress. Special education teachers often, but not always, use the content standards to determine individualized goals for their students, but these same standards are not applied to the majority of students who do not qualify for special education services. Even if teachers did ensure that every standard was covered in their classrooms, it would only further homogenize and regiment a canned educational approach – one-size-fits-all – which, for the most part, is the ideal in current practice today. If it was not the ideal in current educational practice, then what would be the basis for making comparisons in achievement between individual schools? If all schools were not striving for the same goals, then what would be the point of ranking their actual achievements toward these goals?

The homogenization and irrelevance of much current educational practice may have to be pointed out to adults in books such as this one, but students themselves often express their insight and dissatisfaction of what they see as trivial pursuits. Perhaps the most-asked question in the history of education is: Why do I have to take algebra? A similar question might also be something like this: Why do we have to go over the same algebra concepts year after year? These are legitimate questions.

Teachers and administrators often find themselves in a position where they are called upon to answer such questions, but the answers are almost always the same. In an online article for Purplemath.com entitled "Why do I have to take Algebra?" mathematician and teacher Elizabeth Stapel manages to echo the usual responses to this question perfectly, so don't be surprised if they sound familiar:

1. "If you want that great job, that interesting career, that open-ended future, you're almost certainly going to need some mathemati-

cal skills. And algebra is the basis, the foundation, the tool-box for those skills."

2. "...to get the job you want, you need to demonstrate proficiency in basic job skills. To demonstrate that proficiency, you need a degree. To get the degree, you need algebra. In other words, you do need this stuff for your job."

3. "...You didn't learn your alphabet all those years ago because you knew you'd be reading Moby Dick this semester. In the same way, you don't take algebra now because you know that you'll be factoring quadratics in ten years."

4. "...Nobody can say with assurance what skills will be needed twenty years from now. But what intelligent person would want to cut himself off from future opportunities and growth by refusing to expose himself to at least some of the knowledge which will be foundational for whatever is yet to come?"

5. "...The lessons and patterns of mathematics are important too. If all you take from algebra is a comfort with variables and formulas, an ability to interpret graphs and to think logically, and a willingness to use abstraction when you try to solve problems, then you have gained some incredibly useful life skills, skills that will open doors, give you options, and allow you to make your own informed choices." [26]

In the first two responses, Stapel reiterates the response that many students will recognize: If you want a decent job, you are going to have to take algebra. But her argument is that to get the job you want, you have to show that you have basic skills and in order to show that you have basic skills you have to get a degree. The degree that shows you have basic skills includes algebra and that's why you have to take algebra. This is not particularly sound logic unless you define basic skills as including algebra and for many jobs, such skills might really not be needed. Basic skills can only be defined as basic skills if they are the "basis" for all jobs, not just specified ones. Students often see through this argument and find it unsatisfactory.

The third response makes a poor comparison between learning algebra and learning the alphabet. One doesn't learn the alphabet because they might have to read Moby Dick in a classroom years later; one learns the alphabet so that they can expand communication skills to include written text as well as verbal interchanges. It facilitates human communication in all aspects of our lives at every stage of our lives. Algebra may facilitate computation that can be used in specialized jobs around the house or in certain professions, but it doesn't have the same impact on life as a whole as learning to read and write does. This argument also falls short and does little to convince students that learning algebra and then going over it again throughout junior and senior high school is a valuable undertaking.

The fourth point that Stapel makes cannot be argued with. It makes absolute sense to expose oneself to at least some of the knowledge which will be foundational for whatever is yet to come but that doesn't explain why algebra must be focused on for so many years or why reviewing algebra concepts repeatedly is particularly pertinent. Again, students often see the ineffectiveness of the argument they are being presented with.

Stapel's fifth point also seems logical because it is true that gaining some comfort with variables and formulas, an ability to use graphs and think logically are useful life skills that could open doors down the road. But again, this does not explain why concepts must be reviewed ad nauseum for years and unfortunately, most teachers do not explain broader extensions of mathematical importance. Thinking logically by performing mathematical calculations does not naturally translate into thinking logically in other situations that do not involve math. If there is a transferable connection or skill, it is never explained for practical purposes by teachers in high school math classes.

When one looks at actual mathematics curriculum, one often sees mathematical concepts and practice presented in ways that do not reflect real-life use of the skills that are considered so important. This is perhaps the biggest reason algebra and math in general can be a hard sell to students. For example, in a junior high school mathematics text currently in use in many schools across Canada, one doesn't have to go far to find examples of questions or tasks that do little to advance appreciation for the subject. Consider each of the following:

"Work with a classmate to determine how much time each step takes when you walk at your normal walking pace. Give your answer to the nearest tenth of a second."

"The 2 youngest astronauts chosen in 1992 were Julie Payette, aged 28, and Chris Hadfield, aged 32. What percent was Julie's age of Chris's age?"

"Twenty-two out of 25 Canadians put on their right shoe first. What percent of Canadians put on their right shoe first?" [27]

Needless to say, these are not real-life questions, but they are the kinds of questions that will be generated in an artificial setting like a classroom. They are questions set apart and removed from real life experience because the classroom and the subject itself are removed from real life experience. Students realize that such questions are not related to real life problems and therefore question the validity of doing such exercises. I had difficulty seeing the value of advanced mathematics as a young person going through the system too. When I took the initiative to take math more seriously as an adult, I chose to read a book about the history of mathematics. From there I gained an appreciation for the need to understand and develop advanced math concepts. All of a sudden it made sense that to understand and make use of observable events like the configuration of the night sky, one would need mathematics. All of a sudden, it made sense that if you wanted to set up trade agreements, build pyramids, or determine the cost of a war with a neighbour, one would need mathematics. If one wanted to make comparisons that involved value, measure distance or calculate probabilities, one would need mathematics. The problem is that in a classroom where subjects are taught individually and connections between subjects and disciplines are rarely mentioned, let alone taught, it becomes very difficult to see the big picture of interconnectedness that is real world and real life. Consequently, students are asked to do a great deal of busy work that has little to no relevance to what they might use mathematics for later in their lives.

Other subjects are treated much the same way in school classrooms. For example, it might be common for students to write a history exam and be asked what year did Samuel de Champlain found Quebec City – something most students forget easily enough not long after completing the history class. (Most likely they are also given options to guess from in a multiple choice exam. Do you know what year Champlain accomplished this: 1521, 1567, 1608 or 1693)? But how many students have learned why Champlain was successful or what contributions he made that we can learn from today? Champlain stood apart from other explorers of his day because of the respect he showed the Native peoples he encountered in the New World and the respect he in turn was able to garner from them. He was a master negotiator. Yet it would be unusual for a history teacher to ask students, especially on an exam, how the negotiation techniques Champlain used with native people might be applied to negotiations with others in situations of conflict today – whether it is across the world or just in the schoolyard.

Many times we don't even tell the truth in history classes. This is an outright shame as understanding our past is an essential component to understanding ourselves and the world around us. In 1995, an important book was published in the United States entitled: Lies My Teacher Told Me: Everything Your American History Textbook Got Wrong. [28] Its author, James W. Loewen spent two years at the Smithsonian Institution researching twelve current American history textbooks at the time and eventually came to the conclusion that the authors of the textbooks generated factually false, Eurocentric, and mythologized views of history. Accusations against all of these history textbooks include "blind patriotism, mindless optimism, sheer misinformation and outright lies." [29] In the second edition, Loewen added six more textbooks into the collection for criticism and pointed out that historical myths continue to be perpetuated today. Think about it: To what extent are history books that consistently utilize such "blind patriotism, mindless optimism, sheer misinformation and outright lies" likely to present a clearer view of events like 9/11 or the Iraq War than what has been fed to the American public as these events were unfolding?

It should be noted that history – more than any other subject taught in schools today – is dominated by the use of textbooks. In science, the subject matter is supplemented with lab work in many schools and in English, there is the study of actual written work by authors, not just commentary about them in textbooks. But history is almost entirely taught out of textbooks that filter it through commentary about history or presenting a chosen list of "facts" that usually include dates, names, wars and government actions. I can never remember reading an actual historical text in a history class – although the United States Constitution is one document that is usually printed at the back of many American history textbooks as a supplement. The whole point of studying history is that it is essential to understanding ourselves and the world around us, but "textbooks almost never use the present to illuminate the past," and "conversely, textbooks seldom use the past to illuminate the present." [30] Therefore, despite the fact that teachers like to repeat the oft-stated phrase that if we don't learn from history, we are doomed to repeat its mistakes, what lessons are we actually learning from history in our public schools?

History textbooks are not historical documents themselves. They are commentaries about people and events chosen by the writers and editors to represent a very definite perspective. In the case of American history textbooks, James Loewen has very effectively demonstrated that "we have been duped by an outrageous concoction of lies, half-truths, truths, and omissions that is in large part traceable to the first half of the 19th century." [31] A very good example is the figure of Helen Keller. Every North American elementary student has heard of Helen Keller and can tell you that she was a deaf and blind girl who overcame her handicaps with the help of her teacher, Anne Sullivan. Yet no textbook ever mentions what she did with her freedom from these disabilities once she learned to communicate and write. American textbooks never mention the Helen Keller who became a radical socialist. Her many writings could not have been "missed" by those researching the histories they were writing for students in textbooks. Helen Keller's real life story was interesting, dramatic and important but it does not fit the ideals that America wants to instill in its students. Therefore the facts of most of her life are omitted. Instead, students learn about a sanitized Helen Keller who became a mythic figure "who overcame." Teachers tell students to think of what she accomplished, but they are never told what she actually did accomplish over a period of decades. This is intentional. One good example is that of Mel and Norma Gabler. They became famous for beginning a campaign against American public school textbooks in 1961 because they regarded them as "anti-family" and "anti-Christian." Norma Gabler once testified that textbooks should "present our nation's patriots in a way that would honor and respect them." [32] In order to do that, one has to sanitize historical figures and events by omissions, half-truths and sometimes outright lies. Textbook authors and editors are motivated to skew the truth for many reasons. These include pressure from textbook adoption committees, the wish to avoid ambiguities, a desire to shield children from harm or conflict, the perceived need to control children and avoid classroom disharmony, and pressure to provide answers. [33] In the case of Helen Keller, textbook writers and editors seem to think that they can only present her as an inspiration as long as she remains uncontroversial. Helen Keller herself once said that "people do not like to think. If one thinks, one must reach conclusions....Conclusions are not always pleasant." [34]

In the United States, the sorry state of learning history has become evident even amongst prominent politicians who seek to run the country. In early June, 2011, former Alaskan Governor and presidential candidate Sarah Palin offered her version of Paul Revere's freedom ride to warn that the British were coming. She explains it like this:

"He who warned, uh, the ... the British that they weren't gonna be takin' away our arms, uh, by ringin' those bells and, um, by makin' sure that as he's ridin' his horse through town to send those warnin' shots and bells that, uh, we were gonna be secure and we were gonna be free ... and we were gonna be armed." (35)

Palin and other politicians have been widely criticized for their lack of knowledge of American history in recent years. In January, 2011, Minnesota Congresswoman Barbara Bachmann spoke about the founding fathers of the United States and their tireless work to abolish slavery:

"It didn't matter the color of their skin, it didn't matter their language, it didn't matter their economic status, it didn't matter whether they descended from known royalty or whether they were of a higher class or a lower class, it made no difference. Once you got here (to the United States), you were all the same. Isn't that remarkable?...That is the greatness and essence of this nation. We know we were not perfect. We know there was slavery that was still tolerated when the nation began. We know that was an evil and it was scourge and a blot and a stain upon our history. But we also know that the very founders that wrote those documents worked tirelessly until slavery was no more in the United States." (36)

Of course, these comments indicate serious ignorance of colonial history of the United States. It did matter what the colour of people's skin was and many of the founding fathers Bachmann states "worked tirelessly until slavery was no more in the United States" were slave owners throughout their lives and political careers – most notably George Washington and Thomas Jefferson. In fact, until it was amended after the Civil War, the United States Constitution in Article 1, Section 2, defined African Americans as only 3/5ths of a person. [37] Interestingly, when I first moved to the United States in 1988, I was expected to pass an exam on the U.S.

Constitution in order to meet requirements for acquiring a California State teaching license. It did not seem particularly difficult to study for but over the 19 years I spent teaching in the U.S., it seemed that very few students could even state that there were seven articles and 27 amendments in the document, let alone what any of the articles or amendments addressed. Most of the time I lived in California was spent working with students in grades 11 and 12; one would think that an effective education would have produced students who would have had some idea about their own constitution by that time, but they did not. The kind of history that Palin, Bachmann and others like to dispense publicly presents a generally erroneous but startling indication that what one learns or does not learn in formal public schooling has relatively small bearing on what one is qualified for after such schooling has been completed. But more importantly, the kind of history that Palin, Bachman and others actually do dispense publicly is a generally accurate reflection of the blind patriotism, mindless optimism, sheer misinformation and outright lies that Loewen has revealed is the content of American history textbooks in general. One only has to look at the changing historical representation of Louis Riel in various texts over the decades to see that misrepresentation also happens in Canada.

In this section so far, we have seen that: education in North America is not particularly successful at achieving desired literacy rates; that mathematical concepts and practice are presented in ways that do not reflect real-life use of the skills that are considered so important; and that history is significantly and deliberately misrepresented. English (language arts in general), Math and History are considered -- and have always been considered -- three of the four most important subjects to be taken in formal education. Along with science, these are the subjects that are considered the very foundation of formal education and preparation for the future. I have saved commentary about science instruction and curriculum for last because many assume that scientific instruction in schools – more than any other subject -- is practical, hands-on, and relevant. It is easier to question the relevance of studying Shakespearean plays, mathematical probability or much of the history we are presented with, but lab work in science lends credence to the notion that it is practical preparation for a wide variety of possible professions. Science has fuelled the many changes that, as was mentioned at the beginning of this chapter, have continuously restructured how we live our lives, communicate, raise our children and even how we think about and perceive ourselves over the past century and more. Therefore, how we teach and learn science may have the most far-reaching influence on how our society continues to develop. So do students today benefit from a rich science curriculum? Are they able to seamlessly integrate what they learn in school with the fast-paced scientific changes that occur in society at an accelerating rate?

Perhaps one of the best sources of information about the effectiveness of science education comes from the National Academies Press in Washington D.C. The NAP was created by the National Academies to publish reports issued by various scientific institutes, all of which operate under a charter granted by the United States Congress. These include the National Academy of Sciences, the National Academy of Engineering, the Institute of Medicine and the National Research Council. More than 200 books a year are published by the NAP on a wide range of issues in science, engineering and health. These publications express the most authoritative views on important issues in science and health because the institutions represented by the NAP attract the nation's leading experts in every field to serve on their committees. When America needs definitive information on anything from space science to animal nutrition, they turn to the National Academies Press. [38]

In 2005, the NAP published America's Lab Report: Investigations in High School Science. In a clearly damning report, the authors of the book report that neither a basic understanding nor an appreciation of how science has shaped society and culture is being cultivated during students' high school years. They even point out that in the 30 years between 1969 and 1999, high school students' scores on the science portion of the National Assessment of Educational Progress remained stagnant. Interestingly, the NAEP is in effect, "the nation's report card." The publication clearly states that major reforms in science education are needed to increase scientific understanding among students. The reform is needed across the science curriculum, including lab work. Even though scientists, educators and education policy-makers agree that high school graduates today need science education more than ever, very little research has been done to even inform debates about science instruction or to guide the design of laboratory instruction in high schools. [39] As a teacher who taught physical, biological and earth sciences to students in self-contained high school classes in California, I can tell you that high school science instruction in the United States is virtually indistinguishable from the high school science instruction I received in Canada myself decades earlier.

As with the teaching of subjects at school in general, the teaching of science is disjointed. Explanations are given but connections are not made. What happens in a given process is explained in words and sometimes pictures in science textbooks, but explanations of how and why are often not. This promotes a learning culture of memorization rather than understanding. Students are expected to remember the facts of what happens in a given process, but are rarely, if ever, expected to explain how and why the process works in situations other than the one or two examples provided. Students are usually expected to regurgitate the specific example given in a textbook. And in the end, this is more often than not reinforced by using multiple-choice or single-phrase rote testing responses to measure student "understanding" of subject material. Multiple-choice testing rarely requires more than a memorization of specific facts. Even questions that are supposedly designed to measure comprehension typically offer four or five choices to choose from. A one-out-of-four or five guess can hardly measure comprehension accurately.

A good example of disjoined information in a science text is not difficult to find. In a chapter on matter and chemical change in one text book currently in use in Calgary, Alberta (among many places), is a section on ionic compounds. The short, two-paragraph section begins with an explanation of what an ion is (a good idea before discussing compounds). It reads as follows:

> *When an atom gains or loses electrons, the atom is no longer neutral. It has become an **ion**, which is a particle or group of particles with a positive or negative charge. Atoms are neutral because they contain equal numbers of positive and negative charges. A sodium atom contains 11 protons and 11 electrons. If sodium loses one electron (as shown in Figure 2.43), it has 11 protons but only ten electrons, so the ion is positive.*

The electron rearrangement leaves the chlorine atom with a slight negative charge and the sodium atom with a slight positive charge. There is no longer an equal number of electrons and protons in each atom. The sodium will no longer have its original properties, however, and neither will the chlorine. Instead of two elements, the atoms now form a compound – sodium chloride, or NaCl, which is common table salt. (40)

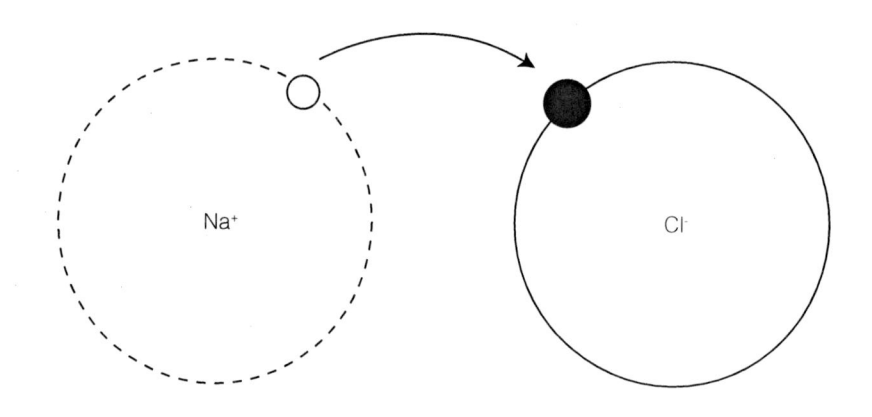

Na⁺   Cl⁻

The only other information about ionic compounds given in this section include a statement that ionic compounds dissolve in water resulting in the formation of both positive and negative ions, and that "charged particles can carry an electric current through water." It also provides a brief explanation of how ionic compounds are named. There is no explanation of how the particles might become charged in order to carry an electric current. Hopefully this is done orally in class before the student is expected to read through the section and then answer a few questions relating to the information given. (Many times this is not the case, however, and students are left to read the section and then do the lab questions on their own).

The diagram accompanying the two paragraphs quoted above shows two atoms with one losing an electron and the other gaining an electron. This can be somewhat confusing to students as the text specifically refers to a sodium atom that has eleven electrons and loses one. The diagram shows the loss of the electron but does not show the other ten electrons. Although the example given concerns simple table salt, the text then jumps directly to the brief information about charged ion particles conducting electricity. The accompanying activity on the following page is also disjointed. There are only four questions for students to answer. The first simply asks them to count the number of ions in a model and then state how many there are. The two types of ions are represented by black and white circles. If the student can count to eighteen, then he or she should get the answer correct — pretty tricky stuff. The last question asks students to match ionic compounds with specific everyday uses. Three compounds are listed and three everyday uses are listed. Students only have to guess between the two lists of three items (not particularly stimulating and really just amounting to "busy work," a regurgitative process that does not encourage real thinking or problem-solving). A classroom lab investigation is suggested to examine a number of substances to see which are ionic and which are molecular (looked at in a previous section), but such a lab may or may not be conducted depending on whether the teacher chooses to assign such work and if the classroom has the materials available to conduct the lab work.

Ions are not mentioned again for another 130 pages in the text and then only in a reference to ionization during a brief discussion about "static cling." When students are presented with this term, it is after spending weeks going through several chapters and topics discussing other terms and concepts. There is no explanation of ionization; students are expected to remember that they heard the term ion and ionic compounds (but not ionization) weeks earlier. Do they remember? Would they bother to look it up? Could they make the connection? The answer is likely no because there are no questions in the new section about ionization to reinforce ideas that might have been learned earlier. Without specific questions they "have to" respond to, it is doubtful that most students would bother looking up the previous information to verify their understanding. Often students go through the motions to acquire credit for the class but many, if not most, are not interested or engaged. Any connection between the two textbook passages may or may not be brought up in class discussion — if there is any class discussion when students come to this portion at all. And once teachers and students have bypassed a particular chapter, answered various textbook questions and possibly a quiz or test about a given topic, that topic, chapter and section are usually closed to further discussion. After all, the teacher is pressured to cover all of the textbook contents during the school year (typically 180 to 200 days, depending on provincial or state guidelines). The only possible exception would be if a review were conducted before the final exam for the course (likely to be a multiple choice exam with the exercise teaching to the test). Throughout the rest of the text, the term "ion" is only mentioned once more some 40 pages later when it states that Michael Faraday was the first person to introduce the term along with other new scientific terms. Many topics are handled in this way and leads one to wonder how even a few students manage to get any semblance of a worthwhile science education at all.

The National Academies Press emphasized in its report that "science education would not be about science if it did not include opportunities for students to learn about both the process and the content of science." This involves laboratory experiences to supplement classroom discussion that is primarily text book driven. Yet the NAP also expresses concern that lab experiences have historically been disconnected from the flow of classroom science lessons and that teachers and lab manuals often emphasize procedures to be followed instead of focusing on clear learning goals. This often leaves students uncertain about what it is they are expected to learn from the experiences. The truth of the matter is that students are not helped to fully understand the scientific process because most of them only participate in a limited range of laboratory experiences. Some students don't even have access to any type of lab experience at all.

Teachers themselves have difficulty bringing their students to a good understanding of scientific concepts. As already mentioned, their efforts are spent following the curriculum as set out by pedagogical frameworks. They are time-constrained to make sure that students have a clear understanding of the many concepts they are expected to cover and therefore are unsuccessful at doing just that. Students do not have a clear understanding of most scientific concepts. It isn't just that teachers' hands have time constraints, following framework guidelines or having limited lab resources to supplement classroom instruction; the NAP reports that the undergraduate education of future high school science teachers does not prepare them with either the pedagogical or scientific knowledge required to carry out appropriate teaching strategies. Many high school science teachers have not advanced their education beyond a bachelor's degree and once on the job, they lack good opportunities to improve their science teaching. "Professional development opportunities for science teachers are limited in quality, availability, and scope and place little emphasis on laboratory instruction." [41]

Part of the problem is the system itself. How schools are organized constrains their ability to address the need for improvement. All of the participants in the school experience – administrators, teachers and students – are accustomed to scheduling routines for all subject classes and have their own schedules and time constraints that limit experience beyond the tolling of classroom period bells. They are also bound by the specific allocation of actual space to work in, the amount of supplies that can be purchased due to budget constraints in general, and actual teaching approaches that are not designed to accommodate individual learning differences among students. When all of these routines and constraints become rigid, only existing knowledge and teaching practices are reinforced. That limits the motivation and ability of both teachers and administrators to try out newer, more current, and newly discovered approaches to teaching science, especially within the context of the all-important lab experiences that are supposed to supplement classroom instruction. [42]

Advanced placement science classes in high school often provide little to no advantage over regular science courses either. Advanced placement textbooks used to be intimidating thirty years ago when many had over thirty chapters and 800 pages to cover within a school year. Commensurate with the explosion of research into cells and genetics in recent decades, advanced placement texts in biology alone have expanded to include more than fifty chapters and 1,400 pages to cover. Not surprisingly, science texts – just like history texts – have been criticized for overwhelming students with facts to memorize and then rushing through important topics. PowerPoint lectures are now the norm in many science classes – advanced or general. That only allows for discussion in point form and students rush to take notes so that they can memorize the material for quizzes and exams. [43]

It is not surprising that many students might find it difficult to take a genuine interest in science. To what extent are they given the opportunity to explore any aspect of a science course in depth? One advantage a science class has is that it is better-equipped to accommodate different learning styles and should therefore be more successful in garnering student interest;

lab activities do provide the additional hands-on approach that might capture that interest. Yet rushing through material, not making essential connections, and reliance on a dry, one-size-fits-all approach to teaching science negates any advantage that might have been exploited through the use of labs. Furthermore, if teacher training, as mentioned above, does not prepare future teachers with either the pedagogical or scientific knowledge required to carry out appropriate teaching strategies, then a routinized, textbook-dominated, boring approach to teaching their subject will not indicate that they have any more enthusiasm for it than their students appear to have. European research published in July, 2011 indicates that

> "the shrinking number of students in Europe who choose to study science is influenced by how school and teachers shape their attitudes...Based on the findings, students start off their education by having a narrow or inaccurate view of science and technology. Their development is impacted by two factors: the school and how teachers are trained."
> (44)

There is no reason to believe that the situation in Canada and the United States is any different. There may be some differences in statistical results between European and North American schools, but all western education is similarly structured to teach to the test with the hope and expectation of raising statistical outcomes. As we have seen, high school success rates are not climbing as the result of this approach to teaching and learning in general. Testing and the curriculum, as we have been discussing in this chapter, are important factors preventing higher statistical outcomes, but the roles of everyone involved in schooling also plays a part.

Roles and Rules

Whether you went to school thirty, forty, fifty or more years ago or still go to school today, the concept of us and them is still a familiar one when one considers or discusses students and teachers. It might even be safe to say that everyone who has ever gone to school has a story about their experience that reflects this concept of us and them. As someone who has been both a student and a teacher, I can state with assurance that it would be equally familiar to hear someone begin a sentence having negative connotations with either of the following introductions: "I once had a teacher who..." or "I once had a student who..." Both of these possible sentences would undoubtedly focus on some aspect of a relationship or situation between a teacher and student that emphasized opposition, dislike or even direct confrontation. This is so familiar that virtually nobody reading these statements would feign surprise in any way. Everyone has a story if not many stories portraying students and teachers in opposition to one another.

The flip side of this observation is that there are also many among us who have exceptionally fond recollections of some teachers or some students and for good reason. There are many teachers who care about students and many students who can point to teachers who made a difference. Yet, any human connection that might be made between teachers and students is made despite the system and framework in which people who are either teachers or students have to work. The traditional classroom is not conducive to natural interaction. The roles of the participants and the rules that govern them provide an environment that is counterproductive to the learning process.

In the morning, students arrive at their school conscious of the fact that they are expected to be there by a certain time. The exact time is announced by a bell, much as it might be in a factory and just as it has been in North American public schools for the past 160 years. The students usually make their way to a homeroom where attendance can be taken so that documentation for revenue purposes is attended to. Once that business is completed, the bell rings again indicating that students will begin their first class of the day. In elementary schools students may stay in the same classroom all day while in junior and senior high schools, students will make their way from class to class much like a product is developed as it continues down the production line. When the bell indicates the beginning of a class, students know from their earliest education training that they are expected to be quiet and wait for the teacher's direction. Similarly, when the bell rings, the teacher of each class knows that he or she is expected to "take charge" of the students' learning. Many teachers might greet their class with a "good morning" or even address various students individually, but throughout the many years of compulsory school education, it would be more likely to hear an introduction such as this: "Okay class, the bell has rung, let's get started."

If that sounds a little like the start of a race or the beginning of a game defined by time limits, it may be because there are similarities. There are x-amount of minutes during which the class will be "conducted." In elementary and many junior high schools, that measure of class time is usually somewhere between 40 and 50 minutes. There are specific structures of bell schedules and they are usually referred to as regular bell schedules or block schedules. Block schedules refer to extended periods that in some high schools may last as long as 110 minutes per class. The fact that there are structures for bell schedules implies standardization, another feature of industrial mass production mentality. Once classes have begun, there really is a race against time to accomplish specific lesson objectives for the day. That may involve some class discussion but in many classes like history, math, science or language arts – the main subjects that are taught in public schools – students can expect to hear the introductory words of the lesson sound something like this: Turn to page 63 or 127 or 204 or whatever. Similarly, at the end of a class, it would not be uncommon to hear a teacher say something like "there's the bell; that's it for today." We have already discussed the inadequacy of much school curriculum in practice today. Yet even if there were real teaching moments in a classroom on a regular basis, the momentum gained by capturing student attention and dancing toward some magnificent learning crescendo and that elusive "eureka" moment could easily be destroyed by the sounding of the bell. And that's what it is often referred to as – a period. One could easily make the comparison with a game contestant trying to achieve an objective but falling short because the time ran out first.

During the class, students may be following along as the teacher reads from a text – or worse, as he or she makes all of the students take turns reading from the text. When this occurs, as it often does in many classrooms, something other than learning takes place. Most of the students are not concentrating on what is supposed to be learned by following in the book. Some of the students are worried about being embarrassed by having to read when it comes their turn because they are painfully aware that their reading skills are not quite up to par with that of some of their classmates. Some students who may want to put forward their best effort, and who feel capable enough to read, find it difficult to pay attention. Other students are reading so slowly and/or being interrupted with corrections by their teacher, that the more capable students find it difficult to maintain their train of thought and/or are bored to tears. Under such circumstances, no momentum toward a crescendo of learning can ever be achieved. The focus continues to be the reading of the text and not on the understanding of the text. Although the teachers who follow this regimen may understand how painful the process is for everyone involved, they often continue to employ the same techniques for "getting through the curriculum" day after day, week after week, and year after year. Often, the teacher as well as the student is so hopelessly bored that the sounding of the bell is welcomed like some intermittent reprieve from the latest round of slow torture.

Who wouldn't want some reprieve from torture? Boredom is the number one reason why students will "act out" in class. Inability to perform is a close second. Although acting out is considered to be an undesirable quality generated by "poor students," schools bear a significant amount of the responsibility for the existence of poor students. Boredom is the number one reason students often do not like school because it affects both those who are capable and those who are not. The capable students become bored because they do comprehend and quite simply aren't challenged. They will begin talking to peers or act out just to entertain themselves or because they are trying to stay awake. The students who are less capable will begin talking to peers or acting out because they have a long history of feeling inadequate and would rather draw attention to themselves for acting out, being defiant or noncompliant because it is a lot cooler in the eyes of their peers than simply being seen as incompetent. Their inability to perform has been fostered by schools themselves because schools continue to move students to the next grade whether they have achieved the objectives of the previous grade or not. Cumulatively, this becomes a worse problem as a student enters the next grade level. Although there may be some legitimacy to the argument that holding a student back could have adverse effects on that student's self-esteem, one must also ask the question: How does moving elementary students ahead until they are illiterate and innumerate high school students actually help their self-esteem?

When students do act out, are defiant or noncompliant, they are routinely subject to discipline in schools. Although such coercion techniques like the strap are no longer used as they were for decades before the 1970s, "the consistent strategy has been to punish or exclude those who violate the rules." [45] In many classrooms, even an initial transgression – as interpreted by the teacher – will result in sending a student to the principal's office to face disciplinary action. This might include simply being spoken to, being warned about future violations with a list of possible consequences, calling home to parents, suspension from school, and worst-case scenario, expulsion. The path to these consequences can begin simply by meeting a teacher's disapproval in some way. In school systems – as they have existed for a century and a half now – the teacher still controls the classroom atmosphere of "learning." The teacher dictates what is to be done and how. The teacher also controls the outcomes of student performance by making judgements about "effort" and "compliance" through grades. The teacher makes decisions about whether a student may speak or not, and even if a student may get a drink or go to the restroom.

Part of the problem in schools is that teachers may have the authority to control all of these things, but in fact there is often little control. Students understand how the system works and yet many still violate the rules by acting out, being defiant and non-compliant. In most schools there is an ongoing revolving door of students into and out of an office for disciplinary reasons throughout the day. This shouldn't be surprising to anyone. How many adults would like to be told what to do and when, whether they can speak or not, when they can go for a drink or to the bathroom or not, and be assigned grades for both their effort and behaviour? Would they put up with it on a daily basis for thirteen years straight without complaint? Would they continue to robotically perform according to the whims and wishes of every instructor – however good or bad the instructor may be and however meaningful or meaningless the instruction may be -- simply because that person was the instructor? Unlikely. There are reasons why teachers and students are often pitted against one another.

A central issue here is respect and for the most part in schools, respect is expected to flow in one direction. This is emphasized throughout the day at most schools where it is still both expectation and policy that teachers will be referred to by title: Mr., Mrs., or Miss so-and-so. There are no policies about how students will be referred to and so they are routinely referred to by their first names. The implication is subtle but the unmistakeable understanding by many students is that respect flows in only one direction and that it is due simply because a label demands it. Most people believe that teachers should be afforded respect by their students but the best way to get it is not by labelling it. Respect is most genuine when it has been earned.

The culture of schools has become the defacto idea of what learning is all about – and that is a fundamentally incorrect assumption. When someone – anyone – tells another person that it would be good or important for them to learn this or that, the person being given the advice inadvertently conjures up the image of having to go to a school and follow a course of study. He or she automatically thinks of textbooks, scheduled classes, lectures, homework, tests, grades, passing or failing and ultimately, when they will be finished. Although some students are more conscientious than others, most only hope for and strive to achieve the bare minimum that will get them by. They know that whether they get 60 percent or 99 percent, the "pass" they achieve is the key value of undergoing the process in the first place. Most students believe that passing the course is what is important. It doesn't matter if they know 39 percent less of the material than Johnny does as long as they pass. The passing grade in each course is enough to help them earn the degree (i.e. ticket they need to move into a professional area of "expertise"). It is just as possible to earn a bachelor's degree by achieving the minimum required grade in each course as it is to earn the maximum grade possible. "Earning" a high school diploma can be achieved the same way but what does this say about the quality of most of our graduates? Most employers are not interested in whether a potential hire achieved 60 percent or 99 percent in all of their courses of study; they are only interested in verifying that the potential hire has a high school diploma or a bachelor's degree. They too are just looking for the piece of paper that certifies achievement and expertise. All of these people are jumping through the hoops set up by the system but in this case, certification is not a guarantee of either achievement or expertise. Using a term popular in the game of Monopoly, simply passing a course of study – whether it was achieved minimally or to the highest possible standard – is the card that allows the student to pass GO and collect x-amount of dollars. The actual scores are virtually meaningless unless the student who "achieved" them wants to go on and jump through more system hoops in the form of further education. That is the only time when scores are really necessary. The whole system is contrived to advance the system itself and little more.

Yet learning before 160 years ago when compulsory schooling began was very different. The basic structure of education was learning from someone who was already proficient in the skill being sought. One didn't need a professional teacher to learn how to read; one only needed to be guided by someone else who knew how to read. Learning to write a sentence didn't involve dissecting it into a collection of nouns, verbs, adverbs and so on – as if that is the only way to learn how to write. One even has to question whether or not it is any way to learn how to write. Babies learn how to speak simply by imitating the examples they have around them. Does anyone think that they would learn more efficiently by having them sit in a classroom with other babies and dissect sentence structure? Of course not. So why do we believe and practice the concept that the only way to learn anything at any age is to take a course and dissect information until we no longer see the relationship it has with other information we dissect in other courses? It is possible to do well in language courses and be considered proficient by the scores one achieves in those courses, yet it doesn't – and can't – guarantee that the person who earned those scores is actually a proficient speaker of the language studied. I studied French in school for four years and achieved passing grades but it wasn't until I moved to Montreal and immersed myself in learning French in a practical manner that I actually became conversational with others who were native speakers.

In our modern society, taking a course of study is the only legitimate way to have proficiency recognized, even if proficiency doesn't actually exist once the course of study has been completed. This is why in North America we still have many high school graduates who are functionally illiterate and innumerate. Interestingly, it has been reported that Ted Kennedy's office once released a paper claiming that in the State of Massachusetts (where compulsory schooling first began), the literacy rate before compulsory schooling was 98 percent. After compulsory schooling began, the literacy rate never rose above 91 percent. [46] This is further evidence that 160 years of compulsory schooling as the only legitimate means of recognizing an "educated" individual is quite simply, not legitimate. Neither is it efficient, reliable or even particularly competent at doing so.

The reason this is the case, along with its roles and rules, is found within the structure of the system itself: It alienates and labels its students by separating them into age groups; separating them from diversity and interaction with society at large; expecting them to memorize and regurgitate isolated facts; imposing mindless rules like not wearing hats; dictating their every move and expecting canned responses; expecting them to sit still for hours upon hours; enforcing the implication that respect flows in one direction; testing them on a lot of mindless facts that will not help them to adapt to a rapidly changing world once they leave school; and then grading them on thirteen years of effort to make sure they understand what their value and potential, or lack thereof, might be in the future.

The Bigger Picture

No one would doubt that there are many teachers who work very hard to help their students learn and achieve. I have personally worked with numerous teachers whom I consider dedicated, conscientious and caring individuals. They believe wholeheartedly that compulsory formal education as a system is what their students need and that those who fall through the cracks – and there are many cracks – simply don't realize the importance of what they are rejecting. That is why they continue to give homework, continue to follow the system's curriculum and continue to test their students. After all, didn't they jump through those hoops and achieve what schooling has always promised them? Haven't they learned to be successful? Aren't they living role models to students of what proper schooling can achieve?

Of course the answer to these questions is that they have jumped through the system hoops, they have achieved and are successful in the current system, and they are examples of what formal compulsory schooling can achieve. But is this the best that can be achieved? Being schooled is not the same as being educated and this is an important point. Being educated means being able to think for oneself, being able to problem-solve, and being able to think outside of the proverbial box. Being schooled means being able to jump through the hoops – maybe the ones on page 47 if not the ones on page 226 – as long as one achieves the magic score of 50 or 60 percent in required courses to achieve the minimum necessary and acquire the piece of paper that now says they are proficient. Being schooled means living, breathing and working inside the same box we expect others to live, breathe and work in and that is why the model is perseverated. We as a society believe that formal compulsory schooling is the only means toward success but this is an illusion of sorts. We may acknowledge that people like Thomas Edison, Henry Ford, The Wright brothers, Abraham Lincoln, Charles Dickens or Mark Twain – all people who succeeded without formal compulsory schooling – were successful, even exceptionally so, but we consider them examples from the past. We separate the possibilities of yesterday from the possibilities of today and perhaps rightfully so because the system itself determines to a large extent who can or who cannot become successful. Yet even in recent times there are bright examples of people who achieved without graduating from formal schooling in the fields where they became successful. In fact, these examples did not complete high school. It includes business leaders and entrepreneurs like Richard Branson, James H. Clark, Soichiro Honda, Ray Kroc, David Murdock, Vidal Sassoon and Marcus Loew. It includes film directors like John Huston, Peter Jackson and Quentin Tarantino, anthropologist Margaret Mead (who was mostly homeschooled), and it includes many from the fields of music, drama, journalism, politics, science, sports, comedy, and many uncategorized fields of expertise.[47] Even Albert Einstein was mostly self-taught. He studied Judaism and learned to play the violin at home, taught himself Euclidean geometry at the age of 12, and was not particularly interested in what he was offered in formal schools of study. He continued to show little respect for teachers, was not a regular attendant at lectures and spent a considerable time studying physics on his own.[48] Learning and education are important, but formal compulsory schooling is not necessary for success. For many students, it may even be detrimental.

Let's take a look at the design and purpose of the system of modern education itself. Much of this comes from the United States where, in Massachusetts as we have already mentioned in this book, modern compulsory schooling in North America began. Compulsory schooling did not just arise and become the megalithic enterprise it is today from nowhere. It had to be considered, planned and then implemented. It had to have a design and a purpose. Although ideas about formal schooling were conceived decades earlier, it wasn't until the early twentieth century that mass compulsory schooling really took the shape that it has retained to this day. At that time many prominent writers, scholars and thinkers weighed in on their views about the subject, even though today most people are unaware of the views and debates that raged during that time. Until the twentieth century, there were still many who opposed compulsory schooling and there were even armed conflicts in response to its implementation.

If one was to poll people on the streets of cities and towns in North America and ask them why modern compulsory education exists, most would respond by saying something to the effect that it provides equal opportunity for all. Many might add that it is designed to make good people, citizens and to assist everyone in reaching their potential. One of the famous writers who weighed in on the topic early in the debate was H.L. Mencken, a journalist, essayist, English language scholar and critic of American life and culture. In April, 1924, he made a statement about public education in The American Mercury, a magazine that featured some of the most important writers in the United States through the 1920s and 1930s. He wrote that the

> "erroneous assumption is to the effect that the aim of public education is to fill the young of the species with knowledge and awaken their intelligence, and so make them fit to discharge the duties of citizenship in an enlightened and independent manner. Nothing could be further from the truth. The aim of public education is not to spread enlightenment at all; it is simply to reduce as many individuals as possible to the same safe level, to breed and train a standardised citizenry, to put down dissent and originality. That is its aim in the United States, whatever the pretensions of politicians, pedagogues and other such mountebanks, and that is its aim everywhere else." [49]

One might find many comments such as these by prominent writers in opposition to modern compulsory schooling at the time, but to verify the intent behind modern compulsory schooling, one can go directly to the source: A book published in 1918 by Alexander Inglis entitled Principles of Secondary Education, (and corroborated by published bulletins from the

Bureau of Education, then part of the U.S. Department of the Interior), is quite clear about the purpose of modern schooling. In Principles of Secondary education, Inglis, for whom an honor lecture in education at Harvard is named, [50] establishes the purpose for education through six functions. Anyone can read the entire original text online at the Internet Archive, a resource for historical collections that exist in digital format.[51] John Taylor Gatto, once named New York State's Teacher of the Year and author of several books on education summarizes each of Inglis' six functions as follows:

1. The adjustive or adaptive function: Schools are to establish fixed habits of reaction to authority. This, of course, precludes critical judgement completely. It also pretty much destroys the idea that useful or interesting material should be taught, because you can't test for reflexive obedience until you know whether you can make kids learn, and do, foolish and boring things.

2. The integrating function: This might well be called "the conformity function," because its intention is to make children as alike as possible. People who conform are predictable, and this is of great use to those who wish to harness and manipulate a large labor force.

3. The diagnostic and directive function: School is meant to determine each student's proper social role. This is done by logging evidence mathematically and anecdotally on cumulative records. As in "your permanent record." Yes, you do have one.

4. The differentiating function: Once their social role has been diagnosed, children are to be sorted by role and trained only so far as their destination in the social machine merits – and not one step further. So much for making kids their personal best.

5. The selective function: This refers not to human choice at all but to Darwin's theory of natural selection as applied to what he (Inglis) called "the favored races." In short, the idea is to help things along by conspicuously attempting to improve the breeding stock. Schools are meant to tag the unfit – with poor grades, remedial placement, and other punishments – clearly enough that their peers will accept them as inferior and effectively bar them from the

reproductive sweepstakes. That's what all those little humiliations from first grade onward were intended to do: wash the dirt down the drain.

6. The propaedeutic (one that serves as an introduction) function: The societal system implied by these rules will require an elite group of caretakers. To that end, a small fraction of the kids will quietly be taught how to manage this continuing project, how to watch over and control a population deliberately dumbed down and declawed in order that government might proceed unchallenged and corporations might want for obedient labor. (52)

Formal compulsory schooling today exists as part and parcel of our everyday life and society. It is such a familiar part of the fabric of our culture that we cannot imagine being without it in the form that it exists today. The widespread proliferation of mass formal education has so permeated our society as part of the process for advancing in our society that we see the connections between being successful in one in order to be successful in the other as being "natural" and even exclusive of other ways to learn and achieve an education. Perhaps the most important thing to remember about the education of our young is that, despite the ongoing rhetoric, it is not intended to be for the benefit of the young as an end product of self-improvement itself. The idea behind education is to prepare the young for the roles they will fill as adults in our society. Society, as we think of it, is the manner in which we organize ourselves so that we can persist as efficiently and productively as possible. Therefore, the whole idea of society must incorporate the idea of economy — the means and method of subsistence for large populations. To spell it out, mass formal compulsory education is a necessary part of managing a large, diversified economy. In order for it to be successful, it must meet the needs of the whole economy, not just the best jobs that can be found within that economy.

Before the industrialized age, there was no need for mass education efforts because until then, most people acquired or manufactured the products they used either themselves or locally from neighbours whom they knew personally — the local butcher, baker, cobbler and so on. People still had to use manpower or animal power to fulfill daily tasks. There weren't any power-machines around to free up as much of our time through mass production as there has been over the past two-hundred years. Therefore, manpower and child power were needed around the home, the farm or the family business if there was one. Most children grew up to follow in their family's footsteps. If a man was a carpenter or a shoe-cobbler, his sons would almost certainly follow the same path he took. Economically, it perseverated the skill set already familiar and accessible. It was cheaper and more prudent to teach your own children what you knew rather than spend or trade goods and services to have another person teach your child or children a new skill set elsewhere. The goods and services one could utilize for such a purpose were needed at home and not available for barter.

Once industrialization began, society began to change rapidly. No one would argue that the industrial revolution marked a significant turning point in human history. Major changes in agriculture, manufacturing, mining, transportation, technology, medicine and many other areas had a profound effect on the social, economic and cultural conditions that existed for thousands of years since agriculture was first developed. People were on the move from rural settings to more urbanized ones. Diversification of skill sets grew exponentially and as things continued to change, so did the conditions that went with them. Now things in our global society change so rapidly that we may consider our lives ones that are always in a state of flux. With the global population also increasing more than seven-fold (so far) since industrialization began, there might be considered good reason to "manage" every aspect of our society and culture. The status quo – whatever that is in whatever time period it exists – is always concerned about keeping the economic and political power that exists intact and this too provides good reason to manage every aspect of our society and culture.

Having stated all of this, let's return to the point that mass formal compulsory education is a necessary part of managing a large, diversified economy and that in order for an economy to be successful, mass formal compulsory education must meet the needs of the whole economy – not just the best employment sectors that can be found within that economy. All of a sudden, the system begins to make some sense. As of November, 2011, the most recent statistics of public school indicators available from Statistics Canada online were published in December 2010 and provide information for the 2008-2009 school year. The "total expenditures in Canada's elementary and secondary schools amounted to $55.0 billion in 2008/2009" and "the graduation rate for publicly funded high schools in 2008/2009 was 74.8 percent." [53] The most recent figures for the United States as of November, 2011 come from the National Center for Educational Statistics and represent the cost of public education for the 2007-2008 school year. During that year, expenditures for public elementary and secondary education were "$506.8 billion." [54] The graduation rate for publically funded high schools was 68.8 percent. [55] Although Canada's dropout rate is 6 percent lower than the United States, both could be rounded off to a 30 percent dropout rate, not unfair since there are differences in such rates from province to province and state to state. Even if you read these statistics a few years from when this book was written, you will find that the dropout rates will remain relatively the same but the cost of formal compulsory education will be higher than it is now. The reasons for this are as follows: Statistically speaking, the dropout rate is not so much a measure of failure as it is a measure of the portion of the population likely designated or allocated for lower-skilled and lower-paying employment in the economy. The cost of managing such a system for determining allocation of human resources increases just like the cost of everything else. If it didn't work, real changes would be implemented to make it work. The fact of the matter is that the education system – as it is and was always intended to be – does work. It very effectively does two important things: 1) It manages the underage segment of the population while parents and guardians contribute to the economy through a formal, compulsory process; and 2) Using an elaborate grading system, it organizes future human resources into a practical, operational method for distribution among the administrative, creative, innovative, entrepreneurial, manufacturing, service as well as various other menial sectors of the economy.

That's right. The current formal compulsory school system as we know it is designed to maximize the efficiency of the economy in the following ways: 1) by effectively mandating that the underage segment of the population unable to contribute, and protected by labour laws from contributing to the workforce, is housed and kept occupied in schools while both parents contribute to the economy (until they reach the age whereby they may enter the workforce and add to the economy themselves); and 2) by preparing, measuring, socializing, and allocating under-aged, future human resources for various positions within the existing structure of the economy once they reach working age.

If one doubts that the modern formal compulsory school system was designed to be this way, it only has to refer to a speech made by Woodrow Wilson, former President of the United States, in an address to the New York City High School Teachers Association on January 9th, 1909, now over one hundred years ago:

> "We want one class of persons to have a liberal education, and we want another class of persons, a very much larger class, of necessity, in every society, to forego the privileges of a liberal education and fit themselves to perform specific difficult manual tasks.....Therefore this is not a subject for cynical comment, this is not a subject for criticism. It is a subject for self-recognition...For a system means a definite thing, it means an organic whole; it means the parts of that whole related to each other in rational fashion, some fixed kind and determined sequence of studies." (56)

Think about everything that has been stated in this chapter so far: Why has the school system remained relatively the same for all of these decades when the world that formal compulsory schooling is supposed to be preparing our students for has changed so radically at an ever-increasing pace during the same period of time? Why do we continue to remove children from the heretofore natural experiences of life in all its diversity to "formally" prepare for "natural" experiences of life? Why is school irrelevant as Marshall McLuhan says? Why does it shield children from the reality of life, as Norbert Wiener says? Why does school educate for obsolescence, as John Gardner says? Why does school not develop intelligence, as Jerome Bruner says? Why is schooling and lack of formal public education based on fear, as John Holt says? Why does it avoid the promotion of significant learning, as Carl Rogers says? Why does it induce alienation, as Paul Goodman says? Why does it punish creativity and independence, as Edgar Friedenberg says? Why do thousands of students continue to drop out of school every day in North America? Why do we continue to test students in ways that do not actually measure what has been learned? Why do we continue to grade students based mostly on test scores in order to categorize them rather than provide them with meaningful learning opportunities to truly meet their individual potentials? Why do we continue to teach so many meaningless facts for simple regurgitation when much of it is irrelevant to future insight or success? Why do we continue to medicate so many children to reinforce compliance when clearly, many of them do not need to be medicated? Why do we take up to thirteen years to "educate" but so clearly fail to produce a higher percentage of literate and numerate students at the end of that process, especially when literacy and numeracy take only about one hundred hours of good instruction? Why do we not produce independent, responsible citizens after raising them in the formal compulsory school process for most of their growing years with the initial purpose of developing independent, responsible citizens? Why is the natural process of learning formalized to the point that only those who have pieces of paper proving they have been through the formal process are recognized as being "educated" and prepared for most positions in the life and economy of our society? Why do we claim to recognize that all students are individual and that multiple intelligences exist if we continue to funnel the vast majority of students through the same processes? And finally, why do we keep spending ever-increasing amounts of money to produce all of these same results?

Despite all that has been stated, the answer is simple: Because the society we live in is getting the results it wants and needs – period. So now we arrive at a place where we must realize and address the issues, obstacles and problems in education. There are many. First we must realize that the education system we have is the way it is for socioeconomic reasons. Second, we must come to see why the system we have is not adequate in broader terms than it is usually presented. That is, we must address the issues of how the current education system impacts the society we live in, who benefits and who doesn't. Third, we must explore new ways of meeting the needs of more people in our society while reducing the inequalities that are currently produced. This requires a complete rethinking of how we create educational experiences. It also requires a complete rethinking of how we certify educational experiences. But in order for us to really create an educational system that can match the rhetoric of the education system we have today, we have to rethink the kind of society and economy we want to meet the needs of all the people who are part of our society.

References and Footnotes

1. Postman, Neil and Weingartner, Charles (1969), <u>Teaching as a Subversive Activity</u>, Delta Books, Dell Publishing, New York, pg. xiv.

2. Wingert, Patrice (June 14th, 2010), The (Somewhat) Good and (Mostly) Bad News About High-School Drop Out Rates, Newsweek, Retrieved online March 19th, 2011 from: http://www.newsweek.com/blogs/the-gaggle/2010/06/14/the-somewhat-good-and-mostly-bad-news-about-high-school-dropout-rates.html.

3. **Editorial Projects in Education** Is the independent, nonprofit publisher of Education Week and other high-quality print and online products on K-12 education. Information retrieved online April 10, 2011 from http://www.edweek.org/info/about.

4. Gilmore, James (2010), <u>Trends in Dropout Rates and the Labour Market Outcomes of Young Dropouts</u>, Statistics Canada publication, Labour Statistics Division, retrieved online April 5th, 2011 from: http://www.statcan.gc.ca/pub/81-004-x/2010004/article/11339-eng.htm.

5. Alliance for Excellent Education Fact sheet (2009), High School Dropouts in America, pg. 2, retrieved on April 5th, 2011 from http://www.all4ed.org/files/GraduationRates_FactSheet.pdf.

6. Jerald, C. (2006), <u>Dropping Out is Hard to Do</u>, The Center for Comprehensive School Reform and Improvement, Washington D.C.

7. Balfanz, R. and Legters, N. (2006), <u>Closing Dropout Factories: The Graduation Rate Crisis We Know and What Can Be Done About It</u>, Education Week 25, no. 42: pgs. 42-43.

8. Allensworth, E. and Easton, J. (2007), What Matters For Staying On-Track and Graduating in Chicago Public High Schools: A Close Look at Course Grades, Failures and Attendance in the Freshman Year, Chicago, IL: Consortium on Chicago School Research at the University of Chicago, University Publications Office.

9. Gerver, Richard (2010), Creating Tomorrow's Schools Today, Continuum International Publishing Group, London, pgs. 67-69.

10. Meece, Judith L., Blumenfeld, Phyllis C., and Hoyle, Rick H. (1988), <u>Students' Goal Orientations and Cognitive Engagement in Classroom Activities</u>, Journal of Educational Psychology, Vol. 80, pgs. 514-23.

11. Description of the CTBS (Comprehensive Test of Basic Skills) was found online and retrieved on May 15th, 2011 from: http://www.kids-iq-tests.com/CTBS.html.

12. Information retrieved online from the Nelson Education site on May 15th, 2011 from: http://www.assess.nelson.com/group/ctbs-khs.html.

13. Kohn, Alfie (2000), <u>The Case Against Standardized Testing</u>, Heinemann, Portsmouth, New Hampshire, pg. 10.

14. Kohn, Alfie (2000), <u>The Case Against Standardized Testing</u>, Heinemann, Portsmouth, New Hampshire, pg.13.

15. Piaget, Jean (1948), <u>To Understand is to Invent: The Future of Education</u>, Grossman Publishing, New York, pg. 74.

16. Gatto, John Taylor (1992) <u>Dumbing Us Down: the Hidden Curriculum of Compulsory Schooling</u>, New Society Publishers, Gabriola Island, British Columbia, Canada, pg. 12.

17. Article on <u>Education and Skills Overview</u> published by The Conference Board of Canada, a not-for-profit applied research organization, found online May 23rd, 2011 at: http://conferenceboard.ca/hcp/overview/Educationskills.aspx.

18. National Assessment of Adult Literacy (2003), <u>State and County Estimates of Low Literacy</u>, published by the U.S. Department of Education's National Center for Education Statistics, retrieved online May 23rd, 2011 from: http://nces.ed.gov/naal/estimates/overview.aspx#2.

19. Education Portal (2007), <u>Grim Illiteracy Statistics Indicate Americans Have a Reading Problem</u>, retrieved online May 25th, 2011

from: http://education-portal.com/articles/Grim_Illiteracy_Statistics_Indicate_Americans_Have_a_Reading_Problem.html. The original information reported here came from caliteracy.org, the National Institute for Literacy – Stats and Resources, found online at: http://www.caliteracy.org/nil/.

20. Bobbitt, John Franklin (1918), <u>The Curriculum,</u> published by Houghton Mifflin, Boston.

21. information taken from an article entitled Curriculum, found online June 1st, 2011 at: http://en.wikipedia.org/wiki/Curriculum#cite_note-0

22. Dr. E.P. Scarlett High School Registration Guide 2011-2012, Calgary, Alberta, Canada, pg. 5.

23. Null, J. (1999), <u>Unacknowledged Changes in the Curriculum Thought of John Franklin Bobbitt,</u> Journal of Curriculum Supervision, 15, Fall, pgs. 35-42.

24. California's Common Core Content Standards for English Language Arts & Literacy in History/Social Studies, Science, and Technical Subjects prepared by the California State board of Education, pg. 31. Updated October 15th, 2010. Retrieved online June 11th, 2011 from:http://www.scoe.net/castandards/agenda/2010/ela_ccs_recommendations.pdf

25. Parsavand, Shirin (2009), California Literacy at Bottom, taken from the Press-Enterprise online edition, Riverside, California. Retrieved online June 11th, 2011 from: http://www.pe.com/localnews/inland/stories/PE_News_Local_S_literacy09.56ff1c.html

26. Stapel, Elizabeth. "Why Do I Have to Take Algebra?" <u>Purplemath</u>. Retrieved online June 7th, http://www.purplemath.com/modules/why_math.htm.

27. Knill, Dottori, Timoteo, Collins, Forest, Kestell, and Macdonald (1996), <u>Mathpower 8,</u> McGraw-Hill Ryerson Limited, Whitby, Ontario, Canada, pgs. 45, 127, 25 respectively.

28. Loewen, James W. (1995), <u>Lies My Teacher Told Me: Everything</u>

Your American History Textbook Got Wrong, New Press, 384 pages.

29. This quote is taken from the product description of the book by one of its distributors, Amazon. The quote was retrieved online June 23rd, 2011 from: http://www.amazon.ca/Lies-My-Teacher-Told-Everything/dp/product-description/0684818868.

30. Loewen, James W. (1995), *Lies My Teacher Told Me: Everything Your American History Textbook Got Wrong*, New Press, from the preface, pg. 2.

31. Loewen, James W. (2007), *Lies My Teacher Told Me: Everything Your American History Textbook Got Wrong*, Touchstone revised paperback edition, New York, pgs. 32-33.

32. Quoted from Kline, Margery (1984), *Social Influences in Textbook Publishing*, Educational Forum 48, No. 2, pg. 230.

33. Loewen, James W. (2007), *Lies My Teacher Told Me: Everything Your American History Textbook Got Wrong*, Touchstone revised paperback edition, New York, pgs. 28.

34. Quoted in Kozol, Jonathan (1975), *The Night is Dark and I am Far From Home*, pg. 101, and in Loewen, James W. (2007), *Lies My Teacher Told Me: Everything Your American History Textbook Got Wrong*, Touchstone revised paperback edition, New York, pgs. 28.

35. This quote was copied directly from an online article written by Brad Bechler for politics.gather.com and retrieved June 24th, 2011 from: http://politics.gather.com/viewArticle.action?articleId=281474979405121. The quote was mentioned in numerous places the day after Palin made the faux pas including political commentary television programs like Hardball and The Last Word on MSNBC.

36. Kessler, Glenn (2011), *Bachmann on Slavery and the National Debt*, taken from a regular editorial in the Washington Post entitled "The Fact Checker" published on January 28th. Retrieved online June 27th, 2011 from: http://voices.washingtonpost.com/fact-checker

/2011/01/bachmann_on_slavery_and_the_na.html.

37. The United States Constitution, Article 1, Section 2, retrieved online June 27th, 2011, from: http://www.usconstitution.net/const.html#A1Sec2

38. Information about the National Academies Press can be found on their website at: http://www.nap.edu/about.html.

39. Singer, Susan R., Hilton, Margaret L., and Schweingruber, Heidi A. (2005), America's Lab Report: Investigations in High School Science, National Academies Press, 254 pgs. This information was taken from the executive summary, pgs. 1-12.

40. Lindenberg, Dawn, Jasper, Gord et al (2002), Science Focus 9: Science, Technology, Society, McGraw-Hill Ryerson Limited, Whitby, Ontario, pg. 140.

41. Singer, Susan R., Hilton, Margaret L., and Schweingruber, Heidi A. (2005), America's Lab Report: Investigations in High School Science, National Academies Press, 254 pgs. This information was taken from the executive summary, pgs. 1-12.

42. Ibid. 41: Singer, Hilton and Schweingruber.

43. Drew, Christopher (2011), Rethinking Advanced Placement, The New York Times, January 7th, 2011, pgs. 1 and 2. Retrieved online July 13th, 2011 from: http://www.nytimes.com/2011/01/09/education/edlife/09ap-t.html?pagewanted=all.

44. European study shows when teachers like science, students do too, an article retrieved online July 6th, 2011 from the European Commission's **Europa** portal where you can find out about all the aspects of EU policy and activities. Taken from: http://ec.europa.eu/research/headlines/news/article_09_04_21_en.html.

45. Brendtro, Larry K.; Brokenleg, Martin; and Van Bockern, Steve (1990), Reclaiming Youth at Risk: Our Hope for the Future, Solution Tree Press, Bloomington, Indiana, pg. 30.

46. Gatto, John Taylor (1992), Dumbing Us Down: The Hidden Curriculum of Compulsory Schooling, New Society publishers, Gab-

riola, British Columbia, Canada, pg. 22.

47. One of many lists of high school and college dropouts can be found online. School-survival.net (http://www.school-survival.net/successful_dropouts.php), Life Magazine's 20 Who shook the World (http://www.life.com/gallery/62031/image/111101010/famous-high-school-dropouts#index/0), Education Reform.net (http://www.education-reform.net/ dropouts2.htm), Increase Brain Power.com (http://www.increasebrainpower.com/high-school-dropouts.html), and WCVB television in Boston (http://www.thebostonchannel. com/slideshow/entertainment/23149440/detail.html) are just a few of many online resources where such lists of dropouts can be found. Use Google to find quite an extensive list of other sites that highlight the achievements of people who dropped out of the system.

48. Information found online at: http://www.zephyrus.co.uk/alberteinstein.html, but can also be verified in books and many other sources online. Zephyrus is an all graduate team with experience in research, education and training.

49. Retrieved online November 4th, 2011, from the archives of The American Mercury online at: http://theamericanmercury.org/2010/04/h-l-mencken-on-governments-and-politicians/ as published in an article by the editor entitled: H.L. Mencken on Governments and Politicians, April 22nd, 2010.

50. Gatto, John Taylor (2009), Weapons of Mass Instruction, New Society Publishers, Gabriola Island, British Columbia, pg. xviii.

51. Inglis, Alexander (1918), Principles of Secondary Education, Houghton Mifflin, retrieved online October 25th, 2011 at: http://www.archive.org/details/principlessecon03inglgoog, from the Internet Archive, a non-profit that was founded to build an Internet library. Its purposes include offering permanent access for researchers, historians, scholars, people with disabilities, and the general public to historical collections that exist in digital format. The text was scanned by Google.

52. Gatto, John Taylor (2009), Weapons of Mass Instruction, New So-

ciety Publishers, Gabriola Island, British Columbia, pgs. xviii, xix. The original text describing these six functions in Alexander Inglis' book, Principles of Secondary Education can be found on pages 158 – 164.

53. Statistics Canada (2010), Public School Indicators for Canada, the Provinces and Territories, published online December 20th, 2010. Retrieved online November 28th, 2011 from: http://www.statcan.gc.ca/daily-quotidien/101220/dq101220c-eng.htm

54. U.S. Department of Education, National Center for Education Statistics. (2011). Digest of Education Statistics, 2010 (NCES 2011-015), Table 188 and Chapter 2. Retrieved online November 28th, 2011 from: http://nces.ed.gov/fastfacts/display.asp?id=66.

55. Wingert, Patrice (June 14th, 2010), The (Somewhat) Good and (Mostly) Bad News About High-School Drop Out Rates, Newsweek, Retrieved online March 19th, 2011 from: http://www.newsweek.com/blogs/the-gaggle/2010/06/14/the-somewhat-good-and-mostly-bad-news-about-high-school-dropout-rates.html.

56. Published in High School Teachers Association of New York, Volume **3**, 1908-1909, pp. 19-31 and in the Papers of Woodrow Wilson, **18**:593-606.

3

Education and Society

"Education either functions as an instrument which is used to facilitate integration of the younger generation into the logic of the present system and bring about conformity or it becomes the practice of freedom, the means by which men and women deal critically and creatively with reality and discover how to participate in the transformation of their world."

Paulo Freire

In the last chapter, it was suggested that if we really want to create an educational system that will achieve the rhetoric touted by the current education system, we have to rethink the society and economy we want. We are all familiar with the rhetoric of the current system. However, if you cannot identify such rhetoric from memory, simply go online and find the homepage of any local school. In fact, feel free to look up your own alma mater. Here is an example of a typical mission statement:

> *"We provide quality learning opportunities and options. Our learners take ownership by discovering and developing their potential, passions and gifts. They take their place as lifelong learners and make a significant contribution within a complex, changing world."* [1]

This rhetoric does not include the large numbers of students that fall through the cracks of the system in this particular district in the same way that similar rhetoric does not account for the many students in other districts who fall out in much the same ways. Many either drop out of the system outright, or they drop out of the process while on the roster either through truancy, inattentiveness, misbehaviour, non-compliance, or simply poor grades due to lack of effort. It has already been shown in the previous chapter that many learners do not take ownership by discovering and developing their potential, passions and gifts because they are funneled through the same process in the same way as most other students. The school system is not about, and has never been about, developing students' individual potentials, passions or gifts. The school system, as has already been made clear, is about compelling students to meet the requirements of a streamlined curriculum that for the most part is one size fits all so that they can take their place in the economy.

At least two questions need to be asked at this point:
1. What are the effects of the current schooling system on the society we live in?
2. What social benefits are gained from the current schooling system and by whom?

The current schooling system cannot be seen as an all-inclusive system. Although mission statements may indicate that they produce life-long learners and that students are able to discover their potential within school walls, it is clear that for the high numbers of drop-outs at least, this is not the case. There have been numerous studies documenting the reasons for dropping out of schools. These include the effects of abuse, poverty, emotional issues, cognitive deficiencies and lack of support. Interestingly, much of the prior research that has been done tends to focus on the personal characteristics of the dropout [2] without focusing on what schools might also be doing to contribute to the problem. Let's take a look at what has been well-documented first.

The economic effects of dropping out alone are staggering. Those who drop out of high school and find a job are often restricted to positions that pay lower wages. They are likely to be stuck in dead-end jobs that depend on physical labour, are mindless due to repetition, and offer no opportunities for creativity or problem-solving skills. Most people who do find themselves in lower-paying positions are usually also at the bottom of a career ladder which is difficult to climb because upper level positions are reserved for those who have specialized skills with evidence of formal education. In 2006, the U.S. Bureau of the Census reported that high school dropouts earned an average income of $17,299 per year. Those who graduate from high school can expect to make an average of $26,933 annually. [3] That difference is considerable at close to $10,000 but concernedly, neither wage is very good. According to a National Public Radio report in the United States in September, 2011,[4] the Census Bureau defines a family of four with an annual income of $22,314 as the poverty line. If the average annual wage of a person with a high school education and a family can only hover $4,619 above the poverty level, then imagine how difficult it is for someone who has been greatly disenfranchised by not achieving that high school diploma at all. Clearly, even a high school education is not deemed enough to achieve the proverbial "American Dream" which most people believe includes much more than barely living above the poverty line. After thirteen years of education from grades kindergarten through 12, is this all that formal education can offer young people today? Is this why we should be telling young people that they must complete their high school education? The promise of barely floating above the poverty line is not much of a promise.

Whether one is a dropout or a high school graduate, the effects of the current schooling system affect society as a whole in many ways. The proximity of both dropouts and graduates to the poverty line extends their likelihood of accruing massive debt, often just in an effort to stay ahead of the game. The reality of living from paycheck to paycheck means that depending on shifts in the economy, these populations have a higher risk of depending on government assistance. Many are only a few paychecks away from homelessness. From the vantage point of being a dropout or high school graduate, it may be easy to descend into poverty; economically, it is considerably more difficult to rise above poverty. Without a lot more disposable income than is available to both these groups, limitations are also placed on opportunities to invest money, start a business or even just save for the future. The public schooling system's high school diploma provides little to no advantage over the dropouts it produces in contributing to all of these risk factors to society.

The skills gap is an area where dropouts may be somewhat more disadvantaged in comparison with high school graduates. Many high schools in the United States offer only limited vocational classes and several do not offer any traditional ones at all. Although computer classes might be considered vocational, they have almost singlehandedly replaced traditional vocational classes like welding, electronics, auto shop, carpentry, drafting and other courses that were once prominent features in many high schools. Since computer-related skills are now necessary even in many industries where one would not have expected computers might be integrated, it makes it even more difficult for those who drop out to acquire entry positions in traditional trades. And unless young people can access courses in high school, they may not have the opportunity to gain hands-on experience in a trade of their choice. Many trade careers some might want to get into – like becoming an electrician or welder – also require some proof of formal training like a certificate or a degree. It may be possible to become an expert at these trade skills by learning from someone who is a professional, but unless a degree or certificate is earned formally, many are blocked from pursuing or advancing in careers and salaries that were once much more accessible. This is the result of having a formal education system where everyone is funneled through processes that require classroom participation – whether it is hands-on or not; the subsequent certificate or diploma that is attached to that classroom attendance, participation and almost always, exam results becomes more important and necessary than practical experience. Since those who drop out of the formal education process often never get the hands-on experience they need or do not have the paperwork to verify formal learning experience, the wage-gap between those who pursue formal verification and those who drop out is continued in perpetuity. If and when the one-size-fits-all approach to education in more and more areas is rejected by dropouts, there are less and less avenues through which they can progress into meaningful career opportunities, regardless of what they might know and be able to do. Dropouts become permanently disenfranchised not just from jobs but from opportunities.

We may now live in what has been broadly touted as "the information age" but despite the networking possibilities online, many who drop out from formal institutional learning often have diminished prospects for connecting with others who might have similar interests and career goals. They will also have less chance of finding a mentor in the field of their choice or of connecting with industry contacts. Without access to networking possibilities, it becomes a lot more difficult to be recognized for the skills one might have. Furthermore, by dropping out of the formal settings that are recognized as the means for entering into and then progressing through a trade or other profession, dropouts often are not able to interact with others who are either interested in the same career path or those who are already successful in those career paths. This can further handicap a person because without the opportunity to network with professionals and peers interested in similar career paths, individuals also lose opportunities to learn about various characteristics that might be valued by potential employers. Without knowing or appreciating valued characteristics of potential employees, dropouts also have diminished skills and knowledge about how to compete or be an attractive candidate for specific jobs. Potential employers tend to have job fairs at institutions of formal learning which means that if prospective candidates drop out of the system, then they often will not have the chance to be seen or discovered for the talent, personality or skills they may actually possess. Under the present system of education, these problems are perpetuated and continue to disenfranchise the dropout in our society.

Disenfranchisement from economic opportunities in society can lead to further problems extending into personal and social realms. Both high school and college dropouts exhibit higher incidences of depression or hopelessness about their situation. This has the distinct potential for large numbers of people pursuing destructive coping mechanisms or techniques for surviving. Drugs, alcohol, gambling, video games, shopping, getting into further debt and many other things can all become coping mechanisms. Self-handicapping in such ways is often seen as the process by which an individual avoids effort to prevent possible failure from hurting his or her self-esteem. [5] Disenfranchisement from economic opportunities in society can be a large part of what Vancouver's Simon Fraser University professor Bruce K. Alexander talks about in his book The Globalization of Addiction: A Study in poverty of the Spirit. He makes the case that humans require psychosocial integration which is defined as a "profound interdependence between individual and society that normally grows and develops throughout each person's lifespan. Psychosocial integration reconciles people's vital needs for social belonging with their equally vital needs for individual autonomy and achievement." Bruce makes the case that an enduring lack of psychosocial integration, which he refers to as 'dislocation' is both individually painful and socially destructive. The subgroups and institutions that provide the foundation for psychosocial integration include many features of human society. These may typically include families, children's play groups and organizations, employment contacts and groups, sports teams and various other neighbourhood, recreational, ethnic, religious, local or national organizations, [6] but the one institution that may have the longest and most pertinent effect on a broad cross-section of individuals in our society is school. If school cannot achieve the rhetoric it tirelessly promotes about itself, then vast numbers among us in society who dropout one way or another are not only disenfranchised, but likely to experience dislocation from psychosocial integration which is vital. The costs and burden of such dislocation have profound effects on our society. For example, in the U.S., States with large numbers of high school dropouts typically find it more difficult to attract business, research companies or increasing productivity. [7] Research published in 2005 by Cecilia Rouse, a Princeton University professor of economics of public affairs indicates very specifically that if high school dropouts would have graduated in Colorado, that state's economy would have grown by 4.2 billion dollars. In the most populous state of California, the economy could have grown by 40 billion dollars more than it has. [8] Whether we are talking about Colorado and California or Ontario and British Columbia, the effects of dropping out are similar in any modern society.

The roots of dislocation often begin at school. This is stated effectively in Brendtro, Brokenleg and Van Bockern's 1990 publication, <u>Reclaiming Youth at Risk</u>:

> "If one looks at the structure of a traditional large urban school, one sees that intimate primary relationships have been supplanted by an impersonal bureaucracy. Students and teachers do not relate to one another as whole persons, but in narrow circumscribed roles. Communication is

restricted to what one can and must do in a 50-minute hour where a highly structured setting is a sanction against all but teacher-directed behavior. The only spontaneity is the too-frequent disruption, and the only "we" feeling likely to develop is the "we against they" which divides students and teachers into separate camps. Research shows that at each progressive level of the education system, relationships increasingly lack meaning and personal satisfaction. [9] Not surprisingly, students at greatest risk of dropping out of school are those who have never been friends with any teacher." [10]

This snapshot of the current schooling system in North America encapsulates the very real experience of developing alienation among so many today. The industrialized model of education is a reflection of the industrialized society that created the system in the first place. In our society, goods are mass-produced and then stored in warehouses or on shelves until they can be consumed. So are our students. They rarely have an opportunity to participate as real citizens until they actually become adults, and by then they have not learned to be responsible but in fact have acquired a learned irresponsibility. People cannot sit in classes that are almost entirely teacher-directed year after year and learn to do things for themselves. This is what is so offensive when teachers, administrators and adults in general talk about young people as being "our future citizens." They are people! They should be allowed to be citizens now by learning responsibility, being able to make decisions that affect them beyond just making superficial choices from among highly limited lists of "opportunity."

This has been a problem in education for as long as formal compulsory schooling has been in place – and criticism of this has been around for almost as long. In his 1897 essay entitled <u>My Pedagogic Creed,</u> John Dewey already stated that education "is a process of living and not a preparation for future living." [11] As long as schooling consists of lectures and activities that flow in one direction – from teacher to student, it will be very difficult to engage many students. And as long as the so-called educational process unfolds in this manner, there is only a chance that it will gain leverage if a student's interests coincide with what is being presented. If not, it will, in Dewey's words, "result in friction, or disintegration, or arrest of the child nature." [11] This is why it could practically be considered a crime to "school" students in the manner that we do. During their first five years of life, they are integrated into the social fabric of their families and society learning many new things. It is through their participation and integration that they learn language, cultural traits, acceptable and unacceptable mannerisms, and most of all, ongoing discovery. They are able to ask many questions related to their curiosity and interest that are meaningful to them because they arise out of their curiosity and interest. Then we put them in schools, tell them they must stay there for x-amount of hours per day – an amount which constitutes a majority of the hours that might be expended on any particular focus within a given day, separate them from all but a teacher and a group of other students who are the same age, funnel them through the same process as everyone else (disregarding their uniqueness and penchant for a different combination of what Gardner refers to as multiple intelligences), and finally, we expect them to endure thirteen years of education directed from teacher to student in activities that do not actually prepare them for future life but are separated from any real active social significance. Hence, as long as they are in school, they will always be future citizens. No wonder youth often feel disenfranchised even before many decide not to continue participating in the so-called educational process one way or another.

The potential for disenfranchisement is embedded in the system itself as a means for categorizing and assessing individuals for roles in our society. The basic idea behind the system is simple. Young people are expected to earn a high school diploma because it validates them in our society. Regardless of the skill set they may or may not have learned throughout their public school careers (and as we have already discussed in previous chapters, that is highly questionable), the diploma itself is the prize. It is the great validation of having gone through the system. It isn't important how well you did as you passed through the process, it is important only that you passed through the process – unless of course, you want to continue in the process itself. Then the grades you made count to further categorize your achievements and possibilities for further "achievement." Your grades will then determine your aptitude, the college or university you may apply to, and so on. All of these aspects of the education system serve to categorize and pigeon-hole everyone in a very industrialized manner. It is a system for determining usable units to feed the almighty economy, the centerpiece of modern society.

Regardless of some of the successes that emerge from the system, public school seems to be at least partially designed to baby-sit minors incapable of contributing to the economy until they are old enough to work or move on. Then they can take their place filling the innumerable menial jobs that really require very little education at all, or they can pay for the opportunity to advance their possibilities further. And this is what it is all about in our society and culture – money. It isn't just maintaining or advancing the economy; it is making money from the system itself in every way conceivable. This includes the education system as well. Never mind just looking at the textbook companies, the testing companies (and the support companies that make educational supplies of all kinds), the numbers employed as "professional" educators, support staff, administration, maintenance staff, bus drivers, and on and on. One must also look at how the corporate world benefits immensely from the compulsory captive audience they have exclusive access to for six to seven hours per day, five days per week, at least 180 school days per year. In the United States especially, it is possible to get a sense of just how pervasive corporations are in the public school system just by entering schools themselves. As Julie Light reported for CorpWatch in July, 1998, when entering a school cafeteria, one would "probably find wrappers from Taco Bell, Arby's and Subway, all fast food chains that provide school lunches. The third grade class may be learning math by counting tootsie rolls. Science curricula might well come from Dow Chemical, Proctor and Gamble, Dupont or Exxon." She goes on to say that it doesn't end there. "The 'education industry,' a term coined by EduVentures, an investment banking firm, is estimated to be worth between $630 and $680 billion in the United States." (Remember this statement was made back in 1998). "The stock value of 30 publicly traded educational companies is growing twice as fast as the Dow Jones Average. Brokerage firms like Lehman Brothers and Montgomery Securities have specialists seeking out venture capital for the education industry." [12]

It is clear that corporations are the major beneficiaries of the current educational system. The problem with this is that they have distinct advantages over the very people who should be benefiting from the education they receive. I would not have an issue with corporations receiving some benefit from the education system as long as all of the people being educated were the primary beneficiaries. In other words, people first, then corporations. But let's take a look at who benefits and who does not benefit from the current education system in North America. Many of the points below have already been made but are grouped together and summarized to clearly designate who the real beneficiaries of the system really are. These are as follows:

- The current schooling system in North America disenfranchises too many people from life-opportunities by not leading approximately 30 percent of students to graduation of their formal compulsory educational experience at any given time. This can be quite a problem for those being disenfranchised as it limits income and opportunity and also creates a caste system. On the other hand, it allows corporations to take advantage of a varied workforce, some of whom have little opportunity but to take advantage of lower-paying, less-skilled jobs needed to keep the current economy chugging along. The workers themselves remain poor while corporations benefit from their labour.

- By using a one-size-fits-all approach to education that includes standardized testing as a means of "verifying" what has been learned, the current schooling system in North America fails to teach all students – whom they know have various intelligences and modes of learning but effectively ignore. Success at school often depends on who is willing to jump through the hoops rather than who has the potential for competency. As Tony Wagner points out in his book <u>Creating Innovators</u>, "Statistics show college graduates earn far more than high school graduates. But is that because they are actually more skilled or because the credential has become a simple way to weed through the forest of resumes." [13].

- The current schooling system in North America imposes thirteen years of compulsory formal schooling on students that still fails to produce a respectable number of literate and numerate individuals by graduation. School districts operate like corporations in almost every way but their product is "educated" individuals. If corporations in any other sector other than compulsory education operated the same

System vs. Culture

way and were only 70 percent effective as most school districts are, investment would fall, superintendents (equivalent to CEOs) would be fired and the corporation would be restructured. The point being made here about formal compulsory education is that the product actually includes both graduates and dropouts. Both are required to benefit corporations in the economy that exists today. As we have already pointed out, both dropouts and high school graduates' economic potential hovers within five-thousand dollars of the poverty level. Clearly the beneficiaries here are corporations and not many of the people who either do or do not acquire a high school diploma.

- The current schooling system in North America has become a type of monopoly that is unfairly recognized as the only legitimate form of learning/education. This excludes any expertise a person might acquire outside of the system itself as the system validates only expertise acquired through the processes it provides with certification of some kind (e.g., a diploma or certificate). Professionals not associated with the formal education system cannot certify anyone they may train outside of the system. Therefore, if one chooses not to jump through the hoops of the system itself, they are disenfranchised from opportunities in the fields they want to enter, regardless of their actual expertise. This does not benefit individuals who choose not to go through the formal system but it does help corporations to enlist employees from a narrowed-down listing which saves time, money and other resources.

- The current schooling system in North America appropriates all of the money and human resources for the purposes of "education" by discouraging other institutions and human endeavors from assuming educational tasks and accreditation of any kind. Again, this funnels all candidates into a narrowed-down listing of "qualified" individuals and disregards all other means of acquiring expertise other than through the formalized education system which, as has been shown, tends to benefit corporations much more than it can possibly benefit individuals.

- The current schooling system in North America benefits numerous corporations by legitimizing and streamlining formal educational systems for the production of "professionals" that require standardized tests, curriculums and so on. These all generate economic opportunities in the form of producing testing materials, textbooks, computers, paper, photocopiers, etc., that have built what is now referred to as the education industry. Most people do not benefit and could arguably be constrained and even harmed by standardized testing (which has spawned a whole industry around the concept of test-phobias), and rigid curriculums that rarely allow for any significant creativity or individual thinking.

- If a person manages to get through the system of formal compulsory schooling by: being separated into same-age groupings; by being pitted against other students by competition; by being typecast by grades for activities that often have nothing to do with the skill-set required to be successful after the schooling process is completed; by following curriculum that for the most part is one-size-fits-all; by enduring what is for the most part one-directional instruction from teacher to student; and by having to live up to rules and regulations designed to teach students their place rather than exercise democratic principles like individuality, creativity or even just choice beyond a narrowly-predetermined set of choices; then students will earn a diploma that qualifies them to apply for positions and economic opportunity entitling them to live barely above the poverty line. The only other option in our capitalist society is to pursue even more formal education which would now be paid for out of pocket. Once that more relevant price is paid, students might finally benefit from opportunities they may still not actually be prepared for but are now officially qualified to perform.

The society and economy we have created – and which is fed and bolstered by the current formal compulsory school system we have in place – tends to create a caste system, limits opportunities for many – perhaps even a majority – erodes any true democratic process, and worst of all, makes the natural inclination to learn seem like a boring, worthless enterprise. Does this sound like a system that benefits individual people with "quality learning opportunities and options" and helps them "take their place as lifelong learners making contributions within a complex, changing world?" [1]

Does it sound more like a system that upholds and strengthens the top one percent that the so-called "Occupy Movement" (that began to take hold in 2011 around the world) has been protesting about? When one considers that an ever-increasing amount of money has been thrown at a system that never makes any fundamental changes, one must conclude that change or improvement is not what is sought, only the preservation of the status quo.

The status quo continues to exist because of a flawed fundamental assumption about the current education system and the society it is meant to prepare people to enter. The current education system assumes that learning and social equality can be achieved through the ritual of schooling, even though John Dewey pointed out otherwise in the late 19th century. Ivan Illich elaborated on that theme in 1970 as well and gets right to the point:

> "We cannot begin a reform of education unless we first understand that neither individual learning nor social equality can be enhanced by the ritual of schooling. We cannot go beyond a consumer society unless we first understand that obligatory public schools inevitably reproduce such a society, no matter what is taught in them." [14].

Illich's statement is particularly poignant when one begins to realize what he means by going beyond a consumer society. Education cannot be produced in a consumer society because learning itself cannot be manufactured like other products are. One can prepare broth, add meat and vegetables and put it in a tin container to produce a can of soup, but one can't pour instruction into a person and expect to produce a vessel of enlightened knowledge. Once we believe that schooling can produce "educated" people to be integrated into society, we have learned to need school and by extension, need every institution it prepares us for interaction with. Illich explains that by doing so, "all of our activities tend to take the shape of client relationships to other specialized institutions. Once the self-taught man or woman has been discredited, all nonprofessional activity is rendered suspect." [15]

Education reform is discussed almost constantly, but very little reform ever takes place. Often programs are dismantled in favour of new programs that look suspiciously similar to the ones that were dismantled in the first place. Emphasis is sometimes stressed on "raising the bar" to compete with testing results in other countries, but raising that bar means creating more rigid guidelines for achieving at the level of the bar which is always measured by testing and more testing. The results remain the same because the process is always the same but it doesn't really matter because the testing process does not accurately assess skills required for most jobs or careers a student (potential employee), might train for. Quoting Dewey and Illich might be effective in showing that arguments against the current formal, compulsory school system have been around for a long time because these two men are well-known. However, several educational experts have voiced similar objections and have expanded arguments to include poignant social commentary about the educational system. "The contention is that the purpose of school is to create a form of consciousness that enables the inculcation of the knowledge and culture of dominant groups as official knowledge for all students, thereby allowing dominant groups to maintain social control without resorting to overt mechanisms of destruction." [16, 17 and 18]. This is a concept that is not easy to grasp. We have all been so conditioned to believe that school and schooling as it exists is so good and important that we have come to depend on it to advance our hopes for opportunity in our society. Yet the subtleties of how the process actually works and who it is benefiting are easily lost. It is very difficult to think outside the box when all one can see (and perhaps has ever seen), is the inside of the box. This is why some of us who have gone through the process determined by the box believe that the benefits conferred within it translate into success. It is the only success we know and can know as long as we follow the system. It is also why we marvel at people like Bill Gates, Steve Jobs or Richard Branson – all of whom exited the formal education system before achieving spectacularly at redefining how what we do can be done.

Framing the box itself goes a long way toward determining what can actually be seen from inside the box. The idea is similar to Orwell's concept of Newspeak. When one reduces and simplifies language to a construct that no longer has words for "freedom," "rebellion," and so on, such concepts become increasingly difficult to imagine, let alone communicate. Similarly, when one reduces education to what one can and must accomplish in a particular way through specified means in order to be "certified," then it becomes difficult to see how one can become "qualified" without the system because certification has become synonymous with being qualified. Furthermore, what one is being qualified for is narrowly determined to meet the needs of the current economy. The current education system does not educate for future innovation; it educates to maintain a desired stability in our society and economy that favours the status quo – what is, not what could be. That is why the culture of our educational system continues to be industrial in its approach and has changed very little over the past 160 years.

In order to think and see outside the box, it is essential to turn towards cultural inquiry if we want to truly reform the educational system to empower individuals. It is the difference between looking to make changes at a micro or a macro level. Without a change in our culture and economy, there will be no real changes made to our educational system. Those who have explored real educational reform in such a macro context – M. Apple in Ideology and Curriculum (1990), S. Aronowitz in The politics of Identity (1992), P. Bourdeau and J.C. Passeron in Reproduction in Education, Society and Culture (1977), Henry Giroux in Theories of Reproduction and Resistance in the New Sociology of Education: A Critical Analysis (1983), T.S. Popkewitz in Reform as the Social Administration of the Child: Globalization of Knowledge and Power (2000), M.F.D. Young in Knowledge and Control (1971), and Yata Kanu in Curriculum as Cultural Practice (2006), have disassembled the structure of the current schooling system to reveal it as predominantly representative of the values of particular interest and power groups in our society and economy. According to these and many other theorists, "schools function not only to normalize those whose attitudes, norms, cultural values, practices and behaviours are different from what is constructed as normal, but also to inscribe particular rationalities into the sensibilities, dispositions and awarenesses of individuals to make them conform to a single set of imaginaries about culture and national citizenship." [19]

Inquiry about the current culture in North America leads to recognition of a culture of illusion and even a culture of intentional delusion. The school system that feeds it functions accordingly. We have already explored how the nature of the current compulsory school system that services our children between the ages of five and eighteen functions. Its intentions as stated are illusory in the sense that the promise of education for all is really a practice to designate social and economic position. But what about the higher education system in our society that is touted to prepare people to become specialists (i.e. experts) in various fields? To what extent does it operate differently? Does it empower individuals any better? Do universities honour intellectual inquiry any more than elementary, junior or high schools do? Do they seek to develop individual potential or to produce a product that similarly designates position in an existing infrastructure of human resources?

It can be shown that in North America universities primarily service the established corporate hierarchy. The established corporate hierarchy has very clear objectives, the main one being an unconstrained, unregulated, free market. This is no secret in a capitalist society but it is not as easily recognized in the education system that maintains it. Universities and indeed the entire educational system in North America are there to service capitalist objectives. Capitalist objectives can be, and often are, in conflict with achieving individual objectives which may not be simply to make money. Higher education used to make a difference in developing skills in knowledge and values that are the cornerstone of a civilized society. Higher education and the institutions created to generate and promote ideas, safeguard knowledge, spur innovation, inspire creativity, and enrich culture have instead become business institutions geared toward making careers instead of making minds. According to Frank J. Donoghue, associate professor of English at Ohio State University, education in the liberal arts has been systematically dismantled for decades. He points out that any form of learning not strictly vocational has at best been marginalized and in many cases abolished. Furthermore, he makes the case that students are steered away from asking the broad, disturbing questions that challenge the assumptions of the power elite. Students increasingly do not know how to examine or interrogate an economic system that serves the corporate state we now live in. Donoghue believes that this state of affairs has led many bright student graduates directly into the arms of corporate entities. [20]

Perhaps one of the best examples of how universities have changed from institutions of higher learning to service preparatory schools for corporate interests is the University of California at Berkeley. The university began classes in 1873 at its present location and by 1942 the American Council on Education ranked it second only to Harvard University in the number of distinguished departments it boasted. [21] Berkeley gained a reputation for free thinking and student activism in the 1960s with the Free Speech Movement in 1964 and vocal student opposition to the Vietnam War. [22] This reputation lasted for decades but by the end of the century, an examination of Berkeley's liberal legacy had been debunked. Students there were no longer considered politically active and free speech movements of any kind had given way to a wide array of corporate interests. Modern students at the university have been significantly less politically active, even nonvocal, and one would have little difficulty finding much more moderate and even conservative students enrolled there. [23] Instead of being a hotbed of progressive thinking, Berkeley has become a microcosm of the intrusion of corporations into education. One student has described the situation clearly by stating that "We have bought hook, line, and sinker into the idea that education is about training and success, defined monetarily, rather than learning to think critically and to challenge." [24] American journalist and author Chris Hedges claims that the corporate hierarchy that has corrupted higher education is on public display at Berkeley. He states that:

> "The wealthiest of the elite schools, such as Yale and Stanford, assign dormitories by lottery. They treat their students with a careful egalitarianism, expecting all to enter the elite. Berkeley and many other public universities, however, assign rooms depending on how much a student can pay. They fall into a capitalist logic of "choice." The poorer Berkeley students end up in residences known as "the units" (Unit 1, Unit 2, Unit 3), while the wealthier students and recruited athletes, sustained by family money or athletic scholarships, receive rooms at Foothill or Clark Kerr, a fancy Stanford-style dorm that was once a private school for deaf and blind children. The food is better at the more expensive dorms. Corporations have cut deals with universities to be sole providers of goods and services and to shut out competitors. Coca-Cola, for example, has monopoly rights at Berkeley, including control of what drinks and food are sold at football games. Corporations

such as Cingular and Allstate blanket California Stadium with their logos and signs." [25]

One of the greatest problems with all of this is that universities as institutions of higher learning have become institutions that determine the worth of a student by the wealth of a student. When such institutions develop the ethic of making money so that an elitist system can be maintained, then such a focus does not allow for critical self-examination but only reaffirmation of what already exists – the status quo. Universities have developed both a need and an appetite for acquiring donations. Fund raising events are perennially essential and multimillion dollar endowments must also be sought out continuously. However, universities cannot expect a steady flow of donations of any kind unless they are constantly producing rich alumni.

Aside from seeking private donations and lucrative endowments, universities also seek corporate investment for research and specific programs but corporations will only do this for research and programs that favour their interests. A good example can again be found at Berkeley. They negotiated a deal with British Petroleum for $500 million that allows BP to gain access to the university's researchers and technological capacity. Such resources were built by decades of public investment, so BP can now disassemble other facilities to take advantage of a prestigious facility that was also publicly subsidized. The investment works for both the university and the corporation. The university acquires much-needed funding to continue prestigious programs that lead to jobs for its students, and the corporation, in this case BP, now legitimizes course content tailor-made to prepare potential employees for careers within its own ranks. BP also benefits by receiving intellectual property rights for scientific breakthroughs that might result from the joint project with the university and be translated into future profit. [26]

The now-changed nature and objective of universities will have a long-term impact on society because higher education is seen as little more than a means to gain employment. Very few people choose to attend university or see their learning experience there as part of a larger and more comprehensive intellectual journey. As mentioned in the first chapter of this book, I am happy that I dropped out of high school and spent years learning many things on my own before re-engaging in any type of formal, streamlined education. It has afforded me a different perspective on learning and education. University itself was, to me, a means for gaining more expertise in the area of writing, a passion I had first developed when I was twelve years old. It is true that I enrolled in the Education Department, but that was with the intention of finding a way to go and live in Canada's far north. And as I also mentioned in that first chapter, I may have been six or seven years older than most of the classmates in my freshman year, but I was more enthusiastic about the learning experience than just acquiring grades, and that led me to study several areas of interest — not just the major course of study I had enrolled in. I became interested in learning in earnest for reasons not associated with the process of formal schooling at all and maybe, just maybe, that is one of the reasons why later in life, I am spending my energy and intellectual curiosity to take on a project that questions and challenges the existing structure of the field I work in.

Although many people these days are geared toward just studying what is necessary to get a job and feel justified in doing so because their streamlined efforts often (though not always) reward them with employment opportunities they are seeking, it is a disservice to both individuals and society that most universities have become high-priced training centers. Yet, to a great extent, this is a natural progression of the kind of conditioning that exists right from elementary grades. Most students who actually continue with their education today are conditioned to pursue education for the purpose of taking their place in our society although what is meant and intended by that is not that they take their place in our society (which is much more comprehensive than the simple pursuit of employment), but that they take place in our economy. That is not usually enough to achieve personal fulfillment.

Just taking a place in the economy can never achieve complete fulfillment for humans because humans need more than just money. In fact, without fulfillment of basic human needs and desires, people are less effective at making money. That really doesn't work either for the worker or the employer. It still puts a strain on the almighty economy and efforts to help it grow. In recent years, many companies are discovering that traditional workplaces are far less productive than ones that see employees as more than just a labour resource. There are good reasons for this which, strangely enough, have taken a very long time to be recognized and are still not recognized by a majority of employers. In a 2012 article in the European Business Review, the concept of putting people first is explored:

> "Central to the concept of enrichment is a focus on the well-being of individuals. When work goes beyond the simple execution of tasks and becomes something of greater importance to the employee's life, then the individual is enriched. The emphasis shifts to what is good for the employee and how employee interests are aligned to organizational objectives. The second aspect is the idea of the meaning of work. Businesses may ask, "Why should an organization care about the well-being of its people?" The reality is that people are the lifeblood of any organization. People provide resources to the firm…shareholders provide capital, customers provide revenue and profits, and employees provide labor, innovation, service and a host of other components that make success possible.
>
> Using an enrichment focus means that care for the welfare of people must be central to the organization's culture. Places of employment are real communities for the people who work there. Employees place tremendous value on the relationships they have with their co-workers. The study authors refer to the emphasis on relationships between people as the human value connection. The human value connection encompasses the links between people within an organization, and the links across organizations best represented by the interactions between employees and customers. Yet, despite this obvious fact, leadership and management practices provide limited guidance on how organizations should build healthy communities and foster a culture of caring." [27]

This is a start in the sense that employers are beginning to recognize that workplaces must meet more needs of employees than just giving them a paycheck. It recognizes that enrichment has to be a focus on the well-being of individuals because it is good for all parties. And most of all, it recognizes and understands that people are the lifeblood of any organization. Recognition of the links between us all is essential to building not only fair and equitable workplaces but a fair and equitable society that empowers us all with economic opportunities and also satisfies other human needs. But what human needs are we talking about?

In 1943, Dr. Abraham Maslow wrote an article entitled <u>A Theory of Human Motivation</u>. [28] Although famous in psychological circles, the illustration that represents Maslow's hierarchy of needs may not be as familiar to the general public. It is displayed as a pyramid that shows the most fundamental physiological needs at the base and works its way up to self-actualization at the top.

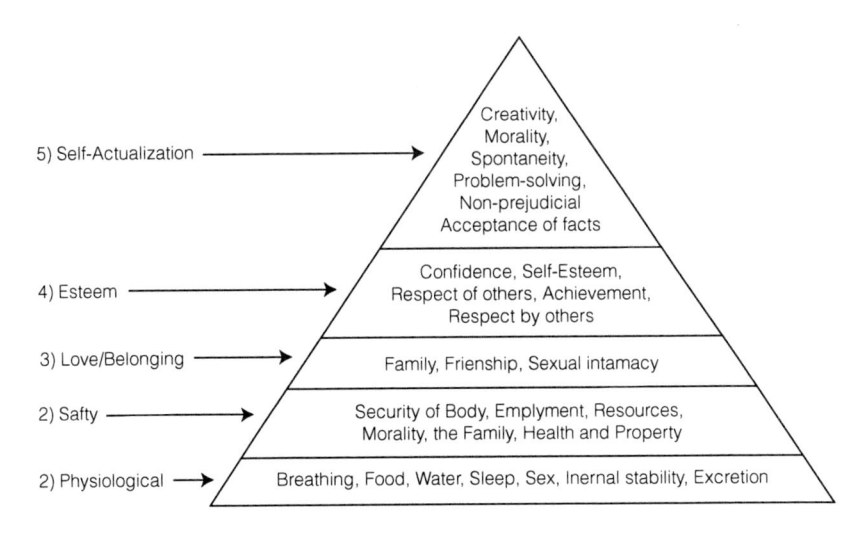

```
5) Self-Actualization  ———→   Creativity,
                               Morality,
                               Spontaneity,
                               Problem-solving,
                               Non-prejudicial
                               Acceptance of facts

4) Esteem  ———————→   Confidence, Self-Esteem,
                      Respect of others, Achievement,
                      Respect by others

3) Love/Belonging  ——→   Family, Frienship, Sexual intamacy

2) Safty  ——————————→   Security of Body, Emplyment, Resources,
                        Morality, the Family, Health and Property

2) Physiological  ——→   Breathing, Food, Water, Sleep, Sex, Inernal stability, Excretion
```

Maslow himself did not illustrate his hierarchy of needs visually as a pyramid, but the pyramid affords everyone an instant appreciation of the hierarchical nature of human needs. The first level is simply basic to survival. Everyone needs to breathe, eat, drink, sleep and so on before any other considerations can be made. The second tier of needs may not technically be essential to survival, but without having these needs met, they tend to become primary motivations for much of our behaviour. Without the security of feeling safe, having a job to make money, the support of friends and family, or a place of one's own to be safe and feel secure, it becomes very difficult to be productive in the society we live and interact within. In the 1990s, James Carville, a Democratic advisor to Bill Clinton coined the popular phrase, "It's the economy stupid." Well contrary to what seems to be the prevailing wisdom, it isn't the economy stupid, it's people. Even some companies are beginning to recognize that a happy staff is a more productive staff. And as some high tech companies like Microsoft and Apple have demonstrated, a more people-oriented work structure produces innovation. It isn't ridiculous to surmise that a people-oriented society rather than an economically-oriented society could better produce solutions that bind us together rather than problems that divide us.

The highest tier on Maslow's hierarchy of needs focuses on the concept of self-actualization. This concept may have been brought most fully to prominence by Maslow, but the term was originally introduced by Kurt Goldstein, a pioneer in modern neuropsychology, for the motive to realize one's full potential. He became known as an organismic theorist for his work stressing the organization, unity, and integration of human beings that is expressed through each individual's inherent growth or developmental tendency as outlined in his 1934 publication. [30] From Goldstein's perspective, it is the organism's master motive, the only real motive:

> "the tendency to actualize itself as fully as possible is the basic drive...the drive of self-actualization." [31]

We all know instinctively that self-actualization has a high level of importance – to be able to achieve what we can – is the stuff of dreams. Right from when we are born, we have that drive to try this and explore that, a drive that helped us to achieve the abilities of locomotion and communication – amazing and complex feats. Communication spurred us on to numerous questions – many that not only satisfied us, but those around us who loved participating in our growth. Interaction and innovation have a subtle association with the desire each of us has to be interconnected on many levels (and appropriately described as needs by Maslow). Children are driven to seek new knowledge and skills from those they know and trust. Those who help them also benefit from sharing what they know or have experienced. Influencing others positively creates bonds and enhances the sense of self-worth by both parties involved. Since we are both individuals and integral members of a collective social grouping, positive interaction of this nature provides an extension of self to encompass the grouping to which we belong. By recognizing one another's worth, by respecting individuality, by sharing for mutual benefit, we become connected. This is very different from the stratification that emanates from a system based on the accumulation of wealth through competition (which by its very nature, breeds opponents). One creates differences, disparity, inequality and greater need; the other builds connections between us that can lead to solutions of common problems. Make no mistake: the society we want is reflected in the education system we have developed to sustain it. If we believe that we can create a better society than we have now – and surely anyone can see areas where improvement is greatly needed – then an education system to build such a society must also be created. The two are entwined and inseparable.

This isn't simply a matter of looking at institutions in our society that need change – in this case, the educational institutions that have played a large part in developing the society we live in continue to play a large role in its maintenance. This is a matter of determining the future we want for our children and our world. Our society is truly becoming global and the westernization of the planet may not be the best way to preserve our species for many reasons. In the words of Ivan Illich already over 40 years ago:

"I believe that a desirable future depends on our deliberately choosing a life of action over a life of consumption, on our engendering a life style which will enable us to be spontaneous, independent, yet related to each other, rather than maintaining a life style which only allows us to make and unmake, produce and consume – a style of life which is merely a way station on the road to the depletion and pollution of the environment. The future depends more upon our choice of institutions which support a life of action than on our developing new ideologies and technologies. We need a set of criteria which will permit us to recognize those institutions which support personal growth rather than addiction as well as the will to invest our technological resources preferentially in such institutions of growth." [32]

Despite the world of production and consumption in which we live, most of us must comprehend that happiness and fulfillment do not come simply from such pursuits. Being human must encompass more than activities like production and consumption that can be achieved by mere machines. The institutions we develop must be able to broaden the scope of our potential. This cannot be accomplished by institutions which tend to mainstream us all through one-size-fits-all processes that only serve to create division and disparity. This is the problem in our society and it is also the problem of the schools that prepare us for such a society. As Illich so poignantly emphasizes, our future depends upon our choice of institutions.

We have come to a crossroads in our developing global culture. Many things have evolved since Illich wrote about the kind of institutions we need to be spontaneous, independent, yet related to each other. The crossroads we have arrived at is one where we either create a world that is sustainable while affording each of us the individuality to contribute on unique levels not experienced or even foreseen before now, or we perseverate a world where individuality is thwarted in the pursuit of an almighty economy that tends to best serve the top one percent in a direction that is, in absolute terms, not sustainable – period. Yet when Illich discussed institutions we need to be related to each other, there was no way he could have anticipated the development of the Internet. In fact, before the wide proliferation of computers in the mid-1990s, the consensus among experts and the general population alike was that the widespread use of advanced technology, especially computers, was expected to isolate people from one another, not bring them together in the way it has done so spectacularly in the last 20 years.

The Internet has proven to be an amazing tool for bringing people together. Email, social networking and many other kinds of digital opportunities online to create, improve or even rediscover long-gone social connections have made a huge impact on people's lives. In addition to making connections that are now easier to make and maintain, the Internet has also lowered traditional communications constraints of cost, time and distance. It is much easier and cheaper to send an email, post a blog or communicate directly through Skype or Google Voice. Several years ago, when such services first began, I enjoyed reconnecting with past friends on Classmates.com. It was a wonderful opportunity to reestablish friendships with people whom I had once been close to but drifted apart from in ways that were quite natural throughout history until the advent of this revolutionary medium. Until the Internet, it was normal for people to follow the progression of their lives and move from one place to another, taking opportunities or suffering setbacks that eventually found them in a place where many of the people they had surrounded themselves with had changed along with those moves, opportunities and setbacks. Later in life, it might have been a common occurrence to wonder whatever happened to so and so, what they were doing or even if they were still alive. Now anyone can check to see if an old friend has a Facebook account, has an email listing, or if any information can be retrieved simply by Googling the person one is looking for.

The Pew Research Center, a nonpartisan, nonprofit "fact tank" that provides information on the issues, attitudes and trends shaping the world issued a report in 2010 that cited "a significant majority of technology experts and stakeholders participating in its fourth Future of the Internet survey as saying the Internet improves social relations and will continue to do so." [33] The potential is incredible. Perhaps one of the most startling examples of social networking that has brought people and ideas together is the so-called Arab Spring of 2011. By connecting in ways that would have been unheard-of, unthought-of, and even impossible only a few years earlier, people were able to organize themselves and actually bring down governments that had been in power for decades. Hosni Mubarak's government in Egypt, which stood for 30 years, fell in only 18 days. And although there was more violent resistance to such change in neighboring Libya, its despot Muammar Gaddafi fell in months under the same intense pressure.

Support for initiatives like the Arab Spring and many other issues, especially human rights, is constantly being organized by groups like Avaaz. org, a global movement that connects people around the planet in order "to bring people-powered politics to decision-making everywhere." The Süddeutsche Zeitung, which is published in Munich and is Germany's largest national subscription newspaper, describes Avaaz as "a transnational community that is more democratic, and could be more effective, than the United Nations." The name of the organization, Avaaz, simply means "voice" in several European, Middle Eastern and Asian languages. It first came online in 2007 with what was considered a simple democratic mission: To "organize citizens of all nations to close the gap between the world we have and the world most people everywhere want." The organization collects and disseminates information about regional, national and global issues that encompass such topics as corruption, poverty, conflict, climate change, media freedom, real democracy and human rights. It organizes letters of protest and makes it very easy for interested individuals to participate and lend their voices in support or criticism of inappropriate objectives being acted out wherever they are being acted out. (34)

The great thing about Avaaz.org, SumOfUs.org and other similar organizations is that they are transnational grassroots movements that enable people to help make a difference right from home, their workplace or wherever they may be just by using their cell phones. Within hours, thousands of digital signatures can be accumulated to present a united front for or against important issues that are often not being dealt with by elected members of local, regional or national governments – the entities that are supposed to represent the rest of us. Instead, many members of government here in the Western democracies behave much like non-elected members of governments elsewhere. They often only address the issues that put their parties and themselves in advantageous positions that, yes, help to retain the status quo that has brought our world and global civilization to the brink of disaster where it is right now. The current global economic crisis is the direct result of collusion between large corporations and governments and has led to more of the same situation which has become a time-honoured cliché: The rich get richer and the poor get poorer.

Although Ivan Illich is not alive to speak about the benefits of organizations like Avaaz, I expect that it is just the kind of institution that fits his description of the need we have to be spontaneous, independent, yet related to each other. If governments and corporations were really acting in our collective best interests, they would not have to fear the kinds of opinions we might express about their actions as revealed by people like Julian Assange, Bradley Manning or Edward Snowden. If there was more transparency, we could then see the truth behind the efforts being made on our behalf or be able to detect the corruption that instead skews advantage in favour of the elite at everyone else's expense. Furthermore, when given an opportunity to think and behave responsibly, many of us are more than capable of doing so. Perhaps the Internet has been a major force in helping us come to realize that social organization and stability does not have to be a top-down enterprise. When there is real and open dialogue that is clear and accessible to all, then people can participate in making good choices collectively. Is it not ironic that in Western democracies, the concept of free will, democratic rights and choice are touted as sacred, but real free will, democratic rights and choice in many areas of our lives are severely limited? This begins right at school where, as has already been discussed at length, none of these choices exists except in word. We expect our students to be able to function as adults in the real world after we have isolated them from any real responsibility throughout their "training" years in school.

The role of schools in promoting the true nature of the democratic process has been lost. Schools, quite simply, do not prepare students to make informed decisions that promote positive public values that work for the common good. Schools neither help us to realize, nor enable us to think and behave responsibly. Schools and schooling tend to do one thing really well: that is, to stratify society into consumable units to be absorbed into, and possibly spat out again, as dictated by the whims of an almighty economy. Any real school reform must address wider issues of the society and culture from which our educational institutions emerged in order to produce something that will be different. Henry Giroux describes this necessity as follows:

> "Public and higher education are crucial reminders of the importance and necessity of having institutions and sites governed by public values rather than limited commercial values. They share an affinity with the social state in which matters of governance are not reduced to individual and corporate interests but are defined as part of the common good. As such, schools are the front line in providing students with the knowledge and skills that enable them to question authority, connect their particular experiences to larger social forces, translate private issues into public considerations, and create a formative culture in which knowledge and reason oppose forms of pedagogy whose ultimate purpose is to create cheerful robots. Educational reform matters, but it cannot be viewed as an isolated issue. It must be linked to the broader crisis of power, literacy, economics, culture, and democracy. Only then will we be given a sense of the larger context in which education must be understood and struggled over." [35]

This is the crux of the entire matter. We absolutely need public institutions that are governed by public values and serve the public good. It is neither "over the top" nor unreasonable to suggest that the very survival of our species depends on our ability to choose a viable and sustainable direction. The society we have produced that worships the almighty economy is one that is based exclusively on corporate and individual interests and one that we cannot continue with ad infinitum. In 2006, Al Gore published a book entitled <u>An Inconvenient Truth</u>. The book accompanied a documentary film that highlighted Gore's campaign to educate people about global warming. [36] It generated a lot of discussion and re-energized the environmental movement temporarily. However, even though Gore was awarded the Nobel Peace Prize for his efforts and lauded worldwide, the entities that really matter in our society – corporations, governments and the top one percent – have effectively ignored his essential, timely and urgent message. Even Canada, an original and once ardent supporter of the Kyoto Protocol, a United Nations framework aimed at fighting global warming, pulled out of the agreement in 2012 because its Conservative government, like most conservative governments, favours corporate and individual interests over social welfare.

When Giroux refers to "the common good," he refers to a concept that describes favourable outcomes that are shared by all and beneficial to all. Although there cannot be a strict definition of what the common good might be in every situation, it has at least sometimes been seen as a utilitarian ideal which represents the greatest possible good for the greatest possible number of individuals. It is also what I mean when I use the term social welfare. This is where any discussion about the common good often becomes a virtual taboo subject, especially in the United States where the common good or social welfare is often unfairly equated with some specific forms of socialism and communism practiced during the 20th century. Many here in Canada and elsewhere are likeminded. Within the past year in Calgary, Alberta, where economic activity is centered around the petroleum industry, I was sitting with a group of friends and acquaintances having a few drinks at a community center on a Friday night. The topic of discussion strayed into the realm of social programs and consciousness versus individual rights and unfettered access to the market. Some of the people around the table worked in the oil industry; others were educators – a good mix of private and public sector personalities. Not so surprisingly, the educators tended to be individuals who could most accurately be described as left-leaning liberals favouring effective social programs and responsible government intervention in areas where many individuals might have some difficulty achieving success on their own. Equally unsurprising was the fact that those who worked in the oil patch or with companies servicing the oil patch could most accurately be described as right-leaning conservatives. The conversation meandered around uses and abuses of social programs and what could be done to address abuses. While most Canadians have traditionally favoured the kinds of social programs – especially universal medical coverage – that Canada has supported for decades, some – particularly those who earn more than the average family does – were more closely aligned with American Republicanism. They believe that everyone has a responsibility to take care of themselves and that social safety nets – even universal medical care – are unfair to hard-working people. When one person tried to argue the benefits of responsible social programs to a population as a whole, another participant became so irate that he blurted out the question: "So, are you a f%$#ng socialist?" It wasn't so much a personal question or criticism as it was an attempt to clarify the other's endorsement of a taboo position.

In our culture and society, any kind of social thinking is becoming unpopular to the point where it may even become anathema. As long as we continue thinking in this way, our culture and society will continue going down the path of individualized consumerism – a culture which emphasizes the importance of accumulating more than one's neighbours and which disproportionately benefits corporations and the top one percent. If this is what we want – and it seems to be – then the education system we have in place is an excellent one for advancing such economic objectives. It is already doing the job these entities want and will continue to do so until all concerned rise up and speak out.

At the beginning of this chapter, we began with a quote by Paulo Freire which basically stated that education either functions to facilitate integration and conformity into the present system or it becomes the practice of freedom. I have attempted to show how the current education system only fulfills one of the two possibilities and that it is one of integration and conformity. To assess benefits, it was necessary to ask two questions: 1) What are the effects of the current schooling system? 2) What social benefits are gained and by whom? The answers to these questions can be gleaned from the 27 points that were made in the subsequent discussion. These points were as follows:

1. The current system of education produces a significantly high number of dropouts.

2. All research on the reasons for dropping out seems to have been focused on the dropouts themselves and not the contribution to this problem that the education system itself makes.

3. Acquiring a high school education does not create much of an advantage for graduates over non-graduates.

4. The proximity of both high school graduates and dropouts to the poverty level extends the likelihood of both groups accruing massive debt as well as suffering other setbacks.

5. The present system of education disenfranchises dropouts perennially in various ways. Such disenfranchisement leads to other social problems in our society.

6. The roots of dislocation often begin at school because primary intimate relationships have been supplanted by an impersonal bureaucracy.

7. The industrialized model of education that we have is a reflection of the now outdated and outmoded industrialized society that created the system in the first place.

8. The current education system does not teach responsibility; schools only allow students to make superficial choices from among highly limited lists of opportunity.

9. The potential for disenfranchisement is embedded in the system itself as a means for categorizing and assessing individuals for roles in our society. People are either validated or invalidated by the system.

10. Regardless of some successes that have emerged from the current educational system, public schooling is at least partially designed to babysit minors while their parents contribute to the economy

until the minors themselves are old enough to contribute one way or another (which is determined by their validation or invalidation by the system).

11. The education system as it exists today is an industry in itself which creates jobs, money and a caste system of professionals and non-professionals to be used by the almighty economy. This is why any real reform is difficult and unfortunately, a cynical statement of likelihood.

12. The current system imposes thirteen years of compulsory schooling and produces a high number of students who are validated by a diploma or certificate but are still functionally illiterate and innumerate. Validation without real-life results makes the whole system incompetent.

13. The education system has become monopolistic and is unfairly recognized as the only legitimate form of learning/education. In real life, there is never only one legitimate form of learning and so the current education system should never be recognized as though it is.

14. The current schooling system appropriates all money and human resources for the purpose of a generally one-size-fits-all program while severely inhibiting other institutions and human endeavors from assuming legitimate educational tasks and accreditation of any kind.

15. The current schooling system benefits numerous corporations by legitimizing and streamlining formal educational systems for the production of professionals that require standardized tests and narrowly-focused curriculums.

16. The society and economy we created and which is maintained by the structure of our education system limits the opportunities of many, creates a caste system, erodes the democratic process and makes the natural inclination to learn seem like a worthless, boring enterprise.

17. Education cannot be produced as part of the framework of a con-

sumer society such as ours because learning itself cannot be manufactured like other products are.

18. Education reform is discussed constantly but very little real reform ever takes place. School is very much like it has been for well over a century.

19. The current education system has made the concept of certification synonymous with being qualified. It isn't.

20. Even universities primarily service the established corporate hierarchy. Universities often determine the worth of a student by the wealth of a student.

21. Corporations have their feet planted into every aspect of the current education system and that is primarily for the purpose of profit. Corporate involvement does not necessarily benefit the actual recipients of the education system unless they jump through the appropriate hoops to gain validation.

22. Schooling has become geared toward studying what is necessary to get a job. This strongly favours corporations and the economic system rather than individuals who could arguably make better choices for themselves about where and how they will contribute to the overall good of the population in our society. Schools have simply become a way to divide the population into various economic roles that serve the existing economic powers – corporations.

23. Just taking a place in the economy can never achieve human fulfillment. Personal fulfillment is a central component to the well-being of individuals and therefore an important component to the well-being of society.

24. Addressing how we implement education in our society is a matter of determining the future we want for our children and our world.

25. We have come to a crossroads where we either create a world that is sustainable while affording each of us the individuality to contribute on unique levels not experienced or even foreseen before -- or – we perseverate the current world where individuality is thwarted in the pursuit of an almighty impersonal economy that

tends to best serve the top one percent in a caste-creating situation that is, in absolute terms, not sustainable.

26. The role of schools in promoting the true nature of the democratic process has been lost. The education system actually limits our ability to do so.

27. The implication of all the above points is that we need to create public institutions that are governed by public values and serve the public good by providing favourable outcomes that are shared by all and beneficial to all. The current education system as the cornerstone of our current society does not – and cannot – produce such outcomes.

These points all lead to very direct answers about the two questions posted: 1) The effects of the schooling system are very favourable to the type of economy we have because it segregates students into castes that can be used in some form of labour whether they graduate or not. It is not very favourable to at least 30 percent of the population that goes through the system because until they jump through the hoops demanded at every level of the system, they will become stuck in lower-paying jobs regardless of the skills they have because they have not been validated by the system as being legitimate. 2) The social benefits that are gained can be many for those who do jump through the hoops, whether their validation and certification actually translates into being qualified in their field of choice or not. We all know people who are incompetent at what they do, regardless of their validated qualifications by certificate or diploma. Conversely, we also know people who would be very capable but are barred from practice because they have not been validated by a certificate or diploma. Corporations and the top one percent reap the benefits of utilizing a wide range of labour developed for their purposes through an educational structure that promotes and maintains the almighty economy as it exists today.

We must ask ourselves a central question related to all of this information: Do we want a society that might be described as an econocracy where the central objective is maintenance of the economy as it exists today at the expense of anything and everything, including human well-being? Most people would need little time to come up with an answer to such a question. Despite the lure of "stuff" as comedian and social critic George Carlin has referred to the many things human seem to want to accumulate (despite the fact they don't need most of it), when it comes right down to it, we all know what is really important. The things that really matter are family, friends, making good connections with people and cooperating with one another for mutual benefit, good physical and mental health, and well, just for fun. In short, we all need and desire to find happiness (A pursuit which is entrenched in some national constitutions but perhaps not so actively supported). While some might interject by stating that happiness can be elusive and that money and the economy are central pillars in modern reality, it might surprise many that even former Federal Reserve Chairman Ben Bernanke in the United States came out in 2012 to endorse a more human perspective on economics itself. It is important to note for those who may not know or care about the Federal Reserve System in the U.S. that it is probably the most important financial regulation system on the planet. In addition to being the central bank of the United States, which at the time of writing this book is still the largest single economy in the world, the Federal Reserve is also assigned the significant but difficult task of maintaining the stability of the financial system and containing systemic risk in financial markets. So what did Bernanke say? The Associated Press reported on August 6th, 2012, that in a speech in Cambridge Massachusetts Bernanke stated: "We should seek better and more-direct measurements of economic well-being. After all, promoting well-being is "the ultimate objective of our policy decisions" In that speech, Bernanke stated that research has found that once basic material needs are met, more wealth doesn't necessarily make people happier. "Or, as your parents always said, money doesn't buy happiness. Well, an economist might reply, at least not by itself." (37)

If promoting well-being is the ultimate objective of policy decisions concerning the economy as Bernanke says, then why do so many decisions about the ongoing global financial crisis seem to hurt so many and benefit only a few? There is – and should be – considerable concern that those responsible for the global crisis are the ones that have been bailed out (through mostly public funds), while at the same time, the financial meltdown has affected the livelihoods of almost everyone else in our increasingly interconnected world. One only needs to look at the harsh austerity measures that have been imposed on countries like Greece in recent years to see how many are being affected negatively. The austerity measures in Greece included a 22 percent cut in the monthly minimum wage, layoffs for 15,000 civil servants, an end to dozens of job guarantee provisions, higher taxes, deep cuts in public spending, and thousands of shop and small business bankruptcies. [38] The global financial crisis may have seen extreme tensions rise in places like Greece because of austerity measures, but there has been considerable unrest in other places around the world because people have begun to wake up to inequality because of unfair institutional practices – hence the Occupy movement that rose to prominence in 2011. We spend so much time thinking and worrying about the economy that our focus tends to hover around the activity of economic institutions like banks, investment firms, the stock market, and so on. But other institutions that support economic institutions – which include governments and education systems – should also be looked at. This is where we need to return to comments made by Ivan Illich that "the future depends more upon our choice of institutions which support a life of action" and Giroux's comments that "public and higher education are crucial reminders of the importance and necessity of having institutions and sites governed by public values rather than limited commercial values." The very institutions that are in place to serve the people should in fact be made to work for all the people, not just a select few.

When we think of institutions, we think about a wide range of structures or mechanisms of social order or cooperation that affect and govern our lives. Institutions are connected with various social purposes that are established or designed to transcend individual human lives, intentions and actions by mediating the rules that govern cooperative human behaviour. Although the term "institution" is often used to describe the customs and behaviours that are important in a society, most of us in the modern world tend to think of specific organizations of government and public service. Examples of institutions we are familiar with that have an extensive effect on our lives include things like: marriage and family; religion; the legal system; hospitals; police and military forces; the monetary system; mass media institutions like television, newspapers and communications institutions like telephone or Internet services; industrial institutions like businesses – including corporations; charitable organizations; advocacy groups; political parties; and of course, education systems and schools to name a few. Although many of these formal organizations have been deliberately and intentionally created by people and sometimes very specific individuals, generally speaking, institutions develop and function as a pattern of social organization. [39]

As the twentieth century unfolded, especially the second half after World War II, we began to see many time-honoured institutions that we thought were indestructible (like marriage and religion), begin to show signs of significant stress due to forces of change in society. Those same changes in society have also prompted us to deliberately change the form and structure of institutions which we never dreamed would change for generations – even the monetary system. In a world that was dominated by cash just a few decades ago, we now live in a world of electronic credit and debit that has significantly altered the very fabric of the emerging global society of the future. Many of our institutions have changed, but as mentioned earlier in this book, schools and the education system have not changed to meet the needs of people in the modern world.

Society is evolving rapidly. With that rapid change comes great opportunity to reinvent and navigate the direction in which we should go. If the society we have and the direction we are going is not what we want, then what is it that we do want? What kind of society do we want to live in and be part of? What kind of an educational process do we want that will support that?

References and Footnotes

1. Calgary Board of Education Mission statement retrieved online January 3rd, 2012 from: http://www.cbe.ab.ca/aboutus/mission.asp.

2. Bryk, Anthony S. and Thum, Yeow Meng (1989), <u>The Effects of High School Organization on Dropping Out: An Exploratory Investigation</u>, American Educational Research Journal, Fall 1989, Vol. 26, NO. 3, pg. 353. Retrieved online February 20th, 2012 from: https://www.msu.edu/~thum/Papers/Bryk-Thum.pdf

3. U.S. Bureau of the Census (2006), Income in 2005 by Educational Attainment of the Population 18 years and over, Table 8, Washington D.C., U.S. government Printing Office.

4. Fessler, Pam, (Sept. 13th, 2011), Census: 2010 Saw Poverty Rate Increase, Income Drop, article published and reported on National Public Radio. Copy retrieved online February 20th, 2012, from: http://www.npr.org/2011/09/13/140438725/census-2010-saw-poverty-rate-increase-income-drop.

5. Kolditz, T. A., & Arkin, R. M. (1982). An impression management interpretation of the self-handicapping strategy. Journal of Personality and Social Psychology, 43, 492-502.

6. Alexander, Bruce K. (2010), The Globalization of Addiction: A Study in Poverty of the Spirit, Oxford University Press, pgs. 58 and 59.

7. Heath, Diane (2011), Economic Effects of Dropping Out of High School or College, Social Science Medley, an article posted online April 30th, 2011, and retrieved online March 5th, 2012 from: http://www.socialsciencemedley.com/2011/04/effects-of-dropping-out-of-school.html.

8. Rouse, C.E. (2005), Labor Market Consequences of an Inadequate Education, a paper prepared for the Symposium on the Social Costs of Inadequate Education, Teachers College, Columbia University, September, 2005. Retrieved online March 6th, 2012 from: http://devweb.tc.columbia.edu/manager/symposium/Files/77_Rouse_paper.pdf

9. Bronfenbrenner, U. (1986), Alienation and the Four Worlds of Childhood, Phi Delta Kappan, Vol. 67, pgs. 430 – 436.

10. Brendtro, Larry K., Brokenleg, Martin, and Van Bockern, Steven (1990), Reclaiming Youth at Risk, Solution Tree Press, Bloomington, Indiana, pg. 13.

11. Dewey, John (1897), My Pedagogic Creed, School Journal Vol. 54, January 1897, pgs. 77-80.

12. Light, Julie (1998, July 8th), The Education Industry: The Corporate Takeover of Public Schools, CorpWatch. Retrieved online February 28th, 2012, from: http://www.corpwatch.org/article.php?id=889.

13. Wagner, Tony (2012), <u>Creating Innovators: The Making of Young People Who Will Change the World</u>, Scribner, pg. xiv.

14. Illich, Ivan (1970), <u>Deschooling Society</u>, reissued in 2002 by Marion Boyers Publishers Ltd., London and New York, pg. 38.

15. Illich, Ivan (1970), <u>Deschooling Society</u>, reissued in 2002 by Marion Boyers Publishers Ltd., London and New York, pg. 39.

16. Althusser, L. (1971), <u>Lenin and Philosophy and Other Essays</u>, New York, Monthly Review Press.

17. Apple, M. (1993), <u>Official Knowledge: Democratic Education in a Conservative Age</u>, New York, Routledge.

18. Kanu, Yatta, editor (2006), <u>Curriculum as Cultural Practice: Postcolonial Imaginations</u>, University of Toronto Press, Toronto, pg. 5.

19. Popkewitz, T.S. (2000), <u>Reform as the Social Administration of the Child: Globalization of Knowledge and Power</u>, in Burbules, N.C., and Torres, C.A. (editors), <u>Globalization and Education: Critical Perspectives</u>, New York, Routledge, pgs. 157 – 186.

20. Donoghue, Frank J. (2008), <u>The Last Professors: The Corporate University and the Fate of the Humanities</u>, Ford University Press, New York, pg. 91.

21. Article on <u>U.C. Presidents</u>, retrieved online May 23rd, 2012 from University of California History Digital Archives: http://sunsite.berkeley.edu/uchistory/general_history/ overview/presidents/index2.html.

22. Article on <u>Days at Cal-Berkeley in the '60s</u>, retrieved online May 23rd, 2012 from http://bancroft.berkeley.edu/CalHistory/60s.html.

23. Doty, Meriah (February 5, 2004), Examining Berkeley's Liberal Legacy, retrieved online May 23rd, 2012 from: http://articles.cnn.com/2004-01-09/politics/elec04. berkeley_1_free-speech-movement-graduate-student-political-science?_s=PM:ALL POLITICS.

24. Hedges, Chris (2009), <u>Empire of Illusion: The end of Literacy and the Triumph of Spectacle</u>, a quote of Berkeley student Chris Hebdon, Vintage Canada Edition (2010), Random House, Toronto, pg.

95.

25. Hedges, Chris (2009), Empire of Illusion: The end of Literacy and the Triumph of Spectacle, Vintage Canada Edition (2010), Random House, Toronto, pg. 93.

26. Hedges, Chris (2009), Empire of Illusion: The end of Literacy and the Triumph of Spectacle, Vintage Canada Edition (2010), Random House, Toronto, pgs. 91-94.

27. The European Business Review (2012), A New Age: Putting People First, retrieved online May 30th, 2012 from: http://www.europeanbusinessreview.com/?p=1899.

28. Maslow, A.H. (1943). "A Theory of Human Motivation," Psychological Review 50(4): 370-96.

29. Adapted from Maslow's hierarchy of needs as represented in several textbooks and online resources. Maslow did not represent his hierarchy as a pyramid himself, but it is popularly represented as such in explanations given in psychology and education courses at the university level.

30. Goldstein, Kurt. (1934/1995). The organism: A Holistic Approach to Biology Derived from Pathological Data in Man, Zone Books, New York.

31. Goldstein, quoted in Arnold H. Modell, (1996), The Private Self, Harvard University Press, pg. 44.

32. Illich, Ivan (1970), Deschooling Society, reissued in 2002 by Marion Boyers Publishers Ltd., London and New York, pgs. 52, 53.

33. Glassman, Neil (July 7th, 2010), Do the Social Benefits of the Internet Outweigh the Negatives? Pew Report Says "Yes", taken from SocialTimes, and retrieved online June 20th, 2012 from: http://socialtimes.com/social-benefits-outweigh-negatives-pew-report_b16832.

34. Information about Avaaz.org retrieved online June 21st, 2012 from: http://www.avaaz.org/en/about.php.

35. Giroux, Henry A. (2012), Education and the Crisis of Public Values,

Peter Lang Publishing, New York, pg. 44.

36. An Inconvenient Truth, article published in Wikipedia and retrieved online July 14th, 2012, from: http://en.wikipedia.org/wiki/An_Inconvenient_Truth

37. Rugaber, Christopher S. (August 6th, 2012), Ben Bernanke has a question for you: Are you happy? Associated Press. Retrieved online August 6th, 2012 from: http://economywatch.nbcnews.com/_news/2012/08/06/13148811-ben-bernanke-has-a-question-for-you-are-you-happy?lite

38. Understanding Greece's Austerity Deal (February 9th, 2012) a report by the Associated Press. Retrieved online August 27th, 2012 from: http://news.yahoo.com/understanding-greeces-austerity-deal-183717700.html.

39. Basic information about Institutions borrowed from a Wikipedia article entitled Institution. Information was retrieved online August 28th, 2012 from: http://en.wikipedia.org/wiki/Institutions

4

On Teachers and Teaching

"The teacher who is indeed wise does not bid you to enter the house of his wisdom but rather leads you to the threshold of your mind."
Kahlil Gibran

"A master can tell you what he expects of you. A teacher, though, awakens your own expectations."
Patricia Neal

So far in this book we have spent a lot of time looking at the educational system – how it works, what it claims to accomplish and how it fails to match the rhetoric about its mission, student achievement, testing and grades to name just a few. We have also looked at the macro-relationship between education and society as a whole, but until now we have not taken a comprehensive look at the front-line staff of the education system – those who are charged with instructing new generations of learners, those who are expected to be experts in a wide range of areas, those who are expected to be role models, substitute parents, community leaders, child and parent advocates – teachers. At this point, there can be no doubt in any reader's mind that the educational system as it exists in North America is one that is quite flawed, especially if one is to look at the rhetoric all school districts disseminate in comparison with actual outcomes. There should also be no doubt that students are at least prospective victims of a system that claims to recognize individual differences but in fact largely ignores them. Let me state right at the onset of this chapter that teachers are also prospective victims of the system.

Our focus on teachers begins with a statistic as reported in the Washington Post in 2006. In that report, the American public was informed that the "proportion of new teachers who leave the profession has hovered around 50 percent for decades." [1] This statistic is particularly alarming when one breaks down the numbers as shown by many sources. For example, each year in the United States, 200,000 new teachers are hired to begin work on the first day of class in September. Yet by the end of the year in June, 22,000 of them will have quit, never to walk into a classroom again. That's more than ten percent of all new hires in just their first year of teaching. By the end of three years, 30 percent of those new teachers will have left the profession and by the end of five, 45 to 50 percent of them will be finished with their chosen profession. [2] In Canada, the province of Alberta claims to be "Canada's highest-performing province" [3] while sporting almost identical statistics to the United States.[4] While it is certainly arguable that many people who choose to teach should not be teachers anyway – just as in all professions, some people rise to the challenge they have chosen for various reasons and many do not, also for various reasons – but it cannot be arguable that half of all people who choose teaching as their profession will opt out after only five years due to their own inadequacies, misgivings or misunderstanding about the profession itself. It should be noted that many bring a passion for teaching, knowledge of their chosen subject(s), and the interpersonal skills required to be good at what they do. If half of all graduates in the field of teaching are so incompetent that they are being naturally weeded out by the system itself in such a short time, then it would follow that we should be asking a lot of questions about the process of teacher training when after four to six years of education at the university level (Bachelor's or Master's degree), the university system has not detected prevailing inadequacy in such a high percentage of individuals. Although there are shortfalls in the university system – and we will discuss them as they apply to teacher training shortly, it is apparent that there is a more definitive problem than assuming that thousands of misguided would-be professional teachers have simply made the wrong choice and/or that the university system has not been able to detect such misguidedness throughout the years of preparation for which universities are responsible.

The literature suggests several reasons why there is such a mass exodus of teachers – a condition that has existed for decades. One source on the subject published in 2010 outlines eight specific areas that are sources of tension and disillusionment for many teachers. These are as follows: 1) Standardized testing; 2) Working conditions in today's schools; 3) Ever-higher expectations; 4) Bureaucracy; 5) Respect and compensation; 6) Parents; 7) Administrators; and 8) School Boards. [4]

After the effort that has been spent discussing the inadequacies of standardized testing in the second chapter, it is not difficult to see why many teachers would see this as an area of tension and disillusionment. Teaching to the test has become the name of the game because so much importance has been placed on the testing process. State or provincial exams can and often do determine the course of student progress. SATs may be the most well-known standardized test, but for many it is an access point to further testing such as the LSAT, GRE, MCAT or GMAT. Even though most people are cognizant that test results do not reflect intelligence, many are brainwashed by their potential impact. Most teachers realize that teaching to the test is a poor measure of learning but they are compelled by most school districts to prepare their students for such tests because they reflect on the schools and school districts in important ways. Under the No Child Left Behind Act instituted under George W. Bush, States must give standardized assessments to all students at select grade levels in order to receive federal school funding.[5] This generates an incredible amount of pressure to implement a curriculum that is, for the most part, determined by test manufacturers and state or provincial legislators. It also provides very little incentive to become a teacher in a profession that is increasingly centered on test results rather than on actual learning or to work in a system where professionals are manipulated with rewards or punishments for leading their students to expected test results. It is demeaning to both teachers and students and does not achieve the objective of learning, only memorization often unaccompanied by insight or understanding.

It would be an understatement to regard schools as being exclusively about the transmission of knowledge. Schools have always had wider roles, including social functions, which seem to expand more and more as time goes on. The other sources of tension and disillusionment mentioned above which included working conditions in today's schools, ever-higher expectations, bureaucracy, respect and compensation, parents, administrators, and school boards are all issues that come down to issues of respect. Let's be honest, society places a lot of expectations on teachers.

Traditionally, the main characteristic of teachers was that they had to have significant expertise in the subject area they intended to teach, but this is not the only trait required of teachers today. Yet just on this point, teachers cannot be educated in a particular area and expect to be continuously proficient without upgrading the knowledge base they have in their chosen subject areas. The level of academic qualifications required of teachers is always increasing – hence the need for both external professional development which is the responsibility of teachers as well as in-services provided by their employers on a regular basis. More than in most other professions – with the likely exceptions of law and medicine – teachers are expected to continuously upgrade themselves. They are also asked to be knowledgeable and innovative as well as being highly self-disciplined, motivated to perform their many tasks, and dedicated not only to their students, but to their schools, school districts and the principles the system promotes and embraces. In addition to all of this, a new key feature of professionalism in teaching involves the understanding of technology. This involves understanding the potential of technology for teaching and learning and being able to integrate technology into strategies for teaching and learning. Any teacher who remembers having to learn how to use computers as an adult will remember how much pressure and tension that placed on people who had already been in the profession. Given all of these requirements expected of teachers, and also considering the challenges of working in overcrowded classrooms and everything associated with meeting various mandated objectives in the field generally, one can imagine how many people might make the following statement: You couldn't pay me enough!

Such a statement becomes even more understandable when one considers that a significant amount of stress can also be produced when having to deal with large classes of 30 or more students shuffling in and out each period – all of whom have to be accounted for in attendance before teaching can even begin. The classes feature x-amount of time for a teacher to get through the curriculum material and often enough, there are behaviour issues that distract from the teaching/learning experience. In most schools I have worked in, one of the most distracting and annoying aspects of trying to teach are the intermittent announcements from the office or the telephone calls into the classroom from the office, guidance, and other departments or classrooms. Teaching and learning momentum can easily be lost several times during a classroom period and if a period lasts for 50 minutes, then one could reasonably expect a maximum of 35 to 40 minutes of quality teaching/learning experience in the classrooms of most schools on any day of the school year. Many schools also lack up-to-date quality equipment, have ill-stocked libraries or science labs, outdated teaching materials like books and little to no online access. Teachers often experience stress in dealing with large classes, heavy workloads and many have to work in old schools that are run down. Combine these challenges with the fact that most teachers are frustrated by having little control over what they are required to teach and are expected to produce satisfactory student performance on standardized tests, one begins to see how the system itself funnels both teachers and students alike through the same narrow passageway that strangely enough, resembles the proverbial eye of a needle.

As mentioned above, many of the sources of tension and disillusionment that lead to high teacher attrition have to do with respect. In many places outside of North America, teachers are treated with respect. Teachers in North America used to be treated with more respect than they are now, but this is often not the case anymore. In a 2012 article for the Huffington Post, Langston University Chair and Associate Professor of Education Matthew Lynch addressed the issue effectively:

> "Unless you are a parent with a child enrolled in a public school, you are probably out of touch with the substandard quality of today's classroom instruction. This is not due to a lack of passion or purpose on the part of our nation's educators -- on the contrary. The majority of school teachers love what they do and consider themselves blessed to be afforded the opportunity to make a

difference in the life of a child. Their profound impact on the world of academia, and their willingness to sacrifice high-paying salaries should be applauded.

When it comes to the educational crisis, the public usually names budget cuts and poorly crafted bills as our schools' greatest offenders. Many insist the strategies articulated by policymakers are nothing more than glorified lip service and place responsibility on the shoulders of politicians. Others express frustration and point the finger at the administrators of their particular school district. The reality is our country is guilty of becoming increasingly apathetic about education. As a rule, teachers are grossly undervalued; their significance is continually diminished and their contributions go highly underrated." [7]

If the public in North America are becoming apathetic about education, it is probably for the many reasons already outlined in this book and many other sources: They see thirteen years of compulsory schooling promising much but delivering little in at least 30 percent of the population going through the system. And even though the system itself is designed by ivory tower experts, legislated by politicians and run by administrators and huge bureaucracies, it is the frontline staff – the teachers – who are, and have always been, the visible face of our educational system. In June, 2012, Gallup published its 39th poll on confidence in American institutions including education. Confidence in the public education system has gone down from an all-time high of 58 percent noted in the first poll taken in 1973 down to only 29 percent in 2012.[8] At a time when confidence in public education is at an all-time low, it is not surprising that the most recognizable face of the system is also at an all-time low.

Insult is added to injury when many teachers work much more than 40 hours per week but often see paychecks that are far from competitive with paychecks in other professions. Of course the public perception is often that this is untrue and that teachers are overpaid. In 2011, researchers from two conservative American think tanks - the American Enterprise Institute and the Heritage Foundation -- announced a "finding" that "America's teachers are <u>overpaid</u> by more than 50 percent." Although the claim was debunked by the U.S. Department of Education,[9] it demonstrates how high dissatisfaction runs with education in general and how the teaching profession is not only disrespected, but under attack. The idea that teachers are overpaid by more than 50 percent, especially when teacher expectations and responsibilities come under consideration, is ludicrous. The National Education Association (NEA) in the United States published an article on their website about the myths and facts about educator pay. These are the facts according to the NEA [10]:

- According to a recent study by the National Association of Colleges and Employers, the teaching profession has an average national starting salary of $30,377. The NACE also notes that other college graduates who enter fields requiring similar training and responsibilities start at higher salaries. For example, computer programmers start at an average of $43,635, public accounting professionals at $44,668, and registered nurses at $45,570.

- Not only do teachers start at a lower salary than other professionals, but the more years they put into teaching, the wider the salary gap between them and other professionals becomes.

- A report from NEA Research, which is based on US census data, finds that annual pay for teachers fell sharply over the past 60 years in relation to the annual pay of other workers with college degrees. Throughout the United States the average earnings of workers with at least four years of college are now over 50 percent higher than the average earnings of a teacher.

- An analysis of weekly wage trends by researchers at the Economic Policy Institute (EPI) shows that teachers' wages have fallen behind those of other workers since 1996, with teachers' inflation-adjusted weekly wages rising just 0.8 percent, far less than the 12 percent weekly wage growth of other college graduates and of all workers.

- Teachers spend an average of 50 hours per week on instructional duties, including an average of 12 hours each week on non-compensated school-related activities such as grading papers, bus duty and club advising. It is unfair for critics to count only the hours that students are in classes.

- In most school districts, salaries are distributed over the ten months of the regular school year. Teachers receive no pay over the summer months when students are on summer holidays and often have to take second jobs or use their time to upgrade their skills and meet State requirements for doing so.

In Canada, salary comparisons with professionals in other fields requiring similar training and responsibilities are more favourable but not spectacular. In a 2012 set of statistics using the same professional fields made in the NEA comparison above for the United States but looking at monthly averages instead of starting salaries, Canadian teacher salaries average $3,868 per month compared to computer programmers at $3,043, accountants at $4,188 or registered nurses at $3,833, [11] not at the bottom, but not at the top either. Some school districts in Canada like the Calgary Board of Education divide teacher salaries into twelve months rather than ten months like many districts in the United States do. When seen in this light, the average monthly teacher salary of $3,868 translates into $46,416 per year. No one is getting rich at this rate.

It is a shame that teachers as a whole are seen in a largely negative light. Despite the many difficulties and obstacles that are presented by the education system itself, the one truly pivotal resource is the teacher. Now this is where one must pay attention to definitions, because when I refer to someone who is a teacher, I do not mean someone who plays the role of teacher within the educational system and contributes to the manner in which the system often fails our students. When I think of a teacher, I think of someone who, despite the pitfalls of working in the formal education system, wants to work with young people and realizes that he or she is much more than a professional educator working at a "job." Teachers are human beings with enough insight to realize that they are the frontline connection with emerging generations. Teachers seek to make a positive difference in the lives of other, fellow human beings as they too develop into full participants in our culture – a rich and diverse cornucopia of interests as varied as the individuals that make it up. Teachers are people who care about helping young people become proficient at skills they need. Teachers are people who want their students to develop into interested, engaged learners in any of the many things that might interest them. Teachers are those who understand they achieve success only when their students no longer need them. This is why teaching is not and cannot ever be just a "profession."

System vs. Culture

Despite the many limitations of the education system itself, teachers often try to figure out new and unique ways to engage their students. In October 2012, I participated in a four-week workshop called Galileo. If truth be told, I often find it difficult to acquire any enthusiasm for a workshop that appears to tout some new "method" or "program" that will enhance the teaching and learning environment in classrooms. For the most part, almost all such workshops are programs and not a set of interactive ideas or guidelines for promoting real learning in genuinely authentic ways. They are just what they are advertised: programs – which are really just another type of curriculum, but for teachers to follow themselves as they try to engage their students. However, it is very difficult for teachers to successfully implement programs to foster genuine learning, because programs follow methodology rather than the basis of true interaction through a real human connection. One of the interesting things about the Galileo sessions was that teachers came together to interact with one another collaboratively and develop design ideas by focusing on three specific things: What the teacher is doing; what the student is doing; and what is the evidence of learning. [12] I was actually surprised to discover that the presenters of the Galileo sessions even went so far as to say that textbooks should only be considered as resources, not the main source of instruction. Good stuff. This is a move in the right direction. The program is meant as staff development in a direction that is quite different from previous decades of typical one-directional staff development that always mirrored the same process in regular classroom environments for students. As far as staff development goes, Galileo has some good objectives:

- To provide access to alternative ideas, methods and opportunities to observe alternatives in action;
- To involve direct mentoring of teachers in the context of their own classrooms in subject content, teaching strategies and uses of technology; and
- To support ongoing professional conversations between teachers.

If we expect students to learn how to think outside the proverbial box, then it is incredibly important that teachers be guided toward the same objective. This is why a move toward getting teachers to develop innovative curriculum that moves in a direction other than the one-directional fill-the-student-with-information-and-then-get-them-to-regurgitate-it approach is definitely a good direction to go in. Does it mean that I think the Galileo approach is going to singlehandedly save formal education? No, but it is a promising alternative that begins to look at one new way of approaching teaching and learning. It is one new way of getting teachers to think of new approaches to teaching and learning that at least attempts to take into account individual learning and engagement of students rather than having them sit like passive receptacles of often trivial knowledge.

This is just as important for teachers as it is for students. If teachers are following routinized schedules of what they should be teaching by certain dates using textbooks as the curricular determinants of such routinized schedules, teaching is going to be as boring for them as learning is for their students. The truth of the matter in such a situation is that if the teacher is bored by such routinization, then there is little hope that their students will be engaged or "turned on" about anything that might be presented in class. Very little actual teaching or learning will occur. Therefore, teachers should want to be as engaged and challenged as possible themselves. The truth is that they need to be. It is in teachers' own best interests to remain fresh, enthusiastic and vibrant about their subject(s) because the human element in all of this – an interested person who is excited to share information and engage others in what could be described as a passion for the subject he or she is teaching – is the single most important factor influencing others to also become interested and even excited about the subject. This is why a fresh approach to subject matter should be instigated by teachers every time they have a new collection of students to teach. They are engaging a different collection of individuals with different backgrounds, interests, capabilities, and so on. Therefore, perspectives may be different, approaches may be different and style may be different all because the students are different. In a sense, the learning community being guided by the teacher must begin with a good example – the one the teacher sets. Good teachers must also be lifelong learners.

The concept of lifelong learning shouldn't sound too difficult for a set of professionals who believe in what they are doing but it can be difficult for teachers who work in a system that seeks to have absolute control over curriculum and assessment to the extent that most school districts do. I have never understood this. If teachers must go through numerous years of

System vs. Culture

training to get a Bachelor's or even a Master's degree in their field, shouldn't they be considered professional enough at the end of that training to know how to develop relevant and engaging curriculum for the students they teach? Even according to the mores of the current system, the teachers have already jumped through the hoops; why wouldn't they be considered prepared to do the job they are hired to do? To an extent, teachers and students are often treated the same way in formal education systems. Although both are touted to function as capable, independent individuals who can make good choices and contribute to the culture at large, both are constrained by the limited opportunities to actually function as capable, independent individuals who can make good choices within the context they find themselves in. The result is what we have now – a flawed education system where teachers and students are both bound to routinization leading to assessment by test results, failure by up to 20 and 30 percent of those who go through the system to complete their education, and finally, total stratification of society into unofficial castes that often determines the path that people can take throughout their lives. Students certainly deserve much better than that – and so do teachers.

Interestingly enough, both teachers and students are trained and conditioned in the same way. Both are subjected to the generally accepted perspective, especially in the United States, that pedagogy should be reduced to the teaching of methods and data-driven performance indicators that allegedly measure ability and improve student achievement. Teachers are also subject to the same pedagogy that students are. They sit in classes, listen to lectures, and verify their competence by passing exams that are also scored in the same way that high school exams are scored. Even practicums do little to encourage thinking about the design of new ways to engage students. Student teachers often enter classrooms to watch and then emulate the same old way of conducting school and are then evaluated according to how well they actually do watch and emulate the same old way of conducting school. So the question to consider is this: To what extent are teachers prepared to think outside of the box so that they can enlighten continuously new groups of students with individual differences to think creatively, responsibly and cooperatively in a world that is in a constant state of flux? The bottom line is that they are not and are not supposed to be. For the most part, they are expected to perseverate the status quo by being unable to see beyond the status quo. This is unfortunate because many teachers really have a genuine desire to help their students achieve, but they fail to see how the system itself sets up barriers to actually accomplish such a goal. Even the Galileo workshop with its focus on what the teacher is doing, what the student is doing and what is the evidence of learning approach is still subject to the routinization of schooling as it has always been by being subject to period bells, class changes, constant attendance-taking, teaching to the test by professionals at the front of the class trying to pour in knowledge for the purpose of regurgitation, being constantly interrupted by announcements and so on and so on. There is nothing to show that college preparation of would-be teachers does anything to elevate the model of teaching beyond that or that the system really encourages teachers to be anything other than what they have been expected to be for generations – little more than clerks and technicians of regimented pedagogy.

Even given this bleak outlook, it should be stated that there are many teachers who want to see the system improved or reformed. As front line workers with the population to be educated, they realize that there are many pitfalls and shortcomings to what they are trying to do. It is teachers who see the human cost of falling behind, being unmotivated and dropping out. It is teachers who see up front the personal frustration and disappointment of many students falling through the cracks name by name, person by person. Even when teachers see their students excel in a particular situation or series of situations, they know that many of them will have a difficult time jumping through successive hoops of regurgitation and examinations in their attempts to prove that they have actually learned something – even when the measuring system itself is incapable of doing just that. A significant number of students do not succeed and when that recurs over and over again, teachers also feel like they do not succeed. It is little wonder that teachers have a high rate of burn-out. Their task can be Sisyphean in nature – a futile effort.

So far, the image of teachers that has been painted here is in a positive light, but as agents of a system, there are many negatives that have been perpetrated by teachers as well and this is important to look at. If there is one thing I sincerely question about many teachers, it is that they are what I call "rules people." A rules person is someone who adheres to the letter of the law rather than the spirit of the law, even when common sense dictates that doing so would be contradictory to objectives of teaching. Of course my favourite example of this is the hat rule which is still adhered to in most public schools across North America. As everyone knows, the hat rule dictates that students are not allowed to wear hats at school. I have never understood the concept of drawing a line in the sand over the hat rule, especially when one follows the logic of possible consequences for violation of this rule. What is a teacher or principal really prepared to do? Will the student be given a simple warning? If a debate ensues, will the teacher or principal then pull rank and turn it into a defiance issue? Once it becomes a defiance issue, will the next step be a detention or suspension? Are school officials really prepared to impose a suspension – which is often three to five days – where a student then misses what the school district claims is valuable learning time over the argument of a hat? And what if the hat rule is disobeyed over and over after several suspensions? Are teachers actually willing to see an expulsion for such defiance because individual suspensions did not work? I have simplified the issue with my portrayal here, but there are many teachers and principals who would weigh in heavily on the argument that it is about "respect" or is many times about what the hat represents. While discussing this issue with other teachers over the years, I have heard many people falter in their logic over this issue and ultimately simply declare that they see it as a respect issue and that is that – without even being able to explain how it is a respect issue. If we are worried that a hat might invoke some ideology about behaviour like many where I used to work in Los Angeles did – where blue and red hats represent rival gangs like the Crips and Bloods – wouldn't it make sense to emphasize that it isn't the hat or the wearing of a hat that offends, but the behaviour one chooses to exhibit because of social affiliations like violent gangs? When we focus on both the serious and the trivial, our ability to really emphasize what is important or not is diluted because the simple wearing of a hat versus an actual act of violence cannot be equated. In and of themselves, one is harmless while the other is not. As someone who has worked with kids in gangs for years, I can tell you that regardless of whether students in a classroom are wearing hats or not, everyone is aware of one another's affiliations – period. The way in which we deal with personal interactions is what really counts, not how people dress. If our purpose is to educate, then teachers should seek to guide intelligently, respectfully and logically so that others might see the benefit and common sense of following; simply imposing rules because they might reflect one way of thinking will win few adherents. Furthermore, imposing rules that make little sense takes the importance away from rules that do make sense.

Another teacher once objected to my position on this issue by asking: What if a student's hat said Bad Religion on it? For those who may not know, Bad Religion is a commercial punk rock band -- and that was all I said in my initial reply. The teacher told me that a hat like that would offend him personally because he has religious beliefs. Wouldn't that make the hat offensive? It might make the hat offensive to those who seek only to have their own ideas expressed through free speech, but what was this teacher's solution? His solution was to ban hats (with the implication that all hats should be banned because some are offensive). I think the answer is both simple and obvious. As a teacher, why would I want to ban something thereby giving it more importance than it actually has as a simple declaration that the student was a fan of a band? If I say something is unacceptable without offering a logical argument and then impose my authority to enforce the decision, am I creating a learning moment? Yes, but not the one with the result that I might want because I have now placed the student in opposition to me even before a discussion could begin. Why not use the hat as a discussion point to explore different possible views? That approach would stimulate creative thinking from both parties, provide a vibrant and relevant social topic that could be used to engage many students and possibly even convince some to genuinely consider the many ideas being discussed. People can be more readily engaged and convinced of something that is a good idea when they are involved in the discussion rather than locked out of any discussion with rigid and often nonsensical rules. Furthermore, the discussion process itself, when conducted with respect for both sides, can and will lead to relationships of respect rather than rivalry or contempt. That is a very positive benefit. I don't see any positive benefit coming from something that is legislated and enforced rigidly without linking any common-sense to the idea behind the legislation and enforcement. It only sets up oppositional lines which will inevitably engage with no benefit for either side. And when such engagement leads to punishment for students, we are simply teaching them to deceive or manipulate to whatever extent they can. That leads to weaker connections between those who want to teach and those who need to learn to the detriment of all involved, often because the only options we offer students are the very ones we don't want them to exercise. This is just one small example of how such an approach can be harmful in many ways, but first and foremost, it is an approach that breaks down communication and potentially beneficial relationships between teachers and learners.

Teachers should not want to be in the position that former award-winning New York educator John Taylor Gatto described about his own career when he stated that "I don't teach English; I teach school – and I win awards doing it." [13] In his book Dumbing Us Down: The Hidden Curriculum of Compulsory Schooling, he points out that "teaching means different things in different places, but seven lessons are universally taught from Harlem to Hollywood Hills," [13] (and I might add from St. Johns to Victoria to Whitehorse as well). These seven lessons are: confusion; class position; indifference; emotional dependency; intellectual dependency; provisional self-esteem; and that one cannot hide from constant surveillance.

1. Confusion is taught by teachers in classrooms across North America because almost everything is taught incoherently. Each subject is taught as a separate thing without showing the connections between them. School districts often talk about cross-curricular teaching and learning, but there is very little of it going on in most schools. As Gatto points out, "quality in education entails learning about something in depth. Confusion is thrust upon kids by too many strange adults, each working alone with only the thinnest relationship with each other, pretending, for the most part, to an expertise they do not possess…Think of the great natural sequences – like learning to walk and learning to talk; the progression of light from sunrise to sunset; the ancient procedures of a farmer, a smithy, or a shoemaker, or the preparation of a Thanksgiving feast. All of the parts are in perfect harmony with each other, each action justifying itself and illuminating the past and the future." [14] This is something very different from what young people get today. Before the advent of compulsory schooling, there was continuity to life experiences such as described by Gatto. If a student were to ask what was the relationship between the different subjects he or

she was studying, most teachers in North America would probably state something to the effect that each subject was a component of a body of knowledge required to be prepared for, and successful in, life, but those same teachers would have great difficulty showing what the relationship between the components was. The continuity of life-learning before school yields exponential gains in a short period of time. From recognizing faces, gestures and words to learning how to manipulate words, form phrases and present ideas, children learn rapidly and enthusiastically in a constant stream of progressive trials and errors on the road toward maturity. Then we put them in school where they must sit and absorb disconnected facts to be regurgitated for grades through the testing process without actually applying what they know to real-life situations. All of a sudden, the learning process is slowed down considerably and the means of learning is pulled out from under students like a rug on the floor. When up to thirty percent later fail to complete the learning process (as it is delivered to them), and an even higher percentage are functionally illiterate and innumerate, we blame it on them and place them in a caste position where they will likely remain for life. This is all part of the confusion we teach over a period of years. As Gatto points out, as a teacher, "what I do is more related to television programming than to making a scheme of order." [15]

2. Class position is definitely something most, if not all, teachers "teach" from kindergarten through to the end of almost every student's formal public education. At first we teach students that they are to be organized by age, regardless of the fact that same-age children are not necessarily at the same level of maturity or learning. We also teach them that within a classroom setting, they have an assigned seat. If they would like to go to the bathroom, they must ask to do so. Often, if they take a little longer than teachers think they should have, they are grilled about not wasting their time. Even if students would like to respond to academic questioning, they are required to hold up their hand and wait for the teacher to indicate it is their turn, even if and when they are the only one volunteering a response. Indeed, if students need or want anything, they are required to ask -- and if the teacher chooses to refuse a

System vs. Culture

request, the student is expected to accept that as law. As far as place is concerned, Gatto states that "if I do my job well, the kids can't even imagine themselves somewhere else because I've shown them how to envy and fear the better classes and how to have contempt for the dumb classes. Under this efficient discipline the class mostly polices itself into good marching order. That's the real lesson of any rigged competition like school. You come to know your place. [16]

3. Indifference is something that is reinforced by teachers, but it is really set up by the system itself. For example, as teachers we do teach that nothing is really worth spending extra time on, no matter how involved we might be in working towards a solution or completion. We may try to get students to show enthusiasm for a lesson and we may demand that students become involved in the lessons we teach, but when that bell rings, we expect them to drop what they are doing, adjust their frame of mind, go to their next class and begin focusing on another lesson with another teacher who also expects them to show enthusiasm for that lesson and become involved in it — until the next bell. As Gatto states so effectively: "Indeed, the lesson of bells is that no work is worth finishing, so why care too deeply about anything…Bells are the secret logic of school time; their logic is inexorable. Bells destroy the past and future, rendering every interval the same as any other, as the abstraction of a map renders every living mountain and river the same, even though they are not. Bells inoculate each undertaking with indifference. [17]

4. Teachers and the school districts they work for may claim that they are trying to mold their students into autonomous, democratically-minded individuals, but instead, they primarily teach them to be emotionally dependent. Emotional dependency is taught right from the beginning of student school experience using check marks, stars, smiley faces and other stickers, actual smiles and frowns, awards, punishments and privileges. It is not uncommon for teachers to confer favour or to actually yell at students, depending on the situation. Any student's rights may or may not be granted because technically, at least in the United States, student "rights may be granted or withheld by any authority without appeal, because

rights do not exist inside a school – not even the right to free speech, as the Supreme Court has ruled – unless school authorities say they do." [18] Student rights are severely restricted within school settings. [19, 20, 21, 22, 23, 24] I remember an incident that happened at a high school in California where I used to work in the early 2000s. One of the students on my caseload came onto the school grounds wearing a knit hat because it was unusually cold that morning. One of the security guards (yes, one of several full-time security guards along with two full-time policemen stationed at that school), called out from a distance for the student to take his hat off. He did not ask politely. It was a command. The student replied that he would take it off once he arrived at class (the rest of the school was not inside as the classrooms were). When the security guard chased him down, the student emitted an expletive along with his reiteration that he would take it off when he arrived at class because it was cold outside. To make a long story short, the student was dragged into the office and was about to be suspended for three days for swearing and defiance. The student's father was upset and came to the school to defend his son's actions. I supported the idea that the security guard could have made the exception to let the student wear his hat until he got to class, especially since the whole school except the classrooms, offices and gymnasium were outside anyway and it was in fact cold outside. The conversation turned to the expletive the student had used in frustration to justify the suspension. The parent argued that it didn't matter that the student used the expletive, especially since he had been unjustifiably provoked by the rigid security guard. His son had a right to free speech just like everyone else has. He wanted to know why the security guard couldn't speak to his son respectfully if he wanted his son to speak to him respectively. It wasn't a good enough reason to suspend a student for three days. I argued that the student had never been in trouble before and this was his third year at the school. The assistant principal wisely decided to let our arguments persuade him not to suspend the student (as he could also see the parent was irate enough to take the matter much further). I know the assistant principal knew that he was within his rights to suspend the student, as unjustified as that may seem to some; I also knew the law was on his side, but I don't agree with it in principle and I believe that assistant principal didn't actually agree with it in principle either. That situation turned out okay but might not have and probably doesn't in many schools on a daily basis all over North America.

5. Intellectual dependency is something that is cultivated very carefully with students at most schools within the current educational system in North America. Everyone who has ever been through the system knows that good students wait to be told what to do by the teacher and that listening to every dictum that is uttered from a teacher's mouth is what defines a good student. As Gatto points out, the most important lesson taught in schools is that we must wait for people who are better trained than ourselves to provide the meaning in our lives. The teacher is often the first "professional expert" students discover in their lives – the person who can make all of the important choices. The teacher is the person who tells students who and what to study, how to study, when to study and where to study. The teacher even lets students know how to prove they have studied by providing the preferred answer in advance. [25] This is no secret; approaches to education have generally been both hierarchical and authoritarian in nature throughout the existence of formal public education. Furthermore, in our society it is no secret that this is the most important lesson teachers must teach. When Gatto points out that we must wait for people who are better trained than ourselves to provide meaning in our lives, he is not only talking about teachers. He means that: "all good people wait for an expert to tell them what to do," and that "it is hardly an exaggeration to say that our entire economy depends upon this lesson being learned." [26]

6. Despite the fact that in schools and in society at large, we talk about the importance of self-esteem, it should be noted that what we mean is provisional self-esteem, because this is what is taught in schools. Alongside the constant stream of rules and expectations a student must navigate through on any particular day, there are also marks to consider and these are written and dispensed from on

high directly to students' homes. Such progress reports and report cards are impressive these days. Often they are printed like a spreadsheet and delivered with both comments and specific grades using decimals and up to four digits. This very specifically informs parents and guardians exactly how satisfied or dissatisfied they should be with their children. As Gatto makes clear: "The ecology of good schooling depends on perpetuating dissatisfaction, just as the commercial economy depends on the same fertilizer." Interestingly enough, the reports that are printed out by schools take a surprisingly small amount of time to consider, reflect upon and calculate mathematically. The cumulative weight of successive reports has a different effect on students. They often make negative judgments about themselves in one or more areas of study and see them reinforced constantly. This in turn leads to decisions about student futures (both by the school system and the students themselves) that have more negative consequences than positive in many, if not most cases. The effects of such decisions often last lifetimes. Gatto sees the lesson of report cards, testing and grades as one that teaches students that they should rely only on the evaluation of certified officials because people need to be told what they are worth (and in the modern world have it precision-documented). [27]

7. Finally, the seventh lesson taught in schools as revealed by Gatto is that there is no place for students to hide. They are always being watched, redirected and told what to do. Even homework is, in effect, an extension of surveillance into the home. Rarely, if ever, does homework make any difference in the progress of students, especially since they may be tired from a day's worth of regimentation at school and may have little or no assistance at home to do the work "right." Most people get to leave work at work when they go home. The expected situation for both students and teachers is a little bit different, isn't it? Homework, to a great extent, is an extension of surveillance into students' homes, where students might otherwise have the opportunity to interact with and maybe learn something from parents or others (which Gatto points out is considered unauthorized learning). Even between periods at school, only a few minutes are allowed for students to go from one

class to another. They are not encouraged to speak to one another for any length of time. There is little private time and few private places where students can discuss things other than those which are school-related. Of course the lesson of constant surveillance and denial of privacy is that no one can be trusted. This has great consequences for society at large. [28]

If, after a description of each of the seven lessons that are routinely taught in schools across North America, the reader decides that these are not what we want to teach our children in the institutions we place them in for most of their childhood, then we must begin to think about what kinds of lessons we do want to teach our children. The problem with the types of lessons that we currently teach our children is that they are an almost natural consequence of the type of system we have in place. If we are told from on high that we are to gather thirty or more students in a classroom of specific spatial dimensions, thereby strategically placing them in a configuration that is space-optimal – in rows from front to back and numbering five or six rows across, we are creating and enforcing a configuration that is not conducive to the kind of beneficial human interaction that allows for, and encourages, cooperation, problem-solving and creative exploration. We are creating a regimented forum for students to follow one main stream of thinking – listen, pay-attention and attend to what the teacher is telling them. In fact, this method is so regimented that, like an earlier example about mathematics, schools often do not allow or provide the means for students to explore and discover other ways of coming to the same conclusions, school systems and the front line teachers who represent them will reduce a student's "score" if they have not shown their work and prove they could come to the right conclusion in the specific method in which they were taught. Furthermore, if a student wants or more importantly, needs to go to the bathroom, they may or may not be given the opportunity during class depending on the whim of the teacher. This whole way of educating young people has to be rethought: If we don't want our children to be confused about the connections between the many things that should and will be important to them as they mature; if we don't want our children to learn the lesson of bells that nothing is really worth spending extra time on or finishing; if we don't want our children to be told what their place is (which in great part determines their place); if we don't want our children to be emotionally and intellectually dependent; if we don't want our children to have provisional self-esteem based on following what everyone tells them and then enforces them to do; and if we don't want our children to learn that they can't be open and honest with us because we are too busy keeping them under surveillance due to lack of trust; then we have to stop, reevaluate and address the situation that is our modern (although old and outdated) method of educating young people. If we really want answers to questions we may have about our society, what is wrong with it and how it became this way, we have to look at the system where our young people spend most of their time "learning" to develop into the people who end up taking the reins of our society's direction and functioning. In short, if we want learning to change and improve, then teaching must change and improve.

There are probably as many ideas about how teachers should conduct themselves and about what should be taught as there are people available to comment on such ideas. Nonetheless, if the reader has made it this far through this book without throwing it down in anger or disgust, then there must be some common ground between us. There must be some connection between what has been stated so far and the opinions that the reader holds as well. There must be at least some agreement on what is wrong with the present school system in North America and potentially some agreement on what could be right about it should we actually choose to do something about it. The following is a short list of my own conclusions about changes that have to be made, but readers are encouraged to create lists of their own as well. It is my sincere belief that one person is unlikely to come up with a perfect solution; it takes many in tandem to do so. Yet the following basic list is derived from the many points that have been made and illustrated throughout the previous chapters and may prove to be a good start:

- Teachers and students alike must be viewed and treated with equal respect by all, especially one another.
- Students should be given ongoing opportunities to be actively engaged and involved in the direction and content of their own education.
- Students should be taught ideas and skills that introduce a broad array of human endeavors and continued along lines that are relevant to

their own interests and skill development.

- Students should have ongoing opportunities to be active participants in our society as they learn and develop and not just as a future promise.
- Students should be taught concepts and skills that enable them to move beyond emotional and intellectual dependence.
- Students should not be tested or graded to a generalized curriculum standard but evaluated according to outcomes produced – both theoretical and practical.

Teachers know that they have a huge part to play in helping young people emerge into educated, informed, responsible and thoughtful citizens who can ask pertinent questions and seek workable solutions to the many issues and problems that arise in life. This is a huge undertaking and one that cannot be done by teachers alone. As Hillary Clinton once famously stated in a book of the same name, "It takes a village." [29] That is, it takes a concerted effort by all involved to ensure that societal goals are met. In order for all to benefit, all must be enfranchised into a system that really can work to produce more than a stratified caste society. Social problems abound in our culture and society and many of these problems either have a beginning or are well-developed in our system of education. The education system and society are closely entwined. Therefore, if we want to change one, then the other is going to have to undergo profound changes as well. This is not an easy task. In short, any alternative for education requires some serious self-evaluation about who and what we are and who and what we want to be as individuals and as a society. As we build the new global society that is rapidly emerging in the 21st century, we need to make sure that the advances we make are not merely technological or economical; they must be advances in learning, understanding, cooperation and most importantly, humanity. Teachers have been important builders of society for a long time but we have yet to imagine what it is like outside of the box. It is time for us to stop being passive observers of the sweeping changes in our society; it is time to imagine the future and think about how we want to shape that future in meaningful and positive ways.

References

1. Lambert, Lisa (2006), <u>Half of Teachers Quit in 5 Years</u>, Reuters, published in The Washington Post, May 9th, 2006. Retrieved online Oct. 3rd, 2012 from: http://www.washingtonpost.com/wp-dyn/content/article/2006/05/08/AR20060508013 44.html

2. Graziano, Claudia (2005), Public Education Faces a Crisis in Teacher Retention, Edutopia, retrieved online from: http://www.edutopia.org/schools-out

3. Hargreaves, Andy (2012), <u>Celebrating Alberta's Educational Success</u>, ATA Magazine, Alberta's Teacher Association, Fall 2012 Edition, pg. 5.

4. Nolais, Jeremy (February 6th, 2012), <u>Teacher retention a growing Alberta problem</u>, Metro, retrieved online Oct. 15th, 2012 from: http://ca.news.yahoo.com/teacher-retention-growing-alberta-problem-055500764.html.

5. Farber, Katy (2010), <u>Why Great Teachers Quit: And How We Might Stop the Exodus</u>, Corwin Press Inc., 167 pages. Excerpts retrieved online retrieved online October 3rd, 2012 from: http://educationpolicyblog.blogspot.ca/2011/01/why-great-teachers-quit-and-how-we.html

6. No Child Left Behind Act, Wikipedia. Information retrieved on October 15th, 2012 from: http://en.wikipedia.org/wiki/No_Child_Left_Behind_Act#cite_note-3

7. Lynch, Matthew (2012), <u>Lack of Respect for Teaching to Blame for Mediocre US Education Results</u>, Huffington Post, July 18th, 2012. Retrieved online November 5th, 2012 from: http://www.huffingtonpost.com/matthew-lynch-edd/american-students-conside_b_1682100.html.

8. Jones, Jeffrey M. (2012), <u>Confidence in U.S. Public Schools at New Low</u>, Gallup, published June 20th, 2012. Retrieved online November 5th, 2012 from: http://www.gallup.com/poll/155258/confidence-public-schools-new-low.aspx.

9. Duncan, Arne (Nov. 9th, 2011), <u>Teacher Pay Study Asks the Wrong Question, Ignores Facts, Insults Teachers</u>, Homeroom, the offi-

cial blog of the U.S. Department of Education. Retrieved online November 5th, 2012 from: http://www.ed.gov/blog/2011/11/teacher-pay-study-asks-the-wrong-question-ignores-facts-insults-teachers/.

10. Myths and Facts about Educator Pay, an article retrieved online November 5th, 2012 from the National Education Association (NEA) website: http://www.nea.org/home/12661.htm. Note: The actual date of publication of this article is not stated, but another page suggested that the NEA was currently supporting a base starting salary of $40,000 for teachers on their website on the same date. Given the numbers quoted here, the article could date anywhere back to 2002.

11. Canada Average Salaries and Expenditures, a table compiled by WorldSalaries.org. Information retrieved online November 5th, 2012 from: http://www.worldsalaries.org/canada.shtml.

12. Information about the Galileo Educational Network can be found at: http://www.galileo.org/about/index.html

13. Gatto, John Taylor (1992), Dumbing Us Down: The Hidden Curriculum of Compulsory Schooling, New Society Publishers, Gabriola Island, B.C., Canada, pg. 1.

14. Gatto, John Taylor (1992), Dumbing Us Down: The Hidden Curriculum of Compulsory Schooling, New Society Publishers, Gabriola Island, B.C., Canada, pg. 3.

15. Gatto, John Taylor (1992), Dumbing Us Down: The Hidden Curriculum of Compulsory Schooling, New Society Publishers, Gabriola Island, B.C., Canada, pg. 4.

16. Gatto, John Taylor (1992), Dumbing Us Down: The Hidden Curriculum of Compulsory Schooling, New Society Publishers, Gabriola Island, B.C., Canada, pg. 4 and 5.

17. Gatto, John Taylor (1992), Dumbing Us Down: The Hidden Curriculum of Compulsory Schooling, New Society Publishers, Gabriola Island, B.C., Canada, pg. 6.

18. Gatto, John Taylor (1992), <u>Dumbing Us Down: The Hidden Curriculum of Compulsory Schooling</u>, New Society Publishers, Gabriola Island, B.C., Canada, pg. 6.

19. "Ask Sybil Liberty About Your Rights." ACLU Online. 1998 http://www.aclu.org. Retrieved online December 12th, 2012, from: http://skyhawk13.tripod.com/rights1.html

20. Guide to the U.S. Supreme Court. Washington D.C.: Congressional Quarterly. 1979. Retrieved online December 12th, 2012, from: http://skyhawk13.tripod.com/rights1.html

21. Harrison, Maureen and Steve Gilbert. Schoolhouse Decisions of The United States Supreme Court. San Diego, CA.: Excellent Books. 1997. Retrieved online December 12th, 2012, from: http://skyhawk13.tripod.com/rights1.html

22. Hayes, Ron. "What Rights Do Kids Have?" The Palm Beach Post 7 Mar. 1997: p.1F. Retrieved online December 12th, 2012, from: http://skyhawk13.tripod.com/rights1.html

23. Whalen, M. Gwyneth. Student Dress Codes. Caplan and Earnest LLC. Retrieved online December 12th, 2012, from: http://skyhawk13.tripod.com/rights1.html

24. Zirkel, Perry. "Another Search For Student Rights." Phi Delta Kappan May 1994: p.728-730. Retrieved online December 12th, 2012, from: http://skyhawk13.tripod.com/rights1.html

25. Gatto, John Taylor (1992), <u>Dumbing Us Down: The Hidden Curriculum of Compulsory Schooling</u>, New Society Publishers, Gabriola Island, B.C., Canada, pgs. 7-9.

26. Gatto, John Taylor (1992), <u>Dumbing Us Down: The Hidden Curriculum of Compulsory Schooling</u>, New Society Publishers, Gabriola Island, B.C., Canada, pg. 8.

27. Gatto, John Taylor (1992), <u>Dumbing Us Down: The Hidden Curriculum of Compulsory Schooling</u>, New Society Publishers, Gabriola Island, B.C., Canada, pg. 9 and 10.

28. Gatto, John Taylor (1992), <u>Dumbing Us Down: The Hidden Cur-</u>

riculum of Compulsory Schooling, New Society Publishers, Gabriola Island, B.C., Canada, pg. 10 and 11.

29. Clinton, Hillary Rodham (1996), It Takes a Village, Simon and Shuster, New York, 352 pgs.

5

Imagine the Future

"The best way to predict the future is to invent it."

Niels Bohr

In 1516, Sir Thomas More, a lawyer, social philosopher, author, statesman and noted Renaissance humanist coined the word 'utopia.' A utopia is a society that possesses highly desirable or even perfect qualities. [1] The term has been used since to refer to people or communities that have intentionally tried to create an ideal society and also to fictional societies in literature like the island society Sir Thomas More wrote about in his book entitled 'Utopia.' The idea of creating a perfect place stems from knowledge that all human societies up to this point have been anything but perfect. The idea also persists because despite human imperfections, we have seen some advances toward better societies as human history progresses. It could be argued that things are better now than they were before and continue to get better. More people have access to effective medicines and health care; more people have access to a wider variety of healthy foods; more people live in better housing; more people can take advantage of better transportation; and so on.

In 1949, George Orwell, a journalist and writer wrote his famous dystopian novel, 1984. A dystopia, in contrast to the idea of a utopia, is an utterly terrible society where misery abounds for most of its inhabitants. Those familiar with this novel might recognize a now almost universal dystopian image of perpetual war, constant surveillance, lack of life-necessities, pollution and even more sinister possibilities like mind control, virtual slavery, total repression and even societal collapse. Unlike a utopia which is based on attaining the good life, any dystopian dream of improvement is, as Britannica Online suggests in its article on science fiction, overshadowed by propagating a fear of the "ugly consequences of present-day behavior." [2] The dystopian perspective of the future became the dominant perspective of humanity's future as we progressed through the 20th century. Early science fiction about the future as seen in some of the works by French novelist Jules Verne quickly lost their optimism as industrialization spread gaining a greater footing as a global movement beyond its original roots in Britain and later Germany and the United States. Toward the end of the 20th century, it might be fair to state that many, if not most people, viewed the future as being potentially worse and even hazardous. Global warming, overpopulation, ongoing regional conflicts and wars often dominated headlines and continue to do so today. Although mentioning above that it could be argued that things are better now than they were before and continue to get better, it could also be argued that things are significantly worse now that they were before and that some issues and problems are threatening dire outcomes for humanity as a whole. In fact, this latter argument could be made much more effectively than the former.

Much of the world's future scenario does appear to be bleak and losing promise faster every day, but there are often illuminating possible advances reported in several areas of our lives. We are inspired by the kinds of ingenuity and hard work that led to the mapping of the entire human genome, the verification of the Higgs-Boson particle and other scientific advances. They herald great promise for learning more about our environment and ourselves and point to a time when we may be able to overcome problems that threaten us and our future. Yet these grand developments often seem far-removed from the everyday lives of most people. These are things we read about or see on the news. Everyday implications of such promises for the future rarely ever seem to trickle down to the general population. Instead, we have seen in recent years that the middle class itself is in danger, even in the United States where the middle class first came to distinctive prominence. Ever since the so-called Reagan Revolution which has been heralded by American conservatives for three decades, there has been an assault on unions and on many social welfare programs and safety nets that have helped to create and bolster some semblance of equal opportunity for all, however disparate the everyday existence between rich and poor has continued to be. It is easy to see how people feel that all of their efforts are being expended on activities just to keep a roof over their heads, food on the table, clothes on their backs and debt as low as possible. And with the busy lives that people maintain just to accomplish these goals, it is also easy to see why most people have little time to think about, let alone do anything about, those things that are important to us collectively. They are already engaged full-time trying to improve their immediate personal and family situations.

So, in combination with the fact that modern societies seem to have a more dystopic vision of the future and its citizens are so busy with personal matters (both needs and wants), to work together for a common good, it seems to many that the problems of the present and the future are too big for individuals to do anything about. Part of the problem is that it is part of our cultural fabric in North America to think about ourselves rather than our social welfare as a whole community. When we think of global warming, many believe there is little to nothing that the average person can do. When we think of pollution, many believe there is little to nothing that the average person can do. When we think of crime, the economy and many other issues that we hear about on the news on a daily basis, many believe there is little to nothing that the average person can do. Yet this is precisely the point. As individuals, there probably is very little that the average person can do. This is why we need to have a common vision about what truly is good for the greatest amount of people possible. In our society this does not usually happen but must if we are to change direction in several important areas of our lives. Education is one of these important areas. We must be able to recognize the proverbial "big picture" and coordinate our efforts to provide a truly comprehensive education culture that can and will work for people rather than just the economy. If we could actually follow through and think about the students as we often say in our mission statements and elsewhere, it might actually become possible to witness a paradigm shift in education.

By addressing what is important for everyone, we open opportunities to shine as individuals. Referring back to Maslow's hierarchy of needs, if we address physiological, safety, love/belonging and esteem needs, we open the door for all to achieve self-actualization in many areas that could benefit us all – especially in the areas of creativity and problem-solving. Self-actualization is the goal – or mission statement if you will – that even appears in some constitutions of western societies. In the United States, self-actualization could be seen as entrenched in its Constitution right at the beginning of the Preamble. In that document, this is expressed as truths that are self-evident:"That all men are created equal, that they are endowed by the Creator with certain unalienable rights, that among these are life, liberty and the pursuit of happiness." [3] It is interesting that life and liberty are considered "unalienable rights" of "all men" but not happiness – only the pursuit of it, as American historian and social critic Arthur Schlesinger has pointed out. [4] Nonetheless, the pursuit of happiness is inextricably connected to life and liberty and is also associated with self-actualization.

The pursuit of happiness is, in many ways, a misguided pursuit if people are only seeking to find personal or individual happiness, especially through money and materialism in general. It has long been known that people with lots of money are no happier than the rest of us. Money can make life easier but it isn't the source of happiness. In 2010, an international team of researchers from Belgium, Canada, and England led by Jordi Quoidbach produced a new set of studies that reveal how money/wealth often dilutes happiness. In a report made to Psychological Science, the team observed that "although wealth may grant us opportunities to purchase many things, it simultaneously impairs our ability to enjoy those things." [5] Several other researchers in studies over the past 20 years or so (Lyubomirsky, Sheldon and Schkale, 2005; Aknin, Norton and Dunn, 2009; Diener and Oishi, 2000; Veenhoven, 1991; Parducci, 1995; and Gilbert, 2006), also point to evidence that happiness levels have little to do with actual levels of income, especially in wealthier societies, and that experiencing the best of life on a regular basis diminishes the ability to take delight in what one might consider to be mundane joys of life – like a sunny day, a cold beer or even a chocolate bar. [6,7,8,9,10,11]. The reader may wish to argue the point that money can or cannot make a difference in the happiness of a person who has it to some degree, but that is not the main focus of the discussion here.

System vs. Culture

The simple idea being presented is that a society and culture that pursues wealth for its own sake without seeing social benefit in other important ways compromises its humanity to the detriment of all. Hold on to that thought as we progress through some ideas for change.

Let's begin to imagine a future that can both benefit and empower everyone. It is a bold venture to try and imagine an equitable world in terms of real opportunity. Both history and current reality are against such a venture because wealth and social opportunity have historically been the real privilege of a relatively small percentage of the population. In January, 2013, I happened to watch a PBS documentary about Henry Ford which showed the impact that can be made to level out the playing field to the benefit of all. Its impact on me in relation to what I was writing for this project was timely and so I sought to learn more about the documentary and its subject. An article written in the Detroit Free Press about the documentary two days before it aired described Henry Ford as a "visionary who shaped the world like no other figure of his era." [12] This is an important point because he did it in unconventional ways that defied the current way of thinking to produce a more equitable life for more people than just financiers. Just like investors of today, those who supported Henry Ford's ideas wanted to maximize profits from their investments in his company. They were appalled and opposed to his idea of the eight-hour, five-dollar workday for the workers in his factory for just that reason; they believed it would minimize their profits. For the same reason, they were also opposed to his idea of producing a car for the average citizen. His investors wanted him to target wealthy citizens whom investors knew could afford such a product. Yet Henry Ford became very successful when, after producing several prototypes came up with the "Model T." It rolled off assembly lines for 19 years from 1908 to 1927 as the first affordable automobile and helped build the middle class in the 20th century. Henry Ford didn't only help create the circumstances that have allowed huge modern cities to be built because transportation from home to work was made feasible over greater distances; he revolutionized the kind of wealth the average citizen could attain – which in turn was good for his business. It could be argued that ultimately, his model for business made life more equitable for many and is also a model for what might be done today if we put our minds to it. Society can change for the benefit of all as we saw just over a hundred years ago with Ford's initiative. It takes a vision and the will to pursue it.

Education is the main building block of all other aspects of our society. If we want a more just and fulfilling society for the greatest number possible, then education is the place where real change must happen. Navigation through the education "system" must, at the very least, become more diverse to meet the many diverse needs among us. Indeed, the educational system as we know it needs to be replaced by a comprehensive educational culture. It isn't enough to simply allocate a certain time period as the one in which education takes place. In the rapidly evolving world we live in, education is an ongoing necessity that needs to be made accessible in all areas of our lives. With changes occurring at an accelerating rate, this makes sense. It also makes sense to eliminate the many barriers to success that contribute to up to 30 percent of students falling through the cracks and not graduating from high school in North America. An educational culture would broaden opportunity, stimulate creativity, create a mindset that learning can be fun as well as personally rewarding, and turn a dumbed-down population into a force for positive change wherever we happen to live, learn, work or play. An educational culture would provide opportunities for all to be included in the benefits that a society has to offer. So what might all of this look like?

A Look at What a Possible Educational Culture Might Look Like

1. **Mission Statement.** In an educational culture, a Sociocultural Mission Statement rather than a simple educational mission statement might be used to provide a framework for educational attainment as a goal for society overall. Perhaps it would require a legal initiative to entrench the goal of universal educational attainment as a constitutional right. Such a sociocultural mission statement might look something like this:

   The fundamental goal of all education is to enhance both the individual and society to the greatest possible degree by developing the means and incentives throughout society to extend human aspiration, creativity, ingenuity and opportunity for the advancement, benefit and self-actualization of all.

This is, of course, a bold and utopian vision for education in the sense that it reaches beyond anything we have implemented to date, but it is not utopian in the sense that it is impossible to achieve. The legal implications of creating a constitutional amendment to guarantee rights corresponding with such a sociocultural mission statement are admittedly difficult but also not impossible. It isn't my purpose to delve into the legal implications and ramifications of attempting to create constitutional supports for an educational culture here, but simply to outline what an educational culture could look like. A vision must be grasped before it can be implemented.

2. **Resources.** In an educational culture, numerous public and private endeavors and resources would come into play to support educational opportunity, achievement and positive social integration. In effect, educational opportunity and credit is made available throughout society, not just in schools or through formal schooling. Of course, there is the question of how this would all be paid for and it is an important question. While some believe that everything should be left up to the private sector and others believe that the government should take on both cost and direction of education, the most likely workable solution would contain a combination of both government and private sector involvement.

3. **Media Exposure, Access and Involvement.** A culture of learning and achievement would become a dominant theme throughout the media. This would help foster further interest in learning and the development of new opportunities to participate in learning experiences. It would become "cool" to learn. In his book, "Creating Tomorrow's Schools Today, Richard Gerver states that he has "often thought that it would be interesting to ask one of the world's giant advertising agencies to create a campaign that marketed learning to children. It fascinates me that in business and industry a considerable amount of time and resource are put into

marketing products and services to an organization's customer base and customer demographic. In start-up business 20-30 percent of total budget is not uncommon, yet in schools we spend no time considering the same scenario. Our children have become complex consumers, some of the most powerful in the global market-place. We must therefore begin to recognize this." [13] This makes a lot of sense and could spur a whole new industry of relevant, interesting products focused on learning and self-advancement rather than just entertainment reliant on violence and exploitation. We could engage and empower them to become motivated consumers of learning opportunity.

4. **Rites of Passage.** Individual and cooperative achievement, positive social integration and commitment to public service could become revered as important rites of passage linked to opportunity, recognition and privilege as citizens of modern culture and society.

As an educational culture develops, it would become possible to apply what has been learned in real ways that contribute to society as a whole. The idea of people being "future citizens" and always preparing for roles in society that one deems worthy would no longer apply. When a student learns a skill, let's say a mathematical concept, then that student has to show proficiency. This does not happen by passing a test so that the student can see whether he is considered proficient or not and to what degree. That, as we have shown, only serves to show that student what his place is in relation to the places others find themselves in according to their scores. In an educational culture, a student could demonstrate proficiency by assisting others in learning the same skill. This is much more practical and beneficial than writing a test. By demonstrating proficiency in a way that also helps others, a student could acquire distinction, become more self-confident and develop better social skills and self-efficacy. If it is also used as an assessment tool which can be documented in the student's personal electronic portfolio (to be discussed further below), then it would also be practically beneficial to the student who is proving proficiency). You may remember the student mentioned in the first chapter who wrote a computer program called "Sammy and the Fish" for students in kindergarten or grade one. That student was highly motivated by producing something of practical value to others as part of the objective of learning and performing specific new skills for herself. She learned much more by doing it this way than she would have by writing a test to prove that she remembered various principles of writing code. Furthermore, as students become recognized for working well with others by proving proficiency in various areas of learning, new opportunities are developed for students to prove higher levels of learning as well. This might be in another practical area like citizen science (which will also be discussed further below). Learning and competency develop hand-in-hand as one progresses through their education so that there is no "future citizen" but a valuable citizen in training now.

5. **Social Role Valorization.** The concept of social role valorization (as originally formulated by Wolf Wolfensberger), is expanded to include everyone in modern society regardless of how "different" they are or what disabilities they may have.

The concept of social role valorization has been around for over thirty years but is rarely ever mentioned, even in circles where people work with those who are "devalued" in some way. The idea behind social role valorization is to develop or support valued roles for all people in the society in which they live, regardless of disabilities which have traditionally prevented them from being seen as "valued" or "worthy" members of society. In French Canada, where I attended university, the term 'valorisation sociale' has been used to teach about the principle of normalization since at least the early 1980s. Interestingly, whenever I have mentioned the term throughout the course of my career since leaving university, I have never come across anyone who heard of it or knew what it referred to. For someone to be valued or find value in society means to have access to whatever is deemed the good things in life. There may not be any consensus about what this means, but usually some examples of what we consider to be the good things in life include respect and acceptance to quite a degree. Family and friendship come to mind almost immediately, but being afforded dignity through opportunities to acquire an education, being able to exercise one's own potential, having a relatively decent standard of living and a voice in the affairs of the community in which one lives also have significantly important meaning to what it is to "live the good life." An educational culture would embrace this for the benefit of all. It is important for all to be valued and equally important for all to understand that everyone has value.

6. **Cumulative Electronic Personal Portfolios (EPPs)** would become:

    6.1 the legitimate measure of learning that an individual achieves;

    6.2 qualifiers of types of service or employment one is enabled to practice based on evidence of accumulated experiences and achievements that support qualification;

    6.3 consummate resumes;

    6.4 repositories of all relevant information;

Portfolios may also provide the same service for cooperative projects, a public service entity or private corporation (but for our purposes, I am less interested in discussing these at this point). Let's focus on personal portfolios.

Recognition of important achievement for the purpose of professional practice would no longer be exclusively dependent on grades from nationally accredited formal educational institutions or educational systems like public or private school districts. Evidence of learning, achievement or advancement could be documented in many ways from many sources and accumulated in personal portfolios throughout one's life. Standards of evidence could be developed to ensure honest and appropriate documentation, but it is no longer restricted to test scores, grades, certificates or diplomas from formal institutions of learning (although with modifications they may also continue to be legitimate and sometimes preferred standards of evidence).

The electronic portfolio would be the central educational fixture in everyone's life but would evolve – when and as they do – to become consummate resumes and repositories of information linked to numerous social, business, government and other links important in the lives of individual citizens. The various experiences and learning opportunities combined could provide the individual with a rich life evolving from one position to another in a wide range of disciplines that would continue to enhance and reward the individual with interesting and diverse challenges and accomplishments. Enhancement of one's portfolio and the subsequent experiences and opportunities one derives from such enhancement are seen as a type of wealth and could confer status among peers and within society as a whole. What if society were to bestow great importance to portfolios and even exalt them as a form of ongoing "reality" education? Students might actually want to diversify their interests because it would not only help them grow but give them a genuine outlet for recognition. Forget Andy Warhol's concept of 15 minutes of fame. A legitimate, current portfolio with connections to social media outlets could provide ongoing recognition, motivation to learn and to excel because exposure of one's achievements could open doors from many unexpected sources as well as expected ones. Modern technology and social media could easily facilitate this process. They could also help to place students in their own "driver's seat" so to speak. Things that are considered important would include entries that are important to students as well as items that are considered to be important by others and by society as a whole. Portfolios could and would highlight a better-rounded picture of an individual.

7. **Ongoing Learning and Achievement.** School-age children would no longer be considered "school-age" because of a chronological number in age or, as Sir Ken Robinson describes it, "date of manufacture." [14] Children would be credited with learning and achievement whenever they learn, achieve or advance significantly. Evidence and validation of such learning and achievement could be provided in a number of ways from various sources in the children's

individual portfolios. Evidence might include photos of achievement or scans of work that might include text, drawings, paintings or whatever. Photos, scans, audio recordings and video could probably be used to document most types of achievement. Given the prolific spread of portable technology and interconnectedness to other forms of technology, most types of documentation could be easily uploaded and updated. People are able to do these things with email, Facebook, LinkedIn and other forms of social media. There is no reason why electronic portfolios couldn't be instant repositories as well. There just has to be infrastructure to support it. So if there are any tech wizzes out there who might be reading this, go ahead and make your fortune by developing such a program. Call it MyFolio, YourFolio, or whatever you believe might catch on and be used simply by as vast a clientele as other social media outlets currently enjoy.

8. **Progress through an Educational Culture:**

    8.1   During an individual's primary education, students would master necessary basics for developing and integrating into the modern world. Primary learning involves acquisition of the means to advance toward and perform higher-level functions. This would include learning things that are important under the current education system like reading, writing, and arithmetic, but it might also include other fundamentally important concepts like using current technology, developing cooperation skills, understanding and respecting diversity, recognizing similarities, differences and patterns in ideas, themes, phenomena and behaviour, understanding the connection between freedom and responsibility, learning how to communicate ideas, understand priorities (what is more essential or important and what is less essential or important, etc.), and whatever else might be deemed imperative to integrate effectively and productively into society as an emerging citizen. Students would be expected to exhibit proficiency before being able to move on to the next phase of their education. There would be no moving students on until they have mastered the necessary basics of education. There would be no equivalent of students graduating at the high school level with issues of illiteracy and innumeracy as there are today.

8.2 For our purposes here, phase two of the educational process is referred to as the Paths of Intelligences where students have an opportunity to explore their aptitudes and interests. They can then begin to plan a path of exploration and study that takes these into special consideration. In the Paths of Intelligences, students explore the areas of multiple intelligences that include: spatial; linguistic; logical-mathematical; bodily-kinesthetic; musical; interpersonal; intrapersonal; naturalistic; and existential. They might also explore directions of learning that correspond to the five minds of the future outlined by Howard Gardner in his book: The disciplined mind who "has mastered at least one way of thinking – a distinctive mode of cognition that characterizes a specific scholarly discipline, craft, or profession;" the synthesizing mind who can take "information from disparate sources, understands and evaluates that information objectively, and puts it together in ways that make sense to the synthesizer and also to other persons;" the creating mind who can "break new ground" by putting forth new ideas and posing unfamiliar questions – someone who "conjures up fresh ways of thinking, arrives at unexpected answers;" the respectful mind who "notes and welcomes differences between human individuals and between human groups, tries to understand these others, and seeks to work effectively with them;" and the ethical mind who ponders the nature of one's work and the needs and desires of the society in which one lives." [15]

8.3 Phase three is specialization. This too can be accomplished through more than one route. Colleges and universities would continue to be important centers of learning, research and accreditation, but professional-level expertise could also be learned/attained through an on-the-job program, mentorship or other means already recognized or yet to be developed. The important thing is that evidence of learning and expertise be presented, accepted and validated, but such presentation, acceptance and validation does not have to come exclusively from a narrowly-prescribed single source – licensed formal institutions of learning. The culture would allow for such presentation, acceptance and validation to be achieved through a variety of legitimate means, including what might be recognized as acceptable means of learning by potential employers – practical demonstration of achievement, skill and/or potential to integrate and be productive based on other skills documented in portfolios (EPPs).

9. **Insight and Outcomes.** Given all of the above information, a grade-based system would be replaced with an outcome-based system where students (who become by extension, life-long learners in general), would have many opportunities to "prove" development and expertise in any of a number of ways. This should not be confused with some current efforts to promote outcome-based-only solutions that tend to favour only subjects that lead to employment. There are many ways to exhibit understanding and exploration of literature, philosophy and other critical areas of study as well. To boost creativity, students themselves would be encouraged and challenged to develop their own evidence of learning as one of many avenues toward accomplishment. This would promote more metacognitive approaches to evaluating both one's own achievements as well as others'.

10. **Assessment.** Written testing of any kind would have to actually be relevant and proven to reveal competency in order to be legitimate. No longer would such forms of testing like multiple-choice be considered legitimate forms of "proof" that learning has taken place. It becomes recognized that having the opportunity to guess at the right answer with a 25 percent chance of being correct without much effort (when there are four options to choose from), is not a legitimate proof of competency. More outcome-based approaches to assessment would be preferred. Written tests would no longer be the dominant form of competency measurement and might only be supplemental to other forms of legitimate evidence of learning. Such assessment, of course, might depend on what kind of expertise was being measured and whether it was best measured

by a hands-on approach or some other form of measurement. In any case, students should be given opportunities to participate in the design of the assessment to be used so that legitimacy is recognized by both the party seeking verifiable assessment and the party providing it. When both parties are involved in determining standards, there is a clearer understanding of what is involved and expected. Having the opportunity to negotiate assessment measures would provide students with greater opportunities to reflect on the importance of what is being learned, their own learning style and the learning process itself. Tests would not be timed in the same way as they are today because speed shouldn't be prized above other attributes of testing. The amount of time taken to achieve an outcome or proof of competency might be included as part of the description of the outcome, but it wouldn't determine an outcome by disqualifying a student from completing other aspects of the assessment.

11. **Interconnected to Teach and Learn.** A Wiki-Learn online service could be developed to connect prospective mentors, guides and teachers with learners in a wide variety of areas. These prospective educators would state what they have to offer, what their qualifications are in the area(s) being offered, the resources that would be used, the curriculum and program intended, and the methodology that would be used. The outcomes would require a digital component that could be added to the student's portfolio. Prospective teachers would also register with a legitimate government-sponsored agency that monitored claims and qualifications to be accurate. Eventually, much of what prospective educators contain in their own portfolios would determine qualification. A set of criteria could be developed for prospective educators to be legitimate, but the criteria for legitimacy would not rely exclusively on formal training to become a "professional," but would instead focus on the legitimacy of an educator's ability to deliver what is promised.

12. **Entertainment and Edutainment.** In the realm of entertainment, especially in the games industry, developers of challenging games would shift from a focus on realistic violence and exploi-

tation to games of exploration and skill-development in a wide variety of areas that could generate equal interest. A heretofore relatively unexplored area of learning could involve virtual world teaching. According to S. Thompson in an essay included in Virtual Worlds, Real Libraries, this could allow "for some of the advantages of online education by letting students participate at a distance, and it lowers social anxiety by allowing students to be represented by an avatar of their choosing." [16] When I first began reading about the developing idea of virtual reality back in the early 1990s, I can remember discussing the possibilities in a summer school class I taught called Future Studies. I asked the students to imagine learning history in an entirely different way. Instead of reading about Christopher Columbus' voyages of discovery that led to European colonization of the New World, wouldn't it be interesting to become a virtual passenger on Columbus' lead ship, the Santa Maria? Databases of information from a wide range of global sources could be utilized to present a realistic virtual simulation of being on board any one of the three ships sailing under Columbus' command in 1492. Students could even assume roles using avatars that represented known crewmen and Columbus himself. Imagine the questions that would arise, the discussions that could be initiated, the virtual decisions that would have to be made and the learning that would take place in such an exciting environment. This could be one good way of engaging students on multiple levels. While we are likely several years away from any Star Trek-like holodeck, there is no reason why an educational equivalent to multi-user virtual environments like the program Second Life which already exists online could not be utilized. Even more exciting would be a virtual program that allowed teachers and students to work together building databases of information in order to produce virtual environments for any area of study. For example, in the Columbus scenario, if there were no databases of information already accumulated by the publisher of software that displays virtual environments, students could be involved by collecting any information that might be relevant from various sources. Some students might find records of actual crewmen, copies of Columbus' log entries if they exist, the specifications of the ships, possible information about known weather and weather patterns of the time period and so on. Once all of the information was accumulated and entered into the program, it could simulate the scenario based on the information provided. All in all, it would be an amazing learning experience and not so far-fetched. When one considers the time, expense and effort that goes into software to make killing realistic, there is no reason why software couldn't be developed to coordinate databases of information to create virtual scenarios that appear realistic either.

13. Roles and Responsibilities of Places of Learning.

The role of formal schools and school districts in an educational culture:
- Public schooling would continue to be a springboard toward other avenues of educational attainment but their functions would change considerably. Public schooling would remain the default source of primary education for many students (unless other opportunities were chosen and accessed by parents/guardians), and could continue to be utilized as a management source for coordinating other avenues of educational opportunity.
- Current school districts would be mandated to break up and downsize or be dismantled altogether in order to reduce the ridiculous amount of top heavy organization. It would also reduce the intrinsic need of the corporate-like institutions to standardize curriculum and procedures in order to manage. Perhaps "school districts" would only encompass local communities and be run by an elected board from within the local community. No longer would there be large sprawling and unmanageable school districts like the Calgary Board of Education, Toronto District School Board or Los Angeles Unified School District.
- As community-based entities, there would be much higher integration of community resources within the local school district. New opportunities would become open for a wider range of participants in the education process including local craftsmen, public libraries, museums, charitable organizations, businesses and other applicable community resources.
- There should probably be a separate regulatory body to ensure that

students' rights to an appropriate education are being carried out given the wider parameters of delivery. This could be government mandated and overseen by a citizen body to ensure the constitutional right afforded in an educational culture.

- Government funding credits for educational purposes might go directly to families who could then choose which resources their children would utilize. Families could choose to spend these credits (which translate into monetary funding) on formal schools or any of the many other educational resources that would become available throughout the community. It would depend on what was best for each child in any given family.

- Education would continue to be publicly funded but public funding would be extended to include access to what we now refer to as post-secondary education if students can provide evidence of a commitment to learn. (If various countries in Europe including a small island-country like Malta in the Mediterranean that only has a population of 400,000 can do it, there is no reason why rich countries like Canada and the United States cannot do it). Evidence of a commitment to learn could mostly be drawn from the contents of an individual's portfolio. Several conditions might apply, including access to funding for only one degree per academic level. For example, a committed student would be able to access funding beyond basic education for a bachelor's degree, a master's degree and a doctorate in fields of their choice, but they would not necessarily be able to acquire public funding for more than one bachelor's, master's or doctorate degrees. The idea is to help facilitate higher learning but not to fund perennial use of funds for learning without students making use of what has already been learned to become productive members of society. In other words, it is important that individuals be given the opportunity to achieve the highest level of education they can and that money not be a barrier to doing so, but it is also important that individuals not exploit access to public funding for the purpose of making learning a lifetime career without also becoming productive members of society.

14. **Alternative Educational Opportunities.** Other educational opportunities that might be made available in addition to formal

public schooling would include various resources in both the local and global community. Students in the Paths of Intelligences phase of their education (corresponding approximately to junior and high school-age levels in the current system), would have access to internships in various areas of study and interest. For example, a student might have an opportunity to intern for a specified amount of time in a hospital learning any of a number of skills in an assisting role to professionals on the job. It might be in a specific area of interest and study or a broad introductory experience. On the same day or during another convenient time later in the week, the same student might also have a different opportunity to work in a music store both to accommodate a need to make some pocket money and to indulge a developing passion about music. As a lover of the arts in general, the student might also develop his or her own ideas about a project that would meet criteria for exploring academic components required throughout courses of study. Such a project might be to critique various historical films on a particular topic and compare presentations and possible exaggerations or omissions with other sources of historical information. The study could be approached in any of a number of possible ways. All of the student's activities on this project as well as experiences at the hospital internship and music store employment and many other things in this person's life would be documented in the Electronic Personal Portfolio repository as easily as a personal Facebook update is conducted today. Perhaps the number of experiences, learning opportunities and creative activities a student might develop would also be as personally valuable as all of the friends and acquaintances one might accumulate on their Facebook page today. In an educational culture, such things would be valued, admired, documented, interconnected and would confer status and further opportunity.

15. **Volunteering.** Volunteering would become an integral part of every student's education and an expected component within the Paths of Intelligences. It would allow students additional opportunities to explore various avenues of learning while appreciating the important concept of service to one's community. The benefits of volunteering would likely even be greater for the volunteer than

the community which he or she has made a meaningful, positive impact upon. It may also be a better vehicle than formal schools for discovering something that students are unaware they may be good at. The element of choice in volunteering allows students to become actively engaged in the design of their educational experiences; and each new experience would help develop students' planning strategies for further opportunities. One could expect students to expend more thought going into the process as they progress and have more volunteer opportunities. Anyone who comes to realize the positive impact they may have on others and their communities as a whole also come to appreciate the general value of thinking and acting conscientiously. A sense of achievement both in specific areas and as a whole can also increase motivation to learn and achieve more. Accomplishment is often its own reward.

16. Yet there are further benefits to volunteering. It brings together a diverse range of people from many backgrounds. Young people enjoy opportunities to meet and interact with others. Most students today will tell you that the number one reason they come to school is to see their friends (and a disconcerting fact for many is that more students than you think would tell you it is the only reason they come to school). Volunteering can open whole new networking opportunities for students. It not only broadens connections made with others in areas of similar interest and positive cooperation, but it also provides a more multi-dimensional portfolio picture of students for employers who are interested in a potential employee's work-life balance. Perhaps the greatest benefit of volunteering is the realization and understanding that self-actualization through meaningful actions cannot simply be calculated in dollar figures.

17. Not all volunteering opportunities have to be in traditional areas either. While a student may elect to volunteer at a senior citizens center, a shelter or an outreach program for a few hours per week, they may also choose to participate in other volunteer activities as well. For example, Students could become participants in actual ventures involving citizen participation in research. The term "citizen science" is a relatively new term but is a concept that has

been around for a long time. As philosopher Paul Karl Feyerabend has pointed out in his book Science in a Free Society, before the 20th century, science was often the pursuit of gentlemen scientists who were self-funded researchers. The list is impressive and includes such notables as Sir Isaac Newton, Benjamin Franklin and Charles Darwin. [17] Citizen science could not produce such well-known notables by the mid-20th century because most scientific research was being conducted by professional researchers employed by university or government labs. By the mid-1970s, Feyerabend was calling for the "democratization of science" because the almost exclusive professionalization of science research was being called into question.

18. Should an educational culture ever truly emerge, it would dwarf the list of citizen-science activities currently available. Nonetheless, there are many citizen-science activities that can be found online already. Some organizations like the Audubon Society have been offering opportunities since before the professionalization of science. Each year since 1900, they have been conducting a Christmas Bird Count which is a census of birds in the Western Hemisphere by volunteer bird watchers in early winter. [18] Likewise, the American Association of Variable Star Observers invites participation by the public analyzing gathered data. Its website Citizen Sky proudly declares that "*Everyone, regardless of science background, can play a role in the Citizen Sky Project.*" They invite anyone who is interested to "learn about astronomy, observe stars, collaborate, create theories, study data," and even "publish papers." [19] In a world where we are beginning to realize that we are all a part of the many problems we have created, we will need to find ways to participate in solving them. Another interesting citizen science web portal where the public can help analyze data and participate in research is Zooniverse, an entity which is owned and operated by the Citizen Science Alliance. At the time of my writing about this, just under 803 thousand people worldwide were participating in projects through this site alone. [20] Citizen science has many interesting possibilities. Students could actively choose to participate in polls and other data-collection that help society as a whole become aware or more

informed about an infinite variety of variables that affect it. Volunteering can help integrate students as important components of life in modern society – actual productive, participant citizens rather than the "future citizens" they are perceived as in the current education system.

19. **The Role of Government.**

The role of government in North American education is significant. In both Canada and the United States, federal, local and (provincial governments in Canada and state governments in the U.S.), all have roles in education. Control of content and funding both emanate from these branches of government with responsibilities being split between them. In the United States, policies for teaching, employment, curriculum and funding are set through school boards that are elected locally. School boards have jurisdiction over school districts but they receive several directives from state legislatures. Currently, the Department of Education can mandate federal plans for education and also retains the right to withhold funding if it believes that any school district is not complying with such mandates. However, federal funding is only a small portion of the overall funding that schools receive. Regardless, a complete overhaul of how education is directed and funded by governments at all levels in both Canada and the United States would have to occur in order to facilitate an educational culture.

According to the United States Census Bureau, the U.S. has more than 14,000 public school districts and spends more than $500 billion on public elementary and secondary education each year (combined spending of federal, state, and local governments). [21] In Canada, 3.6 percent of its gross domestic product is spent on education. [22] At the time of writing this, the most recent figures for Canada were for 2011 when its gross domestic product was worth 1,736.05 billion US dollars. [23] That works out to $62.5 billion spent on education in Canada that year. Yet much of what is spent on education cannot be said to go directly toward educational endeavors. Much of that money is spent on administrative and bureaucratic costs, operational costs, maintenance and many other things that are not directly related to the education of students.

In an educational culture, many of these costs could be integrated into and absorbed by the various public and private entities and resources that are regulated by government and where educational opportunities could and should occur. Private corporations could be given tax deductions or other benefits in exchange for providing spaces for educational centers and opportunities for learning. Corporations currently enjoy tax loopholes benefitting them with millions and sometimes billions of dollars without having to meet any requirement or expectation of giving something back to the community where they enjoy their business. Likewise, any institution that benefits from public funding would receive such funds conditionally in exchange for providing spaces for educational centers and opportunities for learning. The inclusion of such educational centers and learning opportunities would become a fundamental part of any public or private entity design plan.

Government would also be responsible for monitoring and verifying claims and qualifications for accuracy. Anyone using portfolio-documented achievements to acquire a position as a teacher would have to make sure their portfolio entries are accurate and contain evidence of claims. Perhaps submission of such proofs would be a requirement during the process of acquiring a license to teach what the individual claims he or she has sufficient expertise to teach. A license to teach in the area of expertise would become similar to acquiring a business license for a specific venture.

20. **Curriculum Requirements and Options**

With so many options for learning, many might wonder how curricular requirements could be ensured so that students are taught "essential subjects" like history, math, science or language arts. This is a particularly important question for those whose ideas about school as it exists today are entrenched. Remember that in the chapter on issues, obstacles and problems in education, New York State Teacher of the Year, John Taylor Gatto, was quoted as stating that "reading, writing and arithmetic only take about one hundred hours to transmit as long as the audience is eager and willing to learn." [24] Most, if not all of the fundamental information we consider to be important for students to learn can be learned during their primary education. Until the basics are mastered, there would not be any opportunity to advance to the paths of intelligences.

When I was still a student back in the 1960s and early 1970s, advancement and failing were still options. They were a great motivator to work harder at learning objectives because, if nothing else mattered, no one wanted to be left in the same grade if their friends were going to move on to the next. Doing exceptionally well was a motivating factor as well because students had the option to skip a grade— an opportunity that also seems to have fallen by the way in recent decades. The role of incentive is lacking in this equation. What incentive or motivation is there if one's best or worst efforts still leave them in the same position? We have all heard the argument that failing a student can harm their self-esteem, but the counter argument that students who graduate and still can't read, write or do math effectively has been effectively ignored in terms of how that might affect self-esteem. How much self-esteem can we expect a current high school graduate to have if that student is effectively illiterate and innumerate? With a lack of self-confidence that is reinforced by ongoing inability, the kinds of problems that we see with many young people in society today will continue to grow.

The professional development option I attended in 2012 and 2013 called Galileo (and mentioned in the last chapter), laid out some simple guidelines for creating better curriculum for students. In today's schools there are still numerous restrictions that might impede the idea behind Galileo simply because of the structure of the education system itself, but the idea is a good start. The basic focus is for teachers to become curriculum developers themselves rather than relying on many old methods of teaching. The overall key to success, as Gatto has indicated, is for the students to be eager and willing to learn. If teachers continue to be life-long learners themselves and can therefore maintain a freshness about the content they teach, their enthusiasm will rub off on students as well. And as life-long learners themselves, teachers will find more innovative ways to transmit information, motivate students and create self-discovery opportunities.

Once students advance to the paths of intelligences, there would still be guidelines about directions for learning, but students would be expected to follow individualized paths that accommodate interests related to major themes in science, history social studies and so on. The guidelines would really provide frameworks with the students and their mentors or teachers filling in the details within such frameworks. For example, Canadian students might be expected to have a good working knowledge of their country and be able to demonstrate that knowledge, but whether they acquire their knowledge through textbooks, discussion, film, field trips of various kinds – and many other options – would be part of the individualized program a student pursues using the many resources widely available. The idea isn't so much about how many hours a student spends learning about a topic or subject. It is much more important to expect outcomes to arise from the time that was spent learning. Guidelines shouldn't dictate that a student has to take a particular subject for x-amount of years to be considered proficient because as most teachers know, many students can spend any given amount of time in a class but those students who are motivated, interested and engaged will come out of that class with a significant amount more than those students who are not motivated, interested or engaged. Resulting outcomes should be the target of any directional guidelines, not the amount of time spent. When such outcomes are achieved, then a student can be said to be proficient.

This is one of the reasons why grades really don't tell us much about what a student is capable of doing. A student might be placed in a classroom where he is either engaged or not. At the end of the time allotted for the class, the student is given a score that is somewhat representative of how well that student has jumped through the hoops the teacher wanted him to jump through – but it is rarely ever an accurate measurement of what the student is capable of and could actually achieve if he was motivated, interested and engaged. Curriculum design should be about setting guidelines for achieving at different levels while allowing students and their mentors to collaborate on specifics that will allow them to prove proficiency through some individualized variation that is meaningful to all involved.

21. **Certification**

    Certification, as has already been discussed, is not a guarantee of proficiency. We all know people in various fields, including important fields like education and medicine, where some professionals, as verified by certification, are not as good as others with the same verification. Certification itself, regardless of what it is called, is still a matter of trust between the agency or institution that bestows it on a particular recipient and the person, company or institution that is accepting it as proof or verification of proficiency. If you have read up to this point in this book, then you are very familiar with the argument that certification in the form of diplomas or other types of certificates are not so much proof of proficiency as they are verification that a student has jumped through the various hoops (that include a significant amount of test results measuring very little accurately). As long as testing is accepted as the main form of verification, colleges and universities can continue to rely on them as "accurate" measurement. The sad truth of the matter is that even colleges and universities have a bottom-line to meet financially. It is in their best interests to continue to rely on testing as measurement of accuracy because they need to "produce" graduates both to bolster the reputation of the institution and to continue bringing in more tuition dollars. There isn't a college or university out there that would actually be willing to guarantee their graduates as being proficient in the fields they have been trained in and graduated from because they know that individual differences among the graduates might bring such guarantees into serious question.

    Certification by institutions exists because it is a convenient proxy verification of skills. Certification simply verifies that a student has jumped through the hoops successfully in an area of study that focuses on the field the student is training for. Again, it does not claim practical expertise for any individual student as they may or may not exhibit such expertise when they arrive in the working world. A good example can be found in the world of education where it is a lot easier for a teacher in training to pass an exam on educational practice than it is to effectively manage a classroom. Success at one in no way guarantees success in the other.

Since the institutions that bestow such certification are government licensed, registered institutions of "learning," the verification they extend is accepted by potential employers who may not have the time to scrutinize potential employees' actual qualifications and expertise themselves. One wouldn't expect a potential employer to scrutinize the validity of every course taken by a student in a program of study, hence the proxy in the forms of certificates and diplomas. All parties involved willingly participate in the possible charade of professionalism to find placement of employees to fill positions, but what they end up with may or may not be what they were looking for. An education that emphasized outcomes rather than jumping through such artificial hoops would reduce this common occurrence.

Cumulative electronic personal portfolios as described above could change all of this. Verification of outcomes – however they were achieved – could easily be scanned at a glance by a potential employer. A potential employee with an up-to-date personal portfolio would have everything available for an employer at the touch of a click. During a job interview, the potential employer and employee could discuss the learning outcomes and preparedness of the applicant with the portfolio in front of both of them. The portfolio could always be easily accessible because it would exist and be maintained on a skydrive and backed-up on similarly easy-access digital solutions like thumb drives, CDs, DVDs and smart phones. Several technologies are also Bluetooth-enabled for interconnection to make access easier. Other networking technologies are sure to be developed.

In an educational culture, certification would no longer be the exclusive jurisdiction of legally licensed institutions. Certification would occur when a potential employer and employee agree that the experiences and learning opportunities acquired by the applicant meet the demands of the job to be performed. This might include formal certification or recognition from various institutions of learning, but the ultimate qualifications expected and met would be made based on many more considerations than just formal hoop-jumping. This doesn't mean that standards become compromised. People, companies and other institutions would still be expected to maintain the same (or better) standards for services and products than exist today, but now their options for finding better applicants for positions to be filled would be broadened and opportunity to land such positions would also be broadened. The benefits of more open opportunities for learning and acquiring skills would extend far beyond the numbers we enable and empower through the system in existence today. This is the kind of "trickle-down" thinking that we could all benefit from.

22. Empowerment and Freedom

An educational culture would have to be about how we can empower people to become more informed, enabled and productive. Empowerment is directly associated with greater freedom from which two problems arise – both of which are problems of perception about freedom and empowerment. Those who have the ability to empower others are often afraid that if they do empower others, their own empowerment or freedom will then be compromised. Many people – because very few throughout history have ever been empowered to experience complete freedom – also believe that if people are truly empowered with freedom, then it will lead to chaos because everyone will favour their own interests over the interests of others or of collective society.

Human history is a history of control and fear of true freedom regardless of the rhetoric that lauds this very quality. Dictionaries define "freedom" as "the power or right to act, speak, or think as one wants," [25] or "the absence of necessity, coercion, or constraint in choice or action." [26] These powers or rights are often considered separately depending on what one is referring to. It is possible to refer to free will or liberty as a general concept. Furthermore, it is possible to look at rights in different ways: civil liberties, political freedom, freedom of assembly, freedom of association, freedom of choice, freedom of speech, intellectual freedom, academic freedom, scientific freedom, economic freedom and so on. Yet even though all of these imply the ability to exercise freedom in various areas, it is important to understand that freedom of any kind is intricately connected with responsibility. The dictionary definitions of "freedom" as cited above emphasize what is generally believed throughout society: an unrestrained ability to do what one pleases. Yet, this is not a completely accurate definition of the idea in any society because we all live in society. Society itself is a collective entity that acts and reacts to maintain at least some semblance of balance. For example, people can have political freedom in North America in the sense that they may state their views and have a forum to try and win others over to such views. Yet there are many rules of engagement that limits their ability to always do what they might ultimately want to achieve. Not acquiring enough votes to proceed effectively ends one's ability to make wanted changes that the majority does not agree should occur. Freedom of speech is something that is highly touted both in Canada and the United States. It is possible to say what one wants to another person, but if one chooses to state falsehoods about another publicly, there are also rules of engagement that could have legal consequences. On a less serious level, one is free to share one's ideas about an infinitely wide array of topics, but if others around that person do not agree, checks and balances naturally occur that might prevent that person from advancing at work or in personal relationships to the degree that they might hope to without any consequences. These natural "corrections" help make sure that one person's freedoms do not encroach on others. If we encourage and facilitate the improvement of interpersonal rapport between people, these natural corrections will be even more effective.

Empowerment and freedom can only work well for the benefit of all when all realize that they have a responsibility to keep their own freedom from encroaching upon the freedom of others. Freedom and responsibility cannot be taught in a formal course or be legislated into action. In an education culture, there would be a realization and understanding that schools as they are structured today can provide examples of freedom and responsibility and forums for discussing freedom and responsibility, but true freedom and responsibility can only emerge from actual positive human interaction. It happens by example. It happens by engagement in real community. "It takes," as Hillary Clinton has pointed out, "a village," at least in a manner of speaking.

This is not a new idea. In fact, it is a very old idea. It is the way things generally occurred before industrialization – people interacting with people to teach them the skills they want and need. So as we come close to the central idea of this book – which is that education as it exists today is out of step because we have created a process of educating and learning where we treat one another as we have everything else – in an impersonal, industrial manner – it is important to make the following point: It might be easy to judge this book as one written by a radical liberal who comes almost as close to calling for the deschooling of society as Ivan Illich did over forty years ago, but it is also a book that espouses principles one might associate with a conservative approach because it calls for a tried and true way of addressing the problems in education – through an "old-fashioned" way – through interpersonal associations and relationships that promote well-being in many different ways.

It is easy to see how we got off track by believing that we could apply methods of industrialization to human interaction and learning as well as to methods of manufacturing and production, but the experiment has not yielded the results that people might have expected. Industrialization has led to mass production of goods but the industrialization of education in the 19th century has led to mass production of displaced citizens and an increased, specialized stratification of society. In an education culture where people would be empowered to become more informed, enabled and productive, we should also work together to achieve these objectives for all instead of competing to outdo one another to the detriment of many. The difference between an educational culture that promotes interpersonal cooperation and an educational system built on an industrial model and promotes impersonal competition is this: one has a cohesive influence on society; the other has a corrosive influence on society.

23. **Summary**

In this particular vision of a society that embraces an educational culture, several possibilities were looked at that would enable success for a much broader segment of the population. In a society that was serious about providing real, broadly available opportunities for learning, we might consider a sociocultural mission statement that not only supersedes educational mission statements of the many school districts in North America, but would be entrenched into the very constitutions of both Canada and the United States. The wording might well be different than suggested in this work, but would nonetheless entrench the goal of universal educational attainment into the very fabric of our societal framework. With meaningful education ensured, numerous public and private endeavors and resources would enable educational opportunity, achievement and positive social integration throughout society, not just in schools or through formal learning. A culture of learning and achievement would become a dominant theme throughout the media reinforcing interest in the learning process and the development of new opportunities to participate in learning experiences. Such learning experiences would open doors to individual and cooperative achievement, positive social integration and even commitment to public service – all of which are linked to further opportunity, recognition and privilege. Cumulative electronic personal portfolios associated with individuals from their earliest learning experiences throughout life would document all of the relevant information pertaining to what that individual has learned and is qualified to do. Qualifying experiences and achievement would not only be attained through formal "schooling," but would be credited based on outcomes of learning. Since many experiences and learning opportunities exist on many levels, even the most disadvantaged among us could experience social role valorization and be included in the dynamic of modern society in meaningful ways.

Progress through an educational culture would begin, and be documented, from one's earliest learning experiences in cumulative electronic personal portfolios. These portfolios would, in effect, replace grading as the legitimate outcome-based measure of learning that an individual achieves and would function as consummate resumes and repositories of all relevant information. An individual would have to achieve basic outcomes before advancing to the paths of intelligences where they could explore aptitudes and interests. The ultimate educational goal for everyone would be specialization which could be achieved through more than one route. Ongoing learning and achievement would be encouraged and valued. Assessment would have to be relevant and proven to reveal competency. Most written testing as it exists today would no longer be an acceptable form of skill measurement because of inadequacy on several levels. The portfolios themselves would not provide certification in the traditional, formal sense (which, as described above, is only a proxy form of pseudo-verification), but would provide easy electronic access to legitimate documentation that would establish an individual's qualifications as recognized by a potential employer directly during the interview process.

Society would be interconnected to facilitate teaching and learning experiences with marked benefits for all involved. The benefits of educational experiences that could easily be accredited to portfolios are obvious for learners but would also be beneficial to suppliers and facilitators of such experiences in the form of tax credits and other economic advantages. This is similar to what is provided to individuals, small businesses and corporations in exchange for bolstering the economy. Providing teaching and learning opportunities is also a good way to ensure a capable workforce to strengthen the economy and would be seen as being equally valuable. The added learning and teaching focus in society would also encourage new industries and change existing industries to expand their own objectives. Even the entertainment industry would branch out to encompass edutainment that would permeate society in numerous ways.

The roles and responsibilities of places of learning would also evolve. Formal public schooling would still exist as a springboard toward other avenues of educational attainment but would be fundamentally changed to meet the needs of individuals rather than expect individuals to conform to the structure of mass learning objectives. The boundaries between places of learning and the rest of society would be blurred because legitimate teaching and learning opportunities would not only emanate from established "schools" but be made available throughout society. All educational opportunity that might be considered alternative today would be considered legitimate educational experience if outcomes can be demonstrated or proven in portfolios. Volunteering would also become an integral part of every student's education and an expected component within the Paths of Intelligences. Since outcomes gained from volunteering experiences would have value in one's portfolio in the same way as other more formal forms of educational experience, volunteering would increase and permeate the very fabric of society. So-called "citizen science" opportunities would expand and help integrate as many people as possible into relevant, cooperative ventures that advance human knowledge and society in many beneficial ways.

The role of government in an educational culture would continue as a facilitator of funding and a regulator of legal obligations ensuring opportunity and social role valorization as outlined in the sociocultural mission statement. Government would also be responsible for monitoring and verifying claims and qualifications of teaching and learning for accuracy to protect everyone involved. The guidelines established by elected governments would provide frameworks with checks and balances for legitimacy but would allow significant flexibility to allow teachers, mentors and learners to pursue individualized paths of learning.

The entire objective of developing an educational culture is to provide real opportunities for empowerment and freedom to all. This can only happen if we legitimize the experience of young people so that their advancement and integration into society is real from an early age. Real interaction with people who foster respectful relationships while advancing teaching and learning opportunities throughout society is the way to de-stratify society as it exists today and create a future that is good for everyone. Imagine the future!

References

1. Definition supplied by Wikipedia and chosen for use here because it does not represent a utopia as only being a fictional place but implies that such a society could be a goal that humanity might work toward. Retrieved online January 9th, 2013 from: http://en.wikipedia.org/wiki/Utopia.

2. Science Fiction, an article in Encyclopædia Britannica Online, Encyclopædia Britannica, Inc., 2009, 22 May 2009. Retrieved online January 11th, 2013 from: http://www.britannica.com/EBchecked/topic/528857/science-fiction. It is also referred to in Wikipedia's article Dystopia which was also retrieved online January 11th, 2013 from: http://en.wikipedia.org/wiki/Dystopia.

3. Declaration of Independence (Preamble), retrieved online January 18th, 2013 from: http://users.wfu.edu/zulick/340/Declaration.html

4. Schlesinger, Arthur M. (1964), The Lost Meaning of "The Pursuit of Happiness." Retrieved online January 18th, 2013 from: http://www.jstor.org/stable/1918449, which provided the section from the William and Mary Quarterly, Third Series, Volume 21, No. 3, pg. 325.

5. Quoidbach, Jordi; Dunn, Elizabeth W.; Petrides, K.V.; and Mikolajczak, Moïra (2010), Money Giveth, Money Taketh Away: The Dual Effect of Wealth on Happiness, Psychological Science, a journal of

the Association of Psychological Science, version of record June 16th, 2010. Retrieved online January 27th, 2013 from: http://pss.sagepub.com/content/early/2010/05/18/0956797610371963.full

6. Lyubomirsky S., Sheldon K.M., Schkade D. (2005), <u>Pursuing happiness: The Architecture of Sustainable Change</u>. Review of General Psychology, 9, 111–131.

7. Aknin L.B., Norton M.I., Dunn E.W. (2009), <u>From wealth to well-being? Money matters, but less than people think</u>. Journal of Positive Psychology, 4, 523–527.

8. Diener E., Suh E.M., Diener E., Oishi S. (2000). <u>Money and Happiness: Income and Subjective Well-Being Across Nations</u>. In Diener E., Suh E.M. (Eds.), <u>Subjective Well-Being Across Cultures</u> (pp. 185–219). Cambridge, MA: MIT Press.

9. Veenhoven R. (1991). <u>Is happiness relative?</u> Social Indicators Research, 24, 1–34.

10. Parducci A. (1995). <u>Happiness, Pleasure and Judgment: The Contextual Theory and its Applications</u>. Mahwah, NJ: Erlbaum.

11. Gilbert D. (2006). Stumbling on happiness. New York: Knopf.

12. Hinds, Julie (January 27th, 2013), <u>'Henry Ford' film offers look at man behind machine</u>, Detroit Free Press. Retrieved online January 30th, 2013 from: http://www.usatoday.com/story/money/cars/2013/01/27/henry-ford-film-man-behind-machine/1869009/

13. Gerver, Richard (2010), <u>Creating Tomorrow's School Today: Education – Our Children – Their Futures</u>, Continuum International Publishing Group, London, pg. 21.

14. Robinson, Sir Ken (2010), <u>Changing Educational Paradigms</u> (RSA Animate), video on TED.com; also available on YouTube at: http://www.youtube.com/watch?v=zDZFcDGpL4U

15. Gardner, Howard (2008), <u>5 Minds for the Future</u>, Harvard Business Press, Boston, Massachusetts, pg. 3.

16. Thompson, S. (2008), <u>Teaching in a virtual Setting</u>, an essay con-

tributed to <u>Virtual Worlds, Real Libraries</u> (2008), edited by Lori Bell and Rhonda B. Trueman, Information Today, Inc., Medford, New Jersey, pg. 166.

17. Feyerabend, Paul Karl (1982), <u>Science in a Free Society</u>, London: NLB.

18. Christmas Bird Count, Wikipedia. Article retrieved online March 18th, 2013 from: http://en.wikipedia.org/wiki/Christmas_Bird_Count.

19. Citizen Sky can be found online at: http://www.citizensky.org/

20. Zooniverse can be found online at: https://www.zooniverse.org/

21. U.S. Census Bureau. Information retrieved online April 11th, 2013 from: http://www.census.gov/did/www/schooldistricts/index.html

22. "Draft OECD Briefing Note for Canada". *Education at a Glance 2006.* OECD Directorate for Education. 2006. Retrieved 24 July 2009.

23. Trading Economics, founded 2008 in New York. Information retrieved online April 11th, 2013 from: http://www.tradingeconomics.com/canada/gdp

24. Gatto, John Taylor (1992) <u>Dumbing Us Down: the Hidden Curriculum of Compulsory Schooling</u>, New Society Publishers, Gabriola Island, British Columbia, Canada, pg. 12.

25. An Oxford Dictionary definition of Freedom: http://oxforddictionaries.com/definition/english/freedom;

26. A Miriam Webster definition of Freedom: http://www.merriam-webster.com/dictionary/freedom.

6

Directions

"Most worthwhile achievements are the result of many little things done in a single direction."

Nido Qubein

In the 160 plus years that modern education in North America has existed, we have managed to examine, assess, theorize and re-evaluate how we educate ourselves again and again. This has led us in various different directions, often dictated by the times in which we live. I would like to think that those who had a hand in directing change over the years had the best interests of the whole population in mind, but somehow, as is often the case, special interests come to the fore and the imperfections of one system simply give way to the imperfections of the new system that takes its place. Sometimes new systems seek to go in entirely different directions than predecessor systems but, for the most part, they manage to keep the same basic framework. The times in which we live now are a period of significant and fundamental change in how we live our lives, communicate, interact and engage one another. This requires a significant and fundamental change in how we educate ourselves too.

During my lifetime, there have been a few major shifts in thinking about how we should educate young people. When I was born, no one was thinking about lifetime learning as a concept or goal. The idea of education was one reserved for those who were not old enough to take their place in the working world contributing to the economy. Education was preparation for adulthood. For the Baby Boomer generation to which I belong, completing high school was the desired objective for young people. We were told that in the future, it would be absolutely necessary to have a high school education as a minimum requirement for getting into decent jobs. By the time most of us were teenagers, there were already rumblings about the great changes that were coming and that even a high school education would not be enough for many desirable jobs. The push was always to reinforce the idea that formal education was necessary to advance. Yet even though there were rumblings about further higher education, most high schools still had an array of shops for students to learn industrial skills. In the high school I attended, there were several shops: mechanics; woodworking; electronics, painting and drafting. Most of my fellow students were planning to complete high school (although several did not), but very few I knew had aspirations of going to university. By the time I was in my early twenties, I knew several former classmates who were married and had children, were in jobs that were more or less permanent (like working in General Motors), were either in newly-bought homes or planning to buy a home, and were already saddled with the common adult lifestyle of paying bills and trying to get ahead. They were living the so-called "American Dream" which people in several Western countries have bought into.

For the Baby Boomer generation, times were economically good. This was the aftermath of World War II. Both the United States and Canada benefitted from the influx of skilled and unskilled labour immigrating into North America mostly from war-torn Europe. The United States advanced exponentially as the leading economy in the world and this was particularly good for Canada who was, and remains, the United States' largest trading partner. There was plenty of work in the aftermath of World War II in North America. Between the end of the war and the early 1970s, the United States alone produced roughly half of the world's industrial output. [1] The future was optimistic. In many Western countries like Canada and the United States, government intervention and social safety nets were particularly appealing to the many war veterans who wanted to have the freedom and opportunity they had fought for during the war. In North

America, economic theory was dominated by American John Maynard Keynes and Canadian John Kenneth Galbraith, both proponents of liberalism in socioeconomic policy. [2][3] These economists presented the idea of investment in state-sponsored services not only as a social benefit but also as something beneficial for the economy. Social services were considered helpful to develop stability and pools of talent that could cultivate skills to fuel future prosperity. In the United States, this led to programs like Lyndon Johnson's Great Society which sought to enable social reforms where the main goals were the elimination of poverty and racial injustice,[4] because both poverty and racial (as well as other social injustices) could impede economic performance. In Canada, there was a strong emphasis on the establishment of social services which included a national health program, investment in public housing and the expansion of comprehensive education. Although there seems to be precious little evidence or vestiges of such thinking in more modern times, this was a period of significant confidence in the ability of governments to influence and possibly solve social problems. Such optimism also filtered down to how we looked at education.

A major shift began in the 1980s. In 1981, the government headed by Ronald Reagan in the United States commissioned a report called "A Nation at Risk: The Imperative for Educational Reform." Published in 1983, it generated a lot of discussion both in the United States and across its border. At McGill University where I was an education student at the time, A Nation at Risk came up in discussion frequently. There was much to discuss, but several themes emerged. The report was the first to really galvanize public opinion that public education was in danger and was in fact, failing. The industrial concept of standardization became a mantra calling for common educational standards and increased standardized professional training at the district level. Despite growing awareness of individual differences which were made famous by Howard Gardner's book *Frames of Mind: The Theory of Multiple Intelligences*, which was published during the same year as *A Nation at Risk*, the idea that there should be exacting standards across the board for all students won out. The kind of standardized testing that is railed against in this book and others became, and still is, a dominant part of education today. A third theme, a provision for consumer choice in education eventually led to the concept of charter schools in the United States, an idea that began to pick up speed in the early-to-mid

1990s. Minnesota and then California were the first states to institute charter school laws in 1991 and 1992 respectively. [5] Initially, this idea had mixed reviews because many who had grown up in preceding decades, or taught in schools before this report was published, saw the idea of charter schools as one that would further erode public education by becoming elitist. Interestingly, as pointed out in the first chapter of this book where I described some of my own experiences with efforts to co-found a charter school, real changes were reined in by school districts that controlled the initial establishment and monetary purse of any charter school within their jurisdiction. There might be some variation, but real educational change was not going to be heralded in by the charter school movement. The framework was still going to be the same with most still adhering to standardized testing as the ultimate form of determining success and achievement. After two decades of charter school development and three decades of major standardization in testing of students and training of professionals, there are still many studies that publish damning reports about the state of education, especially in the United States. If anything, it has continued to worsen, yet the overall framework has remained much the same.

The wheels of progress often seem to work slowly, even when there are in fact significant initiatives made to try to change the status quo behind the scene. British sociologist and social theorist Anthony Giddens, who has been a prolific writer about many significant aspects of society and an advisor to former Prime Minister Tony Blair's government, often took part in discussions between Blair and U.S. President Bill Clinton from 1997 onwards.[6] He also participated in talks between Blair and Germany's Gerhard Schröder (who had written a paper called Europe: "The Third Way") which can be "loosely described as a move away from both the radical free market policies of Thatcherism and the old socialist Labour centralized state based on "tax-and-spend"." [7] His work is often "an analysis of the interplay between social structures and people's freedom to act," [8] and as far as Blair and Schröder's ideas about restructuring institutions and public management to engage with a globalized economy in the area of education is concerned, was a proponent of their so-called "Third Way." Whereas attempts in previous decades to structure education were either top down or bottom up, Giddens advocated a more "side to side approach. [8] His approach to promote economic prosperity in participatory democracies included some key components including the following: Investment of life-long learning and training; more family-friendly employment conditions which Giddens believes essential to both a flexible workforce and a more self-reliant autonomous citizenry; a commitment to greater social inclusion; more widespread public participation; a mixed economy that includes both public and private investment in education (as well as other public institutions and areas); and a general understanding that economic equalities must be addressed so that education can achieve to its ultimate potential. [9] These were promising goals, but have they trickled down into practice at the level that will affect actual students? This book is not about policies either in Britain or Germany. If Giddens' participation in talks with Clinton had any effect, I did not see it during the nineteen years in which I taught in the United States (1988 to 2007). Furthermore, the kinds of changes suggested by Giddens would be most welcome, but still they would not be enough. The structure of education itself as we have known it for generations is fundamentally unchanged. We still rely exclusively on formal education delivered through a monopolistic system, testing, grades and other standard features that are in place and have been in place throughout living memory. We still talk about multiple intelligences and individual differences but continue to try and streamline education in a way that continues to work toward a one size fits all approach. Furthermore, we continue to advocate practices that ultimately exclude a significant number of people – those who drop out of the system. The system must give way to an overall culture so that as many people who are part of that culture also have a real opportunity to contribute toward and benefit from it.

In the end, it is an entire culture that must change here in North America (I can already hear the protests that might include terms like "anathema," "abomination," and in the religiously capitalist culture that is North America – "sacrilege"). As has already been made clear in this book, the education system we have is the one we want for the economy we have which requires some to be left out of the American dream (and now I can imagine calls of "treason" as well as many more colloquial comments that would be inappropriate to print within the context of what this book is about). Can change happen? Of course it can. It happens continuously, but we must be more diligent in determining the direction that change will go in.

Much has been said in recent years about progress made in Finland – both economic and educational. It has become phenomenally successful only in the past decade and a half proving that phenomenal change can, and in fact does, happen. We read about it in educational journals and books. It has also trickled down into reports in local teacher's union monthly magazines and guides. Finland's example has in a short period of time been touted as the standard to live up to. Finland's graduation rate is not perfect, but close to it at 95 percent. [11] It is particularly interesting to note that its success occurs within the framework of a strong social welfare state – more so than its North American social welfare counterpart – Canada. Finland's overall economy and culture are also highly publicized as it has been ranked one of the world's most peaceful countries [12] as well as one of the world's most economically competitive countries. [13] Newsweek Magazine declared Finland "the best country in the world" in 2010. [14] Public education is considered to be a universal and constitutional right there and is both well-funded and free from early childhood through higher education (including subsidized meals served to full-time students). This publicly-funded comprehensive education system includes higher education and lifelong (continuing) education. [15] By receiving all necessary resources that include meals regardless of any social class distinction, everyone participates in, benefits from and understands the importance of supporting the social welfare system. 33 percent of the residents in Finland have a tertiary degree [16] which helps to create greater equality and helps to reduce dissension, crime, homelessness, and on and on. What the reader might find particularly interesting after reading up to this point is that Finland does not have a system for standardized testing. The only exceptions are confidential samples for monitoring purposes. There isn't even a native Finnish term for accountability in this respect. [17]

In 2009, Andy Hargreaves and Dennis Shirley published a book with promise for the future of education. In <u>The Fourth Way: The Inspiring Future of Educational Change</u>, the authors assessed educational practice in recent decades and described the various approaches to educational practice as the first, second and third ways. The book highlighted strengths and weaknesses of previous efforts to impact the educational process and then suggested a fourth way.

In the "Fourth Way," Hargreaves and Shirley outline a "way of inspiration and innovation, of responsibility and sustainability," and place particular emphasis in subsequent pages on sustainability as something "not merely to maintain or endure, but also to hold up or to bear the weight of something." Perhaps the most important point they make is that sustainable educational change has nothing to do with bureaucratic policies and interventions that shift from one government to the next. The truly important aspect of education that cannot be replaced is "the value of teachers working closely and effectively with students and colleagues, students learning from and supporting each other, and all of them engaging with parents and communities around purposes they develop and deliberate on together." The authors outline what they describe as six pillars of purpose that characterize an emerging fourth way. These are: an inspiring and inclusive vision; strong public engagement; achievement through investment; corporate educational responsibility; students as partners in change; and mindful learning and teaching. [18] These are notable objectives which Hargreaves and Shirley elaborate on in many positive ways, but in the end we are still talking about a framework for education that relies on the structure of the current school system and monopolizes formal educational opportunity and practice (including testing, grading and other long-utilized forms of funneling students through a one-size fits all approach). Like many people, I would like to think that education could be transformed from within the current structure, but I seriously doubt that the current structure would or even could allow the kinds of changes that are needed to make a real difference. There are some indications that the authors of The Fourth Way realize it will take more than systemic change and that broader social change is required as well. They do point out that some American "exceptionalists" have dismissed the educational success of Finland and Singapore because they claim that the U.S. just isn't like those countries. They also state point blank that the United States real challenge "is not to be an exception but to be exceptional." Yet this is unlikely to happen because the point that must be particularly emphasized is that America has continued to abide by habitual frames of reference that emphasize individualism, markets and competition as the solutions for all challenges. [19] Such approaches have become sacrosanct and have even spilled over to other western countries (like Canada) where the economy, in Americanesque terms, has become more significant than any other perceived parts of life. As long as the almighty dollar reigns supreme and individualistic accumulation of such capital is seen as the ultimate goal in life, there can be little significant chance for working together to achieve real equity and opportunity.

So where are we to go from here? In what direction can real positive change have the best chance of happening? Can the odds against real change be so great that we should just give in and succumb to the educational reality that currently exists? Should we all just throw our hands up in the air and say "there is nothing we can do?" Absolutely not! The way forward for each of us is from the various places where we already find ourselves. It is imperative that we recognize what ideas, issues and details are important to work toward and then do so. If we can all buy into the idea of an educational culture that is equitable for all, then we will all be able to: ask the important questions that need to be asked where we are; to make the important decisions where we are by conducting our efforts according to what is best for each person we interact with regularly; and to help foster the corrective checks and balances that move toward a society that is equitable for all and not focused solely on the needs of an individual, corporation or the economy as an entity in and of itself. We need to work together toward what is good for all of us because only seeking out what is good for us individually often fosters competition and conflict, not cooperation and community. Cooperation and community were more important before industrialization and will again be more important in the interconnected digital world that is emerging. What we do or do not do from this point on will shape and determine our emerging world. Individually there is, as perceived, very little we can do to change what currently exists, but together we can transform the many problems that exist into opportunities for making things right and by including everyone who is here to contribute to and enjoy the benefits of our effort. This is about either developing lives to be lived and guided within structured impersonal systems or living lives within the rich tapestry of interpersonal communication that is culture in much more than just education, but in society as a whole.

References

1. Kunkel, John (2003), *America's Trade Policy Towards Japan: Demanding Results*, Routledge. p. 33.

2. David Gowland (2008), *John Maynard Keynes*, Liberal Democrat History Group, retrieved online May 23rd, 2013 from: http://www.liberalhistory.org.uk/item_single.php?item_id=31&item=biography.

3. Neill, Robin F. (2012), *John Kenneth Galbraith*, taken from the Canadian Encyclopedia and retrieved online May 23rd, 2013 from: http://www.thecanadianencyclopedia.com/articles/john-kenneth-galbraith

4. The Great Society, an overview with links to specific programs and initiatives found on the Princeton University site and retrieved online May 23rd, 2013 from: http://www.princeton.edu/~achaney/tmve/wiki100k/docs/Great_Society.html

5. Charter School Laws Across the United States, a publication of the Center for Educational Reform, retrieved online June 3rd, 2013, from: http://www.edreform.com/About_CER/Charter_School_Laws_Across_the_States/index.cfm.

6. McMann, Shaun (2007), *Anthony Giddens: A Biography*, Open Learn University, retrieved online June 11th, 2013 from: http://www.open.edu/openlearn/society/politics-policy-people/politics/anthony-giddens-biography.

7. BBC News (November 8th, 1999), *World: Blair and Schröder Plan New Way*, retrieved online from: http://news.bbc.co.uk/2/hi/europe/205948.stm.

8. Same as (6) - McMann, Shaun (2007), *Anthony Giddens: A Biography*, Open Learn University, retrieved online June 11th, 2013 from: http://www.open.edu/openlearn/society/politics-policy-people/politics/anthony-giddens-biography.

9. Hartley, David (2007), *The Emergence of Distributed Leadership*

in Education: Why Now? British Journal of Educational Studies, Volume 55, Issue 2. Retrieved online from Taylor Francis Online: http://www.tandfonline.com/doi/abs/10.1111/j.1467-8527.2007.00371.x

10. Giddens, Anthony (2000), The Third Way and its Critics, Polity Books, 189 pages.

11. Organization of Economic Cooperation and Development (OECD) Countries with the Highest High School graduation Rates. Retrieved online June 12th, 2013 from: http://www.aneki.com/oecd_countries_high_school_graduation_rates.html. (OECD countries are primarily Western nations but also includes Korea, Japan and Israel). Can also be found at "Tertiary education graduation rates—Education: Key Tables from OECD". OECD iLibrary. Also retrieved online June 12th, 2013 from: http://www.oecd-ilibrary.org/education/tertiary-education-graduation-rates_20755120-table1

12. The Fund For Peace Failed States Index 2012. Retrieved online June 12th, 2013 from: http://www.fundforpeace.org/global/library/cfsir1210-failedstatesindex2012-06p.pdf

13. The 2012 Legatum Prosperity Index. Retrieved online June 12th, 2013 from: http://www.prosperity.com/

14. Interactive Infographic of the World's Best Countries: Newsweek's List of the World's Best Countries, published August 15th, 2010. Retrieved online June 12th, 2013 from: http://www.thedailybeast.com/newsweek/2010/08/15/interactive-infographic-of-the-worlds-best-countries.html

15. Antikainen, Ari and Luukkainen, Anne (2007), Twenty-Five Years of Educational Reform Initiatives in Finland, retrieved online June 12th, 2013 from: https://docs.google.com/viewer?%60a=v&q=cache:NW7wrxDQqykJ:cc.joensuu.fi/~anti/publ/uudet/twenty_five_years.pdf+Finland+comprehensive+education&hl=en&gl=us&pid=bl&srcid=ADGEEShyRLWPX81y0udhExBjjNgZNoOrvE2rXQOvNKqTZ4z7e0ZO1VpGmK9NqH9B9XR0yqZG_0wrZeyKNeicmAeMPlQSF1cR--W4dI-jXpBovJkFAkH-k7KpCRm-

j4Q3wKBR5qCXeKaci&sig=AHIEtbQ9VORHIoF3tYEMneV7C7InXW3Ysw&pli=1

16. Finland, article in Wikipedia referring to a Finnish source. The Wikipedia article was retrieved June 12th, 2013 from: http://en.wikipedia.org/wiki/Finland#Education_and_science and referring to an article in Finnish stating that 33 percent of Finnish residents have a tertiary degree. That source link is: https://www.tilastokeskus.fi/artikkelit/2006/art_2006-07-06_001.html

17. Sahlberg, P. (2006), <u>Dynamic Inequality and Intervention: Lessons From a Small Country</u>, Phi Delta Kappan, pgs. 105 – 114. Also reported in Andy Hargreaves and Dennis Shirley's 2009 book, <u>The Fourth Way: The Inspiring Future for Educational Change</u>, Corwin Publisher, Thousand Oaks, California, pg. 54.

18. Hargreaves, Andy and Shirley, Dennis (2009), The Fourth Way: The Inspiring Future for Educational Change, Corwin Publisher, Thousand Oaks, California, pgs. 71 to 73.

19. Hargreaves, Andy and Shirley, Dennis (2009), The Fourth Way: The Inspiring Future for Educational Change, Corwin Publisher, Thousand Oaks, California, pg. 75.

About the Author

Frank Pace has been in the field of education for almost 30 years. As a high school dropout with degrees in English and Education Psychology from McGill University in Montreal, he can truly be said to have an alternative outlook on the education process as it exists in North America. He has worked in both the United States and Canada. While working in the Los Angeles area for 19 years, Frank worked with students with significant behavioural problems, many of whom were involved in street gangs, as well as working with affluent students who attended a Blue Ribbon school. Also involved at the forefront of technology in education, he was acknowledged in 2000 as a "visionary mentor" to students there by the La Cañada Unified School District's Institutes for the 21st Century. Throughout Frank's career he has cultivated a reputation for developing innovative curriculum, rejecting formal testing in favour of more hands-on approaches and projects, and for employing classroom management techniques that promote individual confidence, mutual respect and partnership toward the attainment of learning objectives.